CLINICAL AND PRACTICE ISSUES IN ADOPTION

CLINICAL AND PRACTICE ISSUES IN ADOPTION
REVISED AND UPDATED

Bridging the Gap Between Adoptees Placed as Infants and as Older Children

Written and Edited by
Victor Groza and Karen F. Rosenberg

BERGIN & GARVEY
Westport, Connecticut • London

The Library of Congress has cataloged the hardcover edition as follows:

Groza, Victor, 1956–
    Clinical and practice issues in adoption : bridging the gap
    between adoptees placed as infants and as older children / written
    and edited by Victor Groza and Karen F. Rosenberg.
        p.   cm.
    Includes bibliographical references and index.
    ISBN 0–275–95816–7 (alk. paper)
        1. Adoption—Psychological aspects.   2. Adopted children—
    Psychology.   I. Rosenberg, Karen F.   II. Title.
    HV875.G776   1998
    155.44′5—dc21   98–11122

British Library Cataloguing in Publication Data is available.

Library of Congress Catalog Card Number: 98–11122
ISBN: 0–89789–827–3 (pbk.)

First published in 1998

Bergin & Garvey, 88 Post Road West, Westport, CT 06881
An imprint of Greenwood Publishing Group, Inc.
www.greenwood.com

Printed in the United States of America

The paper used in this book complies with the
Permanent Paper Standard issued by the National
Information Standards Organization (Z39.48–1984).

10 9 8 7 6 5 4 3 2 1

This paperback is the 1998 version augmented by chapters 8 and 9.

The editors and publisher gratefully acknowledge permission to use the following material:

Excerpts from *Be My Baby*. Copyright © 2000 by Gail Kinn. Used by permission of Artisan, a divi-
sion of Workman Publishing Co., Inc., New York. All rights reserved.

To the children in my life:

Jason Long, Travis Groze,

Amber Groze and Leah Taylor (1988–1994)

—Victor Groza

To my parents, Eva and Milton Rosenberg,

my husband, Roy, and our children—Ezra, Noah, and Caleb

—Karen F. Rosenberg

Contents

Acknowledgments

There are many people to thank for their help in the development of this book. First and foremost, we want to thank the contributors who worked diligently with us through our many revisions and requests. This book would not have happened without their cooperation and willingness to spend the time to write, revise, and revise again.

Second, we would like to thank Theresa Lydonne Wilson and Deborah Horne, who retyped manuscripts when they couldn't be translated by the computer, made copies, mailed revisions, and provided general clerical support. Special thanks to Theresa for her excellent editing and formatting skills.

Third, we would like to thank our colleagues at the Mandel School of Applied Social Sciences, Roth, Stanley and Associates, and the Focus on Adoption Clinical Treatment (FACT) group for their professional nourishment and sustenance.

Fourth, we would like to thank Lynn Taylor from Greenwood Publishing Group for her patience and support. She was helpful in suggesting that we change our time line; she also offered guidance while we finalized the project.

Finally, we want to thank the adoptees, birth parents, and adoptive families we have worked with. They have enlightened us with their stories and journeys.

CLINICAL AND PRACTICE ISSUES IN ADOPTION

1

Treatment Issues of Adoptees Placed as Infants and as Older Children: Similarities and Differences

Victor Groza and Karen F. Rosenberg

Adoption research and clinical literature divides into several poles, depending on whether children were placed for adoption as infants or as older children. In this chapter Victor Groza, Ph.D., and Karen Rosenberg, L.I.S.W., introduce the general ideas that are developed more fully in subsequent chapters. The analysis is an attempt to bridge the separate practice and research areas, accenting the similarities and differences in the two populations of adoptees. The analysis is based on previous clinical and empirical research. The areas compared and contrasted for these two groups of adoptees include the adoption process, family formation, abandonment, separation and loss, identity development, and attachment. Recommendations are made for practitioners working with these adoptees.

For the most part, adoption has been a very successful social arrangement. There are several ways to measure the successes of adoption. Disruption, which means the removal of the child from the adoptive placement prior to finalization, does not occur in most cases. The most commonly used estimate is that about 15% of adoptions disrupt (Barth & Berry, 1988), which means that most adoptions (over 80%) remain intact. However, ranges from 7% to 60% (Barth & Berry, 1988; Groze, 1986; Kagan & Reid, 1986; Rosenthal, Schmidt, & Conner, 1988) have been reported; the range in rates is attributed to the age of the child, with older children who have behavioral and emotional problems experiencing higher rates of disruption. Even with more disruptions for older, special needs children, adoption disruption research suggests that this problem is uncommon and not normative.

In addition to the research on disruption, success can be examined by postlegal adoption outcomes. Several studies support the notion that adoption outcomes are overwhelmingly positive. In a review of 24 studies of infant adoptions, Kadushin and Martin (1988) suggest that 66% of adoptions are successful. They indicate that only about 16% are problematic. In their follow-up of 800 families who adopted older and special needs children, Rosenthal and Groze (1992) reported that parent-child relations were overwhelmingly positive, and 75% of parents were very or mostly positive about the impact of the adoption on the family. In a subsequent longitudinal of families who adopted older and special needs children, Groze (1996) found that 78% of parents reported the adoption to be very or mostly positive, and by the fourth year of the study 69% felt the same way. In the same study, only 8% of the children ended up in out-of-home placements during the course of four years.

While there is much cause for optimism in adoption, there are also some areas of concern. Several studies suggest that adopted children are overrepresented in mental health services (Brinich & Brinich, 1982; McRoy, Grotevant, & Zucher, 1988). Rosenthal and Groze (1992) found that about one-third of families who adopted older and special needs children participated in individual therapy for the child and about one-fourth of families participated in family therapy after placement. Thus, although adoption is decidedly positive, there is some indication that a significant proportion of adoptees may require mental health or other therapeutic intervention. Many mental health and adoption professionals recognize that there are unique clinical issues for adoptees throughout the life cycle (Grabe, 1986; Rosenberg & Groze, 1997; Rosenberg, 1992; Sandmaier, 1988; Winkler, Brown, van Keppel, & Blanchard, 1988). This chapter explores core issues that may require clinical intervention for two specific groups of adoptees. It focuses on those issues that are common when adopted children present themselves for mental health or other therapeutic services.

THE POPULATION OF ADOPTEES

Several different groups of children make up the pool of adoptees. Each group presents some different clinical and treatment issues. One group are those who live with one birth parent and are subsequently adopted by that parent's spouse, who is not otherwise related to the child (a stepparent adoption). In most states, stepparent adoptions are the most numerous (Barth, 1992). A second group are healthy, white infants who are predominantly placed with white, middle-class families. Many of these adoptions are arranged independently, meaning that children are placed directly in an adoptive family without an agency acting as intermediary. Usually, in independent adoptions the primary intermediary is an attorney. Independent adoptions account for 15% to 20% or slightly more of the adoptions that occur (Barth, 1992; Stolley, 1993). A third group are foreign children who are adopted in the United States. Barth (1992) estimates that about 10% of placements are international adoptions, while Stolley (1993) suggests this figure is about 16%. A fourth group are minority children who enter foster care as infants or toddlers, but who age in foster care because the system has not been successful in developing an adoption plan and resource for them in a timely manner. One study (Schwartz, Ortega, Guo, & Fishman, 1994) indicates that a significant proportion of infants in general, and minority infants in particular, do not achieve a permanent placement within four years of initial placement. Many foster children are adopted by their foster family. Fanshel (1979) found that over 70% of foster families responded favorably to adopting their foster child. In one estimate about 40% of finalized adoptions were by former foster parents (Tatara, 1993). Although only about 8% of adoptive placements are transracial (Stolley, 1993), practice wisdom suggests that a significant proportion of transracial adoptions are foster-to-adopt placements (excluding international transracial and transcultural placements). A fifth group are children who have a physical or developmental disability, who may or may not be infants when they become available for adoption. The sixth group is made up of older children who are often victims of abuse or neglect, and who have spent considerable time in the child welfare system; included in this group are children who are members of sibling groups. The last group of adoptees are children who come to the attention of the child welfare system; some of these children are placed in kinship care, and some are subsequently adopted by the relatives or extended family who have been serving as their caretakers.

While there are many groups of children who comprise the pool of adoptees, the adoption research and clinical literature divides into several poles depending on the type of adoption. While comparing and contrasting the issues between all the subgroups of adoptees has merit, it is beyond the scope of one chapter. Drawing on recommendations from the professional community on trying to integrate various pools of adoption knowledge, this chapter was developed to examine treatment issues of those adoptees placed as infants and those placed as older children. The purpose of this chapter is to bridge the separate practice and research areas, accenting the similarities and differences in two populations of adoptees. It is hoped that it will provide the impetus to integrate the research and clinical literature for other groups of adoptees.

Age of the child at placement was chosen as a topic for several reasons. First, the two writers had professional expertise in this area in both research and practice. Second, most of the studies in adoption use age at placement as one variable in their analysis of the different issues. It seems to be the one variable that is consistently mentioned and examined, regardless of the subgroup of adoptee studied. Third, age of the child relates to child development and a life-cycle perspective in examining issues. It is from these perspectives that the chapter was organized. The areas discussed for these two groups of adoptees include the adoption process, family formation, abandonment, separation, loss, identity development, and attachment.

ADOPTION PROCESS

Three issues in the adoption process will be discussed. First, there are actually two systems of adoption. Most infants enter the adoption process differently than do older children. This difference generates separate issues for the adoptees. Second, children's understanding of adoption and the adoption process differs depending on the age of adoptive placement as well as the developmental age of the child. The third issue in the adoption process is postplacement services, which differ by age of adoption. The following section summarizes these differences, and the clinical implications of these differences are highlighted.

Most infant placements are legally voluntary and are made through attorneys and private agencies (Gilles & Kroll, 1991). Historically in infant adoptions, children were chosen for parents who were infertile resulting in a process that was parent-centered, not child-centered. In most of these placements, potential adoptive parents underwent a home study at some point, but not enough attention was given to preparing the parents for the life-long issues in adoption. For many of these couples (single-parent adoption of infants historically was an anomaly), placement resulted in the expectation that the child would "fix the infertility" of the adoptive parent or parents. As is now well known, adoptive placement does not "fix the infertility"; however, it does allow the parents to have the experience of parenting (Pavao, 1992). As issues of infertility erupt throughout the life cycle, adoptive parents may feel the loss of the pregnancy experience, the loss of the fantasized biological child, and the loss of genetic continuity.

These loss issues can have substantial impact for adoptees since the implicit or explicit expectation of the child entering the family is to fix the infertility. Adoptees often feel that they have an enormous role to fill in order to deny the losses that their parents experienced. The child's role is often to collude with the game of "as if"; that is, the adoptee often feels because he/she has been chosen, he/she has to please his/her adoptive parents by being complicit with the illusions and pretending as if he/she were born into the family. However, as Lifton (1994) writes, there is a paradox in infertility and adoption; that is, "the child who rescues adoptive parents from childlessness is also a reminder of their infertility" (p. 27).

For older adoptees, most children enter the system involuntarily. They become available for adoption after efforts at family preservation and family reunification are not successful. In many ways, adoption of older children is more child-centered. Adoptive families are chosen on the basis of their ability to meet the needs of children. Parents often have been involved in preparatory activities before adoptive placement. In many families who adopt older children, infertility is not the overriding reason for adopting. Thus, the issue of loss from infertility has less significance.

There are also differences in how children understand adoption and the adoption process. Adoptees placed as infants understand the process differently at different developmental levels. When children have little or no information about birth families, they can create fantasy and illusion in place of reality. Some feel as if they have never been born. Some feel unreal and invisible. Others report that they are floating in space, ungrounded. They fantasize that their birth mothers are either the princesses or the paupers and may be preoccupied by fantasy life. They may feel like they were given away because they were damaged. Children placed as infants have no conscious memories of life in other family systems; however, family integration issues arise when they figure out they are members of two different family systems (birth and adoptive). Issues around family integration often surface during adolescence when the adoptee is forming identity and has little information on his/her biological family background (Rosenberg & Groze, 1997). This will be discussed later in the chapter.

Many of the older children have spent an extended period in some aspect of the child welfare system. Often, this time results in multiple-familial placements. One consequence of the process of removal from the biological family, placement in foster care, and then movement to adoption is that children must often piece together the sequence of events with little concrete information from the adults involved. Often, moves are not adequately explained to them. Even in instances where they are told why they can't go home or why they are moving, the information is often not fully integrated. Children's understanding about changes comes in waves and is different at different developmental levels; they have to be told and retold, each time adding a different piece of information or presenting the information in a different way. Their memories are not perfect; some older placed children, like some infant adoptees, make up stories or myths to fill the gaps. It is not unusual for some children to develop stories of being kidnapped (Hartman & Laird, 1990). As with infant adoptees, some older placed children develop stories that glorify the birth parents, and on some level view themselves as the problem and the reason they cannot return home to the birth family. This story is perpetuated when the child is removed from one foster family for placement with another foster or to adoptive placement.

In addition to issues surrounding moving, older children must assimilate several family systems and be integrated into a new family system (Pinderhughes & Rosenberg, 1990). This new adoptive family system is often different from both their birth family system and the foster family systems that have been part of their lives. It is less problematic when they are adopted by the foster family. However, there may be issues of loss of the relationship with biological siblings, who may be in a different location, and loss from a lack of contact with extended family members. So, the adoption process can create or accentuate treatment issues in older children, particularly when the issue is how to live and function in a new and different kind of family system.

Finally, there are differences in the adoption process in the postplacement period. For families who adopt infants, there are few postadoption support services, implying that these services are not necessary. With infant placements, lawyers and private agencies are more likely to perpetuate the myth that adoption is a one-time legal event. "Go home and love the baby as if it were your own" is the message that adoptive parents of infants are given.

Agencies tend to have developed more support for families adopting an older child or a child with special needs. There seems to be an implicit message for families that if they adopt an older child, they are deserving of and will need more assistance. Behavior problems are more likely to be viewed as having to do with the child's history (type of and extent of trauma, number of placements, quality of life before leaving the family of origin) and less likely to be attributed to factors that have to do with the adoption or the task of integrating two or more distinct family systems.

For families who adopt infants who later demonstrate special needs, there is more of a tendency to scrutinize the family as if the family is the cause of difficulties with the child. Depending on the training of the therapist, sometimes adoption is not an issue in the treatment if the child who was placed as an infant. That is not to say that family system issues are not part of the problems for both infant and older adoptees, but families receive different messages and different services are available for adoptees entering the family as infants compared to older children.

FAMILY FORMATION ISSUES

Family formation is also affected by whether the child enters the family as an infant or at an older age. However, there are general family formation issues that transcend differences due to age at placement. As part of family formation, families that reject the differences between adoptive parenting and forming a family biologically are at a higher risk for difficulties (Brodzinsky, 1990; Kirk, 1984). The issue of dealing with difference is described by Kirk (1984) and Brodzinsky (1990). They offer three models to describe adoptive families and how they view themselves as adoptive families. First, there are families that reject/deny the differences and create a less open and less reality-based environment. Second, there are families that insist on differences and ascribe blame for difficulties to genetics or preadoptive history (i.e., "the bad seed"). Third, there are families that acknowledge the differences openly, sharing concerns and feelings about their adoptive status.

Depending on the family style of dealing with differences, families who deny or insist on differences are most at risk for difficulties in the life cycle. In addition, families who acknowledge differences are more likely to be involved in support groups and workshops and to pursue early intervention such as outpatient services; these families are less crisis-oriented in their problem-solving skills. Families denying or insisting on difference are more likely to be involved in intensive clinical services such as residential treatment, juvenile court, and mental health systems. Often, they will wait for a crisis before they begin to look for help.

Denying differences results in children growing up in a family system filled with pretending and a disavowal of reality. For example, the denial can make children feel split off or inauthentic when they bring up or confront their parents about the differences. When children do not feel permission to bring up these issues verbally, they often do it behaviorally. Clinicians also collude with the denial of differences when they fail to explore adoption issues when families present themselves for services and/or genograms are completed without including the birth family and placement history of the adopted child (Rosenberg & Groze, 1997).

Some adoptive families want to deny differences by saying to their older children, "Your life starts now," "What is past is past," or "You dealt with that."

These messages imply that children can dissociate or cut off the part of themselves that symbolizes their history, experiences, genes, and biology. Usually this approach spells disaster. It is a red flag for predicting future difficulties in the placement. It is often a companion to "All we need to do is love you; love is enough." With this notion, parents often imagine that the child will be a loving, happy "orphan" willing and grateful to be adopted. Although love is an essential component of a successful adoptive family relationship, it is often not enough. In addition, the expectation of reciprocity early in the relationship will invariably lead to more feelings of loss and disappointment and ultimately an unsatisfying experience. Older children have great difficulty with reciprocity and may take years to give anything back in a positive relationship to the family that adopts them.

In families that insist the child is different, the myth that prevails and perpetuates is the "bad seed theory." This becomes easier for families to do when the kids behave poorly and the only information they receive about the biological family are its problems and dysfunction (alcoholism, child abuse, poverty, etc.). Child welfare workers acknowledge difference, although difference is often interpreted as the birth family was deficient or had significant deficits. The presentation of birth families as bad and adoptive families as good promotes splitting of allegiances and dual identities in the child, as the child belongs to both families (Sorosky, Baran, & Pannor, 1975).

How the family views its identity as an adoptive family affects family formation, family integration, and adoption outcome. To be successful, there must be a sense of entitlement, claiming behavior, integration of multiple family systems, and acknowledgment of differences (Bourguigion & Watson, 1987).

Social work and legal practice have colluded with the denial of difference by sealing records in all adoptions at finalization. In both infant and older child adoptions, records are sealed at finalization. It is at this point that the judicial system amends the birth certificate creating what some adoption specialists call "legal fiction." Some agencies duplicate records for the adoptive family of older children or the family may have access to records before finalization; however, this does not always mean that the adoptee, at some point, has access to that information. Often, children adopted when older know the names and addresses of birth parents as well as of extended family members. In one study (Groze, 1990), over one-third of older and special needs adoptees had contact with members of the extended family after adoptive placement. However, most older placed children do not have contact with siblings or extended family.

With both infant and older adoptees, as part of denying differences, parents develop dreams and expectations about the child or children they adopt. These dreams can develop into high parental expectations for the "dream" or "fantasy" child. These expectations are shaped and reinforced by socioeconomic status, with middle-class and upper-middle-class families holding high aspirations for their children. If the child fails to fulfill expectations, the parents experience yet another loss. Often, at this stage the family may distance themselves in the relationship with the adoptee and begin to insist on differences.

While there are many similarities between the two age groups of adoptees, there are unique issues for older children. Older child adoptees brings into the family their own family system and known separate history. They enter the family with at least one model of family life that they obtained from living with their birth family. Often, their experience with the birth family involves abuse or neglect. One of the first tasks of adoptive families is to integrate a child with his/her own history and values into the existing family. To accomplish family integration, the adoptive family and the family system the adopted child brings to the family must change to develop a third system, much like the experiences of blended families (Carter & McGoldrick, 1988; Pinderhughes & Rosenberg, 1990). When a family system is too rigid, the tasks associated with integration become problematic.

To create familiarity in the new family, it isn't unusual for the child(ren) to promote coalitions and triangulation to diffuse intimacy and increase their control in this family environment (Groze, 1996). Older children may not have developed the interpersonal and social skills to live successfully with others or may not have a very good idea about how families function. This may be particularly true if the child has spent an extended period of time in group or residential care. These children often have questions about boundaries and may not respect personal space, including property. They may hoard items or not place much value on property. Older children may also have issues concerning roles (Reitz & Watson, 1992). Sometimes the issue is role conflict, particularly for the child who has been the parental child. He/she may not be able to make the transition back to the role of a child. There may also be role ambiguity. This may be particularly true for the child who has been in multiple placements and has occupied several role positions. For example, the child may have been the oldest child in the birth family, the youngest in the first foster family, and a middle child in the current adoptive family. Occupying several role positions in several family systems can be very confusing to the child. Some behavior and adjustment of the child to the family system may be an attempt to discover his/her role in the family system.

The fact that so many older children have access to memories about birth families complicates the family formation issues. As families deal with the issue of integration, they follow one of the three models of dealing with difference as outlined above. For families who accept the difference, integration, while no easy task, is usually resolved without the necessity of intervention. It is more difficult to deny the difference when placing older children, especially when placement is transracial or transcultural, but it can happen and is seen in families that do not encourage or allow adoptees access to their birth culture, religion, or ethnicity. Families who adopt older children and insist on the differences are most likely to be the families where the adoption disrupts or dissolves.

ABANDONMENT, SEPARATION, AND LOSS

Adoptees struggle in their own personal style with the fact that they were relinquished from their birth family. They have lost control over their past; that is, they have lost attachment to the family they are connected to genetically and biologically. This loss of control contributes to feelings of abandonment, separation, and loss at critical developmental points throughout their lives.

With infant adoptees, issues of loss and abandonment are often denied because the abandonment happened so early in the child's life. With the denial of the loss also comes a lack of permission to grieve. This denial has been challenged by the "primal wound theory" (Verrier, 1993). According to this theory, separation of a child from the birth mother results in a separation trauma, that is, a fundamental loss of the birth bond with much significance throughout an adoptee's life. Verrier believes that the younger the child when separated, the more profound the loss. Some adoption specialists feel that adoptees placed as infants struggle with attachment issues even more than older children who have had the benefit of an earlier experience of bonding, because there was a disruption of the birth bond at a preverbal stage. Attachment difficulties develop because children have no words to express what was happening to them, yet they experience the loss and separation from the birth mother.

From a psychosocial perspective, adoptees placed as infants begin to realize during latency that in order to have been the "chosen baby," they had to have been "given up" by someone. As they have a growing awareness of what adoption means, they begin to act out more. This acting out needs to be seen as part of the adaptive grieving process (Brodzinsky, 1987). Lifton (1994) presents a theory of "cumulative adoption trauma," which begins when a child is separated from the birth mother. The trauma continues when the child understands that he/she was not born to the adoptive mother. The trauma endures when the child discovers that he/she cannot gain access to information about the birth parents.

To be placed as an older child is to know significant loss. At a minimum, there is the loss of the biological family when a child enters foster care. This loss is often compounded by separation from siblings and extended family members who may have had a significant place in the child's early life. Siblings are frequently separated when one or more of them are placed in foster care. In some locales, it is not unusual for some children to enter foster care while other siblings remain in the family. To be separated from all that is familiar, from family, culture, and community, is to experience a sense of loss and abandonment.

Many older children have experienced loss in a more conscious and traumatic way. As stated previously, many of them are victims of neglect, physical abuse, and sexual abuse. In fact, if it were not for the traumatization from abuse or neglect, they never would have come to the attention of the child welfare system. Victimization leaves children feeling lost and betrayed.

An issue that complicates the ability to grieve and deal with separation and loss for both infant and older adoptees is that many adoptees feel that because they were "saved or rescued," they must be grateful to their adoptive families. Lifton (1988) suggests a splitting occurs into the "good adoptee" and the "bad adoptee." The good adoptee is compliant with the adoptive parents' expectations and appears happy. This behavior may be a defense against fear of further abandonment. The bad adoptee rebels against adoptive parents. This behavior reflects the adoptee's feeling that he/she must be damaged to have been given up for adoption. The good adoptee may evidence internalizing difficulties (shy, withdrawal behavior) while the bad adoptee is the acter-outer who behaves provocatively. These kinds of behavior (opposition, defiance, aggressive, impulsive or withdrawn, compliant, clingy) are different styles of responding to the pain and anxiety that children feel about loss and abandonment. One type of behavior pushes to be rejected again but this time when it is in their control. The other style guards against being rejected. Both styles of behavior are about the fear of rejection and abandonment and are seen in clinical populations of both infant and older adoptees.

IDENTITY DEVELOPMENT

Identity "provides the ability to experience one's self as something that has continuity and sameness and to act accordingly" (Erikson, 1950, p. 38). Historically, adoption status is one dynamic thought to influence the identity of adopted children. However, several studies (Benson, Sharma, & Roehlkepartain, 1994; Shireman, 1988; Shireman & Johnson, 1976, 1985, 1986; Stein & Hoopes, 1985) concluded that there is little evidence that adoptive status unfavorably affects identity formation. Although research has failed to consistently provide evidence that adoption negatively affects identity, qualitative and clinical work suggests that adoption status does affect identity in adoptees. From a developmental perspective, the task of both kinds of adoptees is to integrate two sets of parental identities into a cohesiveness of self. Both kinds of adoptees have to integrate the paradox of having a biological parent who gave birth to them but could not raise them and an adoptive parent who raised them but did not give birth to them (Rosenberg, 1992). Some infant adoptees have difficulty developing a sense of self when information about their past and their genetics are hidden behind a legal curtain. The lack of information that adoptees have about their biological origins results in a sense of "genealogical bewilderment" (Sants, 1965).

Older placed children also can suffer from a type of "genealogical bewilderment," in part because they lack information but also because they have experiences in multiple family systems. In addition to being a part of multiple family systems, their experiences in these different systems have not been uniform. For example, they were "abused" children in their biological family, the "foster" child in the foster family, and now the "special needs" child in the adoptive family. As part of their experiences in these various family systems they have occupied assorted formal and informal role positions. Thus, as they begin to try to sort out their identity, they may be overwhelmed by the question, "who am I?"

Related to the issue of genealogical bewilderment is the concept of "hereditary ghost" (Frisk, 1964). Hereditary ghosts are members of the birth family who are not physically present and may be unknown, but who can become powerful forces in the dynamics of the family. The reality is that "birth families are a part of the adoptive family whether they are physically present or not" (Campbell, Silverman, & Patti, 1991, p. 334). Hereditary ghosts are a more covert issue with infant placements. Because of the secrecy of the closed adoption system with infants, the "ghosts" (i.e., the birth family) are often felt or implied but not talked about. In older child placements, everyone knows that the child was removed from the family of origin due to neglect or abuse and there is generally acknowledgment of different genetic background.

The denial of the existence of the biological family has a long history in adoption practice perhaps in order to make adoption more acceptable. Professionals who worked in traditional adoption practice contributed to denial by creating anonymity through closed records, amended birth certificates, and the disclosure of limited information to the adoptive family (Rosenberg & Groze, 1997). They propagated the myth of "as if"; this myth indulges the family's fantasy to treat the child "as if" the child was born to the adoptive parents. Older children are in a sense more empowered because families can rarely deny the existence of the birth family; however, there may not be permission to talk about them. The older adoptee is often an active part of the adoption process through the creation of life books, visits with the adoptive family before placement, continued relationship with foster families, and maybe even a continued relationship with select members of the extended family system. They go to court with their adopted parents, talk to the judge, and agree to be adopted. It is important to keep in mind, whether the child is adopted as an infant or when older, that "a family never adopts just a child . . . but rather a whole new extended family system" (Bourguigion & Watson, 1987).

Identity difficulties can develop if an adoptee's lifetime is built on denial, secrets, illusions, and mystery (Winkler et al., 1988). Identity confusion contributes to difficulties in forming intimate relationships and developing a positive self-concept. Identity confusion can promote feelings of alienation and isolation, feeling different, and not having a sense of belonging. The lack of knowledge of who one is, in a genealogical sense, can affect the development of one's identity and one's ability to project into the future.

ATTACHMENT

Attachment is the term for the social, psychological, and affective relationship between a child and one or more specific persons with whom it interacts regularly; it is a mutual and reciprocal emotional connection between a child and a caregiver (Hirschi, 1969; Wilson & Herrnstein, 1985). Attachment serves a variety of functions. It provides the connection, or bridge, across which parental ideas, values, and expectations are passed (Hirschi, 1969). It also serves as the basis for separation and individuation as well as for the development of self-concept (Bowlby, 1988). Factors such as genetic predisposition, parenting/caregiving behavior during the first 18 months to two years, placement history, and the attachment history of the adoptive parents have an effect on attachment. Based on early life experiences with their caregivers, children develop a cognitive model of themselves, their caregivers, and the world around them (Bowlby, 1969, 1973, 1988). This cognitive model is then transferred to other relationships. To develop secure attachments and confidence about relationships, children must receive sensitive, nurturing care (Carlson, Cicchetti, Barnett & Braunwald, 1989). Difficulties in attachment develop when caregivers are unresponsive or unavailable to meet the child's needs or are otherwise rejecting or hurtful in meeting the needs of the child.

Attachment theory emphasizes the role of a child's birth parents in shaping the child's ability to form emotional bonds (Bowlby, 1988; Fahlberg, 1979). For adopted children, attachment theory suggests that the preplacement history of the adopted child can influence later adoptive family relationships (McRoy et al., 1988).

Some difficulties have been noted in the capacity of adopted infants to form different levels of attachment to their adoptive caregivers and other significant figures, both immediately after adoption and for over a decade for some children (Yarrow & Goodwin, 1973; Yarrow, Goodwin, Manheimer, & Milowe, 1973; Yarrow & Kein, 1980). These difficulties in attachment are more pronounced for children who spent some time being reared in institutional settings (Tizard, 1977; Tizard & Hodges, 1978; Tizard & Joseph, 1970; Tizard & Rees, 1974, 1975). Yet others have found no significant attachment difficulties. Singer, Brodzinsky, Ramsay, Steir, and Waters (1985) assessed the quality of attachment relationships in interracial adoptions, intraracial adoptions, and nonadoptive mother-infant pairs. Results indicated no differences between the groups in mother-infant attachment.

Yarrow and Klein (1980) found that infants who moved from a high-quality foster home to an adoptive home with less adequate care demonstrated significant disturbances after the move. Conversely, infants who moved to an adoptive placement with improved maternal care were less likely to evidence disturbances. While any change can be disconcerting, the consequences of change can be mitigated by the quality of parenting. The authors found that older infants experienced more difficulties than younger infants with the change. In addition, separation difficulties associated with adoptive placement are less problematic than separation that results in institutional or hospital placement (Yarrow & Goodwin, 1973).

It is not unusual for older children, many of whom have lengthy histories of abusive or neglectful treatment as well as frequent moves, to manifest attachment difficulties. Barth and Berry (1988) indicate that behaviors indicative of attachment generally increase over time when comparing the first three months of placement to the three months preceding finalization or disruption. In addition, children who had developed secure attachments to prior caretakers experienced more stable placements than did children who had not developed such attachments.

A preadoptive history of abuse or neglect makes it more difficult for children to attach to new caregivers. Groze and Rosenthal (1993) found that attachment was most positive for adopted children with no abuse history and least positive for children with multiple-abuse histories. If children experience frequent moves in foster care, with each loss of family most children experience greater difficulty in "bonding" with subsequent families. Thus, both the child's history before placement and history within the child welfare system can compound the losses he/she experiences and negatively affect attachment behaviors, self-esteem, and capacity to cope. Many older adoptees have specific attachment difficulties, such as lying and stealing, school problems, indiscriminate relationships, delayed conscience development, difficulty expressing feelings, and feeling different.

Attachment theory and research, particularly as it relates to adopted children, needs more refinement and development (see Groze, 1992; Groze & Rosenthal, 1993). There appear to be issues that place some adopted children, regardless of age at placement, at risk for attachment difficulties. There are life experiences of older children who are placed for adoption that place them at high risk for attachment problems. It is not adoption per se that places children more at risk for attachment problems. Rather, genetic predisposition, parenting/caregiving behavior during the first 18 months to two years, placement history, and the attachment history of the adoptive parents have an effect on patterns of attachment.

RECOMMENDATIONS

As a general orientation, adoption services should be child-centered. The only way to assure such a system is to move to agency-based adoption practice, whether in the public or private sector. Families should not have to pay a fee to adopt a child; when families pay fees there is a conflict of interest over whether the needs of the consumer-family or product-child are being met. Private-attorney-arranged adoptions are not well regulated and differ from state to state. To assure that the best interest of the child becomes the guiding principle, agency practice may be the best method of assuring the adoption is child-centered. This would represent a shift from the current operation of most infant adoptions.

Adoptive families need to be prepared for adoption before placement and be given access to an array of adoption services throughout the life cycle. Postadoption services need not be mandated, but should be accessible and affordable for adoptive families. Prevention activities need to target families adopting both infants and older children. Practitioners need to be trained to be sensitive not only to adoption issues, but also to unique issues faced by children and families. These clinical issues include loss and trauma, rejection, guilt, shame, negative self-concept, low self-esteem, identity confusion, isolation, and unresolved grief (Winkler et al., 1988).

The adoption process needs to have the option of being more open (Baran & Pannor, 1993; Berry, 1993). Adoptees have difficulty planning the future when they have little or no information about their past. Adoptees talk about their feelings of alienation, isolation, and disconnectedness. Practitioners need to be trained to assist in search and reunion activities. Training is particularly critical when these activities are undertaken by adoptees who were victims of abuse or neglect. While many adoptees do not search, some do and others express a desire to do so. Clinicians also need to be knowledgeable about post-reunion issues in working with adoptees.

In regard to family intervention, most therapists agree that family secrets and cutoffs have powerful effects on individuals and families. Often, they fail to see these issues in adoptive families. Genograms are completed with adoptive families without diagraming the birth families as part of the history. There are a variety of valuable tools that help adoptees integrate their continuous sense of self, including placement genograms (McMillen & Groze, 1994), life maps (Pinderhughes & Rosenberg, 1990), and famographs (Anderson, 1986). However, many of these techniques are not routinely taught to and employed by mental health, adoption, and child welfare practitioners. Professionals need to become acquainted with these tools and integrate them into their practice.

Some families need help accepting a different model of family life. This includes helping parents recognize that there is sometimes a need for the adoptee to take an alternate course in development (Rosenberg, 1992). A child placed when older may need more structure and a more emotionally close family environment than a typical adolescent. Families may need help in normalizing their feelings, losses, and expectations. Many adoptive families need help in getting beyond denial and the "as if" game. Families may need help dealing with genealogical bewilderment and hereditary ghosts. To do this a therapist must be able to deconstruct the past for the child and the family and put it in perspective. Therapists must be aware of the myths that occur in adoptive families. They need to be able to acknowledge and challenge family myths, including creating new constructs and paradigms that are more functional and serve to strengthen the adoptive family.

In addition to addressing clinical issues, therapists need to work with families to create rituals to celebrate adoption in family life (Rosenberg, 1993). There are several good sources for helping families learn about adoption rituals such as placement-day ceremonies (Severson, 1991). In addition, there are periodicals and newsletters that focus on multiple aspects of adoptive family life such as the *Adoption Therapist Journal, Adopted Child Newsletter, Adoptalk,* and *The Roundtable.*

Regarding the adoptee, adoptees benefit from working on grief and loss issues. The works of Fahlberg (1979) and Jewett (1982) are helpful resources in working with children about loss. Almost any transition, such as starting school, puberty, or divorce, can stir up issues of loss and grief. Children need to be given permission to grieve. Parents and clinicians need to keep in mind that grieving may show itself as acting-out behavior. As part of dealing with loss and grief, children may need to make contact with siblings or extended family members. This may be particularly true for older adoptees who lived with siblings and who were subsequently separated from them.

When doing an assessment with an adoptee, it is always important to ask: Is this an adoption-related difficulty, or is it developmental, or is it an interaction of both? Adoptees may need help in figuring out who they are and in assimilating an identity from more than one family system. Helping the infant adoptee can be more complicated. The infant adoptee has no conscious memory of the mother, only somatic memories or feelings. This can result in a sense of loss and an emptiness, a feeling of not belonging. This is why a search for birth relatives can be so important. A search for the lost mother is really about a search for the lost self, about feeling more whole and more complete (Lifton, 1988). Search should not be seen as pathological. In addition, many of the tools referred to above (i.e., placement genogram, famograph) also are good tools for helping children deal with abandonment, separation, and loss. They serve multiple purposes when applied to adoption issues.

Children, regardless of age at placement, benefit from a lifebook. For the adoptee placed as an infant, the lifebook could be the link to the past that is often denied in the current system of closed adoption. For the older child, the lifebook is a scrapbook that can serve as a reference point as the child builds and rebuilds his/her identity in the context of the past. For both kinds of adoptees, the lifebook may provide the information they need to develop a cohesive identity throughout their lives. In addition, it could be useful if they decide to search for birth relatives later in life.

New models of attachment need to be developed that take into account the unique attachment issues of adopted children. There is a need for new attachment theory development for older children. Most attachment theory and research is grounded in infant and toddler studies; although these studies are helpful, they do not provide all the information in this complicated issue. Some models of clinical work with children with attachment disorders have become popular over the last decade, including holding therapy, rage induction therapy, and regression work (Cline, 1979; Welch, 1988). However, no outcome studies have been conducted on the efficacy of these techniques.

CONCLUSION

This chapter focused on the difficulties encountered by some adoptees and attempted to analyze similarities and differences in the children adopted as infants and children adopted when older. There is significant overlap between the two populations and similar interventions can be used when working with adoptees, no matter the age at placement. The following adoption resources are recommended for those readers interested in learning more about the unique and similar issues for adoptees placed as infants and placed as older children:

Adoptalk
North American Council on Adoptable Children
1821 University Avenue, Suite N-498
St. Paul, MN 55104

Adopted Child Newsletter
105 East Second Street
Moscow, ID 83843

Adoption Quarterly, Innovations in Community and Clinical Practice, Theory and Research
The Haworth Press Inc.
10 Alice Street
Binghamton, NY 13904-7981

Adoption Therapist Journal
House of Tomorrow Productions
209 McKinney Avenue, #200
Dallas, TX 75205

The Roundtable
Journal of the National Resource Center for Special Needs Adoption
P.O. Box 337
Chelsea, MI 48118

REFERENCES

Anderson, J. (1986). Holding therapy: A way of helping unattached children. In P. F. Grabe (Ed.), *Adoption resources for mental health professionals* (pp. 62–69). Mercer, PA: Mental Health Adoption Therapy Project.

Baran, A., & Pannor, R. (1993). Perspectives on open adoption. In I. Schulman (Ed.), *The future of children* (pp. 119–124). Los Altos, CA: Center for the Future of Children.

Barth, R. P. (1992). Adoption. In P. J. Pecora, J. K. Whittaker, A. N. Maluccio, with R. P. Barth, & R. D. Plotnick (Eds.), *The child welfare challenge: Policy, practice, and research* (pp. 361–400). New York: Aldine De Gruyter.

Barth, R. P., & Berry, M. (1988). *Adoption and disruption: Rates, risks, and response.* New York: Aldine De Gruyter.

Benson, P. L., Sharma, A. R., & Roehlkepartain, E. C. (1994). *Growing up adopted: A portrait of adolescents and their families.* Minneapolis, MN: Search Institute.

Berry, M. (1993). Risks and benefits of open adoption. In I. Schulman (Ed.), *The future of children*, (pp. 125–138). Los Altos, CA: Center for the Future of Children.

Bourguigion, J.P., & Watson, K. (1987). *After adoption: A manual for professionals working with adoptive families.* Chicago, IL: Department of Children and Family Services.

Bowlby, J. (1969). *Attachment and loss: Attachment.* New York: Basic Books.

Bowlby, J. (1973). *Attachment and loss: Separation, anxiety and anger.* New York: Basic Books.

Bowlby, J. (1988). *A secure base: Clinical applications of attachment theory.* Routledge, London: A Tavistock Professional Book.

Brinich, P. M., & Brinich, E. B. (1982). Adoption and adaptation. *Journal of Nervous and Mental Disease, 170,* 489–493.

Brodzinsky, D. (1987). Adjustment to adoption: A psychosocial perspective. *Clinical Psychology Review, 7,* 25–47.

Brodzinsky, D. (1990). A stress and coping model of adoption adjustment. In Brodzinsky, D. & Schecter, M. (Eds.), *The psychology of adoption* (pp. 3–24). New York: Oxford University Press.

Campbell, L., Silverman, P., & Patti, P. (1991). Reunions between adoptees and birth parents: The adoptees' experience. *Social Work, 36*(4), 329–335.

Carlson, V., Cicchetti, D., Barnett, D., & Braunwald, K. (1989). Disorganized/disoriented attachment relationships in maltreated infants. *Developmental Psychology, 25*(4), 525–531.

Carter, B., & McGoldrick, M. (1988). Overview: The changing family life cycle—A framework for family therapy. In B. Carter & M. McGoldrick (Eds.), *The changing family life cycle* (2nd ed.)(pp. 3–18). New York: Gardner Press.

Cline, F. (1979). *Understanding and treating difficult children and their parents.* Evergreen, CO: Evergreen Consultants in Human Behavior.

Erikson, E. (1950). *Childhood and society.* New York: Norton.

Fahlberg, V. (1979). *Helping children when they must move.* Detroit, MI: Department of Social Services.

Fanshel, D. (1979). *Computerized information for child welfare: Foster children and their foster parents.* New York: Columbia University School of Social Work.

Frisk, M. (1964). Identity problems and confused conceptions of the genetic ego in adopted children during adolescence. *Acta Paedo Psychiatrica, 31*, 6–12.

Gilles, T., & Kroll, J. (1991). *Barriers to same race placement.* St. Paul, MN: North American Council on Adoptable Children.

Grabe, P. F. (ed.). (1986). *Adoption resources for mental health professionals.* Mercer, PA: Mental Health Adoption Therapy Project.

Groze, V. (1986). Special needs adoption. *Children and Youth Services Review, 8*, 81–91.

Groze, V. (1990). Subsidized adoption in Iowa: A study of adoptive families and special needs children. Part I: The family's response. Part II: The child's response. Prepared for the State of Iowa, Department of Human Services, Des Moines.

Groze, V. (1992). Adoption, attachment and self-concept. *Child and Adolescent Social Work Journal, 9*(2), 169–191.

Groze, V. (1996). *Successful adoptive families: A longitudinal study of special needs adoption.* Westport, CT: Greenwood Publishing.

Groze, V., & Rosenthal, J. (1993). Attachment theory and the adoption of children with special needs. *Social Work Research and Abstracts, 29*(2), 513.

Hartman, A., & Laird, J. (1990). Family treatment after adoption: Common themes. In D. Brodzinsky & M. Schecter (Eds.), *The psychology of adoption* (pp. 221–239). New York: Oxford University Press.

Hirschi, T. (1969). *Causes of delinquency.* Berkeley: University of California Press.

Jewett, C. L. (1982). *Helping children cope with separation and loss.* Cambridge, MA: The Harvard Common Press.

Kadushin, A., & Martin, J. (1988). *Child welfare services* (4th ed.). New York: Macmillan.

Kagan, R. M., & Reid, W. J. (1986). Critical factors in the adoption of emotionally disturbed youth. *Child Welfare, 65*, 63–74.

Kirk, D. H. (1984). *Shared fate: A theory and method of adoptive relationships* (2nd ed.). Port Angeles, WA: Ben Simeon Publications.

Lifton, B. J. (1988). *Lost and found: The adoption experience.* New York: Harper & Row.

Lifton, B. J. (1994). *Journey of the adopted self.* New York: Basic Books.

McMillen, J. C., & Groze, V. (1994). Using placement genograms in child welfare practice. *Child Welfare, 22*(4), 307–318.

McRoy, R. G., Grotevant, H., & Zurcher, S. (1988). *Emotional disturbance in adopted adolescents.* New York: Praeger.

Pavao, J. (1992). Normative crises in the development of the adoptive family. *Adoption Therapist, 3*(2), 1–4.

Pinderhughes, E. E., & Rosenberg, K. (1990). Family bonding with high risk placements: A therapy model that promotes the process of becoming a family. In L. M. Glidden (Ed.), *Formed families: Adoption of children with handicaps* (pp. 209–230). New York: Haworth Press.

Reitz, M., & Watson, K. W. (1992). *Adoption and the family system.* New York: The Guilford Press.

Rosenberg, E. (1992). *The adoption life cycle.* New York: The Free Press.

Rosenberg, K. (1993). Healing our losses. *Adoption Therapist, 4*(2), 4–9.

Rosenberg, K., & Groze, V. (1997). The impact of secrecy and denial in adoption: Practice and treatment issues. *Families and Society, 78*(5), 522–530.

Rosenthal, J. A., & Groze, V. G. (1992). *Special needs adoption: A study of intact families.* New York: Praeger.

Rosenthal, J. A., Schmidt, D., & Conner, J. (1988). Predictors of special needs adoption disruption: An exploratory study. *Children and Youth Services Review, 10*, 101–117.

Sandmaier, M. (1988). *When love is not enough.* Washington, DC: Child Welfare League of America.

Sants, H. (1965). Genealogical bewilderment in children with substitute parents. *Child Adoption, 47*, 32–42.

Schwartz, I., Ortega, R., Guo, S., & Fishman, G. (1994, September). Infants in nonpermanent placement. *Social Service Review*, 405–416.

Severson, R. (1991). *Adoption: Charms and rituals for healing.* Dallas, TX: House of Tomorrow Productions.

Shireman, J. (1988). *Growing up adopted: An examination of some major issues.* Chicago, IL: Chicago Child Care Society.

Shireman, J., & Johnson, P. (1976, March). Single persons as adoptive parents. *Social Service Review, 50*(1), 103–116.

Shireman, J., & Johnson, P. (1985). Single parent adoptions: A longitudinal study. *Children and Youth Services Review, 7*(4), 321–334.

Shireman, J., & Johnson, P. (1986 May/June). A longitudinal study of black adoptions: Single parent, transracial, and traditional. *Social Work, 31*(3), 172–176.

Singer, L. M., Brodzinsky, D. M., Ramsay, D., Steir, M., & Waters, E. (1985). Mother-infant attachment in adoptive families. *Child Development, 56*, 1543–1551.

Sorosky, A. D., Baran, A., & Pannor, R. (1975). Identity conflicts in adoptees. *American Journal of Orthopsychiatry, 45*(1), 18–27.

Stein, L. M., & Hoopes, J. L. (1985). *Identity formation in the adopted adolescent.* New York: Child Welfare League of American.

Stolley, K. S. (1993). Statistics on adoption in the United States. In I. Schulman (Ed.), *The future of children* (pp. 26–42). Los Altos, CA: Center for the Future of Children.

Tatara, T. (1993). *Characteristics of children in substitute and adoptive care: A statistical summary of the VCIS National Child Welfare Data Base.* Washington, DC: American Public Welfare Association.

Tizard, B. (1977). *Adoption: A second chance.* New York: Free Press.

Tizard, B., & Hodges, J. (1978). The effect of early institutional rearing on the development of eight-year-old children. *Journal of Child Psychology and Psychiatry, 19,* 99–118.

Tizard, B., & Joseph, A. (1970). Cognitive development of young children in residential care: The study of children aged 24 months. *Journal of Child Psychology and Psychiatry, 11,* 177–186.

Tizard, B., & Rees, J. (1974). A comparison of the effects of adoption, restoration to the natural mother, and continued institutionalization on the cognitive development of four-year-old children. *Child Development, 45,* 92–99.

Tizard, B., & Rees, J. (1975). The effect of early institutional rearing on the behavior problems and affectional relationships of four-year-old children. *Journal of Child Psychology and Psychiatry, 16,* 61–74.

Verrier, N. (1993). *The primal wound: Understanding the adopted child.* Baltimore, MD: Gateway Press

Welch, M. (1988). *Holding Time.* New York: Century.

Wilson, J. Q., & Herrnstein, R. J. (1985). *Crime and human nature.* New York: Simon & Schuster.

Winkler, R., Brown, D., van Keppel, M., & Blanchard, A. (1988). *Clinical practice in adoption.* New York: Pergamon Press.

Yarrow, L. J., & Goodwin, M. S. (1973). The immediate impact of separation: Reactions of infants to a change in mother figure. In L. J. Stone, H. T. Smith, & L. B. Murphy (Eds.), *The competent infant: Research and commentary* (pp. 1032–1040). New York: Basic Books.

Yarrow, L. J., Goodwin, M. S., Manheimer, H., & Milowe, I. D. (1973). Infancy experiences and cognitive and personality development at 10 years. In L. J. Stone, H. T. Smith, & L. B. Murphy (Eds.), *The competent infant: Research and commentary* (pp. 1274–1281). New York: Basic Books.

Yarrow, L. J., & Klein, R. P. (1980). Environmental discontinuity associated with transition from foster to adoptive homes. *International Journal of Behavioral Development, 3,* 311–322.

2

Infertility and Adoption

Regina Kupecky and Karen J. Anderson

In this chapter, Regina Kupecky, L.S.W., and Karen J. Anderson, M.S.W., offer an overview of infertility, including treatment options, clinical issues, and implications for adoption practice. As little research has been done in this area, they have relied on practice wisdom to examine parallel and different issues surrounding infertility and adoption for families adopting infants and for families adopting older children.

INTRODUCTION

Infertility is an issue that affects adoption, whether it is an infant, older child, or intercountry placement. Much is written about how couples need to resolve their infertility issues before adoption (Fleming & Burry, 1989). Daly (1990) challenges this notion and suggests that while some couples need to experience a sense of infertility closure before they are ready for adoption, other couples experience infertility and adoption in a concurrent manner.

Infertility is about loss—the loss of the ability to conceive children. Like all issues involving loss, dealing with this problem is a lifetime task that is never completely resolved. It can emerge at anniversaries (i.e., the date of a miscarriage or abortion), at life-cycle events (i.e., sister or adopted daughter becomes pregnant or gives birth), at the onset of menopause, and/or on specific holidays, such as Mother's Day. It also changes over time; how a person feels about infertility at 28 is different than how he or she feels at age 48. Infertility can be painful in different ways at different times.

WHAT IS INFERTILITY?

Infertility comprises two categories. Primary infertility is generally described by the medical community as the failure to conceive or carry a pregnancy to term after one year of trying to get pregnant (Menning, 1988). Secondary infertility is the inability of previously fertile individuals to conceive after six months (Corson, 1990). Often, infertility is confused with sterility or impotency. Conception is impossible if a person is sterile. Sterility can result from accidents, diseases—such as ovarian, testicular, or cervical cancer—hysterectomies, undeveloped gonads, or other serious medical conditions of men and women. Impotency, which is found in the male population only, is the inability to achieve or sustain an erection. Impotency is associated with infertility, since erection and ejaculation are essential to sperm production and fertilization of the egg. Impotency can be caused by medical disorders, drug use, and, less frequently, psychological factors. Thus, while impotency results in de facto infertility, they are not the same thing.

Until recently, reproduction was a medical mystery. It was determined in the mid-nineteenth century that sterility could be a male problem (Greil, 1991). An understanding of the menstrual fertility cycle came about in the twentieth century. It was in the 1960s, with the introduction of the birth control pill and the legalization of abortion, that women began to believe that they could take charge of their reproduction. Infertility, seldom discussed in sexual education courses, becomes a control issue for couples who thought they were in control of their reproduction.

The process of conception, though seemingly uncomplicated, is a complex series of events. However, a pregnancy carried to completion is often taken for granted. Considering all the elements necessary for conception and a safe, healthy pregnancy, it is less than a certainty. Reproduction is regulated by chemicals called hormones. These hormones are responsible for releasing the eggs and preparing the uterus for the fertilized egg. During the cycle, the female's egg, no larger than the head of a pin, travels through the fallopian tubes and is fertilized by the sperm. The egg must be fertilized within 24 hours of ovulation. The egg travels through the fallopian tube and implants itself in the wall of the uterus, which has changed to become an ideal environment for conception and development. Conception is possible only four or five days during the month.

Often, people who are not interested in reproduction may not know they are infertile and just assume that their birth control methods work.

One couple shared that they used the rhythm method and had no children for seven years. Their friends, using the same Catholic Church–approved methods, were all pregnant. They couldn't understand why their friends couldn't control themselves and use the method successfully. They would tease, "Can't you count?" Like all people they were horrified to learn it was not that their birth control worked so well, but their reproductive systems didn't work at all. Their "success" at birth control became their "failure" to reproduce.

An interesting facet of infertility is that it is not a problem unless the couple want to become pregnant. Thus, if the female has a hysterectomy at age 16 and, as an adult, never has a desire to parent, she does not have an infertility problem. Likewise, if a man has no sperm due to a genetic problem or an illness that renders him sterile, he does not have a fertility problem unless he desires to produce biologically related offspring.

Thus defined, it is important to understand who is affected by infertility and the reasons why one may become infertile.

WHO IS AFFECTED BY INFERTILITY?

According to the National Center for Health Statistics, 5.3 million, or 18.5%, of all couples have fertility problems. This represents a 14.4% increase since 1965. One in every 6 or 7 couples trying to conceive is infertile or have fertility problems (Menning, 1988). The number rises to 1 out of every 4 among women 40 to 44 years of age (Rosenbaum, 1995).

Given the requirements for a successful conception, problems may occur at any time during the process. Sperm motility, sperm count, hormones, ovulation, age, and disease are frequent causes of infertility. If a woman does not become pregnant, many people will believe that she has a fertility problem. It has only been recently that popular literature and media reports have publicized the possibility that the infertile person in a relationship is the male, and not the female. It is a misconception that infertility is a problem that exclusively affects women. In approximately 80% of infertility cases, one partner would be able to conceive if paired with a likewise fertile partner. In 20% of the cases, both partners have some form of fertility problem.

Male infertility is most frequently caused by low sperm count and/or poor sperm motility/mobility. A normal sperm count is approximately 40 million per milliliter; 20 million is considered to be on the low end for fertility. A normal ejaculation contains between 2 and 5 milliliters of sperm. Sperm motility refers to the ability of the sperm to swim in seminal fluid through the female reproductive tract. Although some men have high sperm counts, their sperm has poor motility, being unable to reach the egg, thus causing infertility. On the other hand, men with low sperm counts and good motility are usually fertile (Corson, 1990; Wood & Westmore, 1984). Other factors, such as a man's age, the sperm's pH, exposure to radiation, disease, trauma, drug use, and hormones, may also lead to male infertility.

Female infertility is most frequently caused by failure to ovulate, endometriosis, obstructed fallopian tubes, sexually transmitted diseases, or age. Age is perhaps the greatest cause of infertility. Since many couples are pursuing careers and marrying at a later age than in previous generations, they often delay having children. At age 38, a woman's chances of successful conception begin to decline; by the time she reaches the age of 40, the odds of becoming pregnant have declined dramatically. Most women will produce approximately two million eggs in a lifetime. Beginning at puberty the number of eggs begins to decline. As the number of eggs decreases, so does the quality, or health, of the remaining eggs (Rosenbaum, 1995).

Endometriosis, another major factor in female infertility, occurs when pieces of the uterus lining (called endometrium), which change during menstruation, break away from the uterus and attach to the surfaces of other organs. Each month as the body signals the endometrium to grow, these pieces grow as well. This condition can result in painful internal bleeding that leads to infertility (Corson, 1990). Endometriosis is frequently referred to as a "career woman's disease" because it tends to affect middle- to upper-income Caucasian women in their thirties.

Sexually transmitted disease is the last major factor in infertility. The sexual revolution of the 1960s led to increased sexual activity and to an increase in sexually transmitted diseases for both men and women, and pelvic infections in women. The increase in pelvic infections led to an increase in tubal scarring and blockages, subsequently resulting in infertility. Infections secondary to contraceptive devices, such as the intrauterine device (IUD), have also been associated with increased pelvic infections, resulting in scarring and blockages. However, researchers believe that the presence of an IUD enhances the risk of infection, but does not cause infection (Corson, 1990).

Perhaps the most frustrating diagnosis for the infertile couple is "unexplained infertility," which occurs in about 10% of cases. After exhaustive routines of semen samples, laparoscopies, temperature records, and medication, it can be devastating for the infertile couple to be told the cause of infertility is unknown. When there is no diagnosis or clear-cut cause for infertility, it is often more difficult for the couple to have closure on infertility. A specific diagnosis often accompanies a specific treatment or cure, if such is possible. New studies have shown that at least 50% of couples who have not conceived will conceive in 5.7 years. The news is even better for women experiencing secondary infertility. At least 50% of women who have been given no reason for their infertility are likely to conceive in 2.7 years (Johnston, 1994).

WHAT ARE THE TREATMENT OPTIONS AND COSTS?

Most couples do not seek medical help for infertility. According to Greil (1991), only about 44% of infertile couples seek medical intervention. The reason for this can be a social class issue: poor people and uninsured working people do not have insurance plans or financial resources to seek medical help for fertility problems. It can also be a value or religious belief that, if pregnancy doesn't occur, then this was meant to be. Medical intervention can be seen as an attempt to interfere with fate, harmony, or God's will.

When a couple explores the choices they have to deal with in infertility, Johnston (1994) writes, "there are few right or wrong answers in weighing options [for medical treatment]. What seems right for one individual may be wrong for another patient with a similar diagnosis. No one can or should make these decisions for you. Partners may find it helpful to ask others for advice, but ultimately you must decide together what will work for you. The most important thing here is that you remain committed to *deciding together* what to do next" (p. 121).

When a couple first experiences an inability to conceive, well-meaning family members and friends often will advise the wife to relax, the husband to wear boxer shorts, get more rest, eat a healthy diet, go on a vacation, or stop thinking so much about having a child, and it will just happen naturally. While good intentioned, this advice rarely results in a pregnancy. When a couple makes a decision to seek professional help or advice, they usually consult their family physician or their obstetrician/gynecologist. In most cases, the couple will be told to continue trying and return in several months if they are not successful. When they return—to a doctor who does not specialize in infertility—the wife will be given instructions to chart her body temperature (to predict ovulation, the most fertile time of the month) and start on fertility drugs. When this produces nothing but diminishing hope, the couple is then referred to a fertility specialist or clinic.

There are many types of fertility clinics: those that are associated with major medical centers, those that are free-standing, and those that are part of a chain. They serve hundreds of patients each year. The costs for infertility assessment and treatment range from $250 to $13,000. Only about half of those seeking treatment have coverage through their health insurance plans. The average patient may spend $2,000 on fertility hormone drugs and between $8,000 and $10,000 for an in vitro fertilization procedure.

A typical visit to a fertility specialist includes a physical exam, a complete medical and social history evaluation, including questions about health, previous and current treatment, life-style, and sexual activity. Generally, the least invasive tests will be completed first, for example, blood work and urinalysis, physical exams, a sperm analysis. Then more complicated, costly, and invasive procedures are pursued, including a hysterosalpingography (dye and X-ray of the fallopian tubes and uterus) and a postcoital test (a sample of mucus is taken from the woman one to four hours after intercourse).

Often, couples experience inhumane treatment and embarrassing situations at fertility clinics. Most men are not thrilled when given a cup and told to go into the bathroom and return with a sample of their sperm. Women are concerned about the discomfort of the physical examination. Questions about the frequency, position, and duration of sex, previous sexual partners, and previous abortions are also embarrassing. However, as uncomfortable as the first step in this process may be, the next steps are even more invasive.

The next step usually begins with painful shots of hormones to induce the female's body to produce multiple eggs. Often, the partner is asked to give these shots. Next is the recommendation for treatment, which will vary depending on the clinic. The three most common forms of assisted reproductive technologies are intrauterine insemination (IUI), invitro fertilization (IVF), and gamete intrafallopian transfer (GIFT). These three means of assisted reproduction can become complex issues for the infertile couple, as they consider donor sperm, donor eggs, embryo adoption, costs, and successes, as well as other pertinent issues.

IUI is a process where sperm is delivered to a woman's uterus by a catheter. IVF was the first technology developed (it is also known as test-tube reproduction) and is the most commonly used method. After fertility, the eggs are removed and fertilized in a Petri dish, and then deposited into the uterus. GIFT is similar to IVF, except that the egg and the sperm are placed into the fallopian tubes where conception occurs naturally.

The results of these procedures are not often made available to consumers. Some clinics have been known to inflate their successes by counting multiple births separately, leading consumers to believe that they were single births. *Consumer Reports* (1996) reports that in IVF, for every 100 attempts by women under age 40, 19 babies are delivered (19% success). For every 100 attempts by women over age 40, 7 babies are delivered (7% success). Begley (1995) noted in a *Newsweek* article that with each IVF attempt, the chances for success decrease from 13.0% on the first attempt to 4.3% on the fourth attempt. Fertility clinics often tell patients that four attempts is the best means to increase the likelihood of pregnancy. Given that many insurance companies will not pay for treatments, this may mean that infertile couples are paying up to $40,000 for four cycles of IVF.

Infertility treatment should first be evaluated by the couple, to determine how reasonable the option is for their life-style and how consistent the option is with their own value systems. Some couples, for example, cannot integrate the choice of using artificial insemination with a sperm donor with their religious or value system. A husband who is unable to impregnate his wife may find the idea of her fertility resulting from someone else's sperm too disturbing. Other religious beliefs preclude various types of intervention, and these value choices must be honored. Once a couple pursues infertility treatment and pregnancy does not occur, or they decide not to pursue treatment, they must decide what to do next. An option for some couples is to remain childless. Others may choose to have a parenting experience through adoption. Some couples have a very clear idea of the next step, while others struggle with the issues. It is very important that the couple continue to make decisions together.

CLINICAL ISSUES IN INFERTILITY

The fundamental issue in infertility is loss. Infertile couples have lost the children of their dreams, genetic continuity, the feelings and experiences associated with pregnancy, and control over their reproduction. It should be noted that infertility becomes a clinical issue only when the "desire" conflicts with the "ability" to have children.

When a clinician works with an infertile couple, it is important that he/she examine and understand the couple's values and feelings about loss, grief, pregnancy, and parenting. It is also important for the clinician to examine his or her own values and feelings. These will be challenged through contact with the infertile couple.

Many people grow up with images of the children they want to have in the future. When partners begin discussing whether to have children, they draw upon their own childhood experiences and together create an image of the children they want to have. Parents of children by birth are the first to acknowledge that their children are a mixture of their parents, their extended families, their own personalities, their environment, and their life experiences.

When couples find they are unable to produce their fantasy child, often the idea or image of the child becomes idealized and the drive to achieve parenthood becomes more desperate. Some couples see it as a failure that they cannot produce offspring that will carry on the family name or tradition. In certain religious traditions, religious identity is passed through the mother to the child. It becomes important to produce a child to continue religious traditions and links with past and future generations.

In much of American culture, pregnancy is the preparation for parenthood and the admission into adulthood. It is a rite of passage. Women are given advice from friends about pregnancy, birth, and baby care. Couples are given showers and co-workers may have a pool to guess the sex of the baby. Pregnant couples shop for baby furniture, car seats, clothes, and toys. They attend childbirth classes and start interviewing child care providers. These tasks become consuming for the couple, and they begin to join with others experiencing similar life events.

The infertile couple has multiple losses to deal with when their peers become pregnant. Often, infertile couples, particularly women, feel devastated after learning their friends are pregnant. They may become angry with peers who complain about pregnancy's problems, such as weight gain, morning sickness, and swollen ankles. Many infertile couples choose to avoid their pregnant friends during this time. Thus, their social lives shrink. They are unable to attend baby showers and face the reality of their losses. They try to avoid questions from well-intentioned friends and acquaintances, such as "When will it be you?" "Aren't you planning to have children?" Feelings of loss and anger lead infertile couples to isolation at various stages during the infertility process.

As far back as puberty, women have spent a great deal of time thinking and fantasizing about reproduction. While the teenage boys were thinking about sex, the girls were often thinking about reproduction. For many women, the emotional issues surrounding infertility become immobilizing. The woman is usually seen as the person "in charge" of fertility in the family. She decides when "it's time to have a baby." American culture still encourages women to reproduce. Even the "superwoman" of the media is shown with a briefcase in her hand and a baby on her hip. A woman's biological clock becomes an issue. If she has used birth control, she begins to regret "lost opportunities." If her infertility is due to abortions, birth control, or STDs, guilt is often a large part of infertility.

Men experience infertility in different ways. As adolescents, they may think about playing ball with their children, but they probably don't, as girls do, spend a whole afternoon naming their unborn children. Male fertility is not tied to a time clock. However, a man's infertility is tied to his sexual ego. A low sperm count implies that he is less sexually interesting, his prowess is poor, or he is less of a stud. It attacks his manhood.

The loss, or potential loss, of parenting is the ultimate devastation for the infertile couple. Many women and men have always thought about being parents. People choose to be parents for a variety of reasons. Some people have personal needs, which are met through reproduction and parenting. Other people want to face the challenge of shaping a child's future. For most people, parenting is a combination of both. When the infertile couple's friends or family members have children, they are again faced with their loss. It is especially difficult when a sibling gives birth. The infertile couple may want to become involved with the new baby but their pain and desperation stop them. New parents and grandparents sometimes become baffled and are unable to understand why infertile couples feel the way they do. Infertile couples find themselves angry at new parents who complain that their baby does not sleep, or that they can't get out any more because of the kids. Even a trip to the grocery store, when they see mothers buying formula or baby food, is a reminder that they are not parents and how unfair the world can sometimes be.

Another major theme in the infertile couple's life is the loss of control. They are unable to conceive a child, yet they have been successful in so many other areas of their lives. At this stage, they begin to accept their world as normal. Sex used to be spontaneous, but now is dictated by temperatures and cycles. They need to schedule working hours around sex during opportune times for fertilization. They have to keep track of temperature readings day after day, only to start the menstrual cycle month after month. While initially frustrating, eventually these experiences are seen as a loss of intimacy and control, which leads to anger. Infertile couples may become angry when they hear a mother yelling at her children in a shopping mall or see a pregnant 15-year-old. They may be angry at the onset of the menstrual cycle. They may become angry at the medical providers when they don't have a diagnosis or a definitive answer. The couple may attempt to organize their diets, activities, and life-style around fertility in order to conceive a child. This type of control is all they have, yet it often leads to more anger and disappointment when a child is not conceived. This sometimes leads to avoiding sex altogether, or over-focusing on sexual activity for reproduction and not for closeness or fun. This can result in further distancing in the relationship and yet another loss—the loss of intimacy.

Partner issues can become major problems between the infertile couple. Most often, only one partner has fertility problems, which could lead to guilt for that person and blame for the other partner. Sometimes they suggest to each other that they should have found different partners. Treatment is also a time when partners experience differences. Each partner may want to pursue totally different options. One person may be ready to stop treatment before the other person is ready to stop. Conflict also occurs when extended family members become aware of their infertility and react in ways that are not helpful. Each partner experiences the loss differently, based upon family histories and life experiences.

Even at the institutional level, infertile couples experience nonsupport, blame, and feelings of shame. One infertile client related the following example:

At her church, the minister asked all mothers and mothers-to-be to stand. She felt sad sitting there but could handle it, until he went into a 10-minute lecture to the selfish women seated who refused to mother a child. Her tears that day ended any comfort her church could give. Instead she quit her church after sending copies of all her medical bills to the minister with a note signed "from one of the selfish women."

Through all of this, infertile couples must be encouraged to deal with infertility, and all of the resulting issues, as a team and to support each other throughout the process. Eventually, infertility studies stop, because of pregnancy, lack of money, or depleted emotions. The monthly cycle of hope, fear, and loss has to end for the infertile couple to begin the healing process. At this point, the decision to adopt can be made. It should be noted here that although feelings of infertility have been resolved, these feelings can emerge again.

A mother of three adopted children said she long ago gave up wishing she could have a baby. She thought all her emotions were over, until she had to have a hysterectomy at age 46. Her thoughts in the operating room were "It's really over, I never will have a baby."

An adoptive father said that his oncologist told him his chemotherapy would make him sterile and asked him if he wanted to freeze some of his sperm in case he wanted a child. He told the doctor, "Forget it, my wife (of 20 years) has an infertility problem and we adopted two kids, I don't care." Years after he was cured of cancer he said, "But you know, later I regretted it. What if I got married again? It was okay to accept when it was her but I don't like being sterile and knowing I'll never have the option of reproducing."

For both this woman and man, their infertility was revisited at later points in their lives.

CHOOSING ADOPTION

Infertility is a condition that can lead to a decision to adopt. About one-third of infertile couples adopt; how many children they adopt and the characteristics of those children are unknown (Menning, 1988). While there is little empirical data, there is much anecdotal information on this population.

Couples who decide to pursue adoption face a myriad of choices, including whether to work through an attorney or an agency, whether to pursue domestic or international adoption of infants or toddlers, whether to adopt older children or sibling groups from the United States or other countries, and whether to adopt children with special needs. These options vary by state; costs for each type of adoption also vary. It is as important for families to choose the right type of adoption and adoption provider as it is to choose the right fertility specialist.

Adoption of infants, either domestically or internationally, is dominated by middle- and upper-middle-class infertile couples seeking children. It is also dominated by Caucasians. In 1994, the cost for infant adoptions ranged from $8,000 to $50,000. While the exact reason for this wide discrepancy is not known, the amount of money is related to the philosophy of the agency or the individual providing the adoption service and, perhaps, the circumstances of the family. The more desperate the family, which often means the older the adoptive couple or single person, and the longer they have waited to adopt, the higher the cost. In some agencies, parental age or marital status disqualifies adopters from consideration for infants.

Adoption of older and special needs children usually involves three groups of adopters. With the increasing diversity in family life-styles, growing numbers of fertile couples have also become adoptive parents. This group of adoptive parents often seek to express social, political, and religious ideologies. They are much more likely to adopt older, special needs children and to adopt across racial lines (Feigelman & Silverman, 1979).

The second group of adopters includes single people and older couples who have been disqualified by agencies and do not have access to infant adoptions. In addition, couples or single people who feel that they are too old to adopt babies, or do not have the financial resources to do so, may choose to adopt older or special needs children.

The third group of adopters who adopt older children are infertile couples or single people. Single-parent adopters may also have fertility problems, although the relationship between single-parent adoption and infertility has not been not well established. Clinical practitioners suggest that up to half of the families that adopt special needs children have fertility problems. It is interesting to note that in agencies that place older children, there is less focus on infertility in the initial interviews compared to agencies that place infants. Also, much of the preparation materials for families adopting older children focus on the child or family, but rarely discuss infertility.

ADOPTION: PRACTICE ISSUES

Infertility and the issues of loss surrounding infertility affect adoptive parents and need to be addressed. Otherwise, there is a risk that these issues will interfere with the parent-child or couple relationship. Infertility is not an incurable, contagious disease to be avoided, but a loss that never completely resolves. However, it does heal over time. Open discussion about loss and infertility during a family assessment for adoption is important, but even more important is the couple's honesty. Adoption allows people to parent and to not remain childless, but it does not cure infertility. It does not cure the longing to reproduce, or the wish to have a child who is genetically linked, or the sadness that a very normal, natural function of the body does not work the way it should. Resolution of the loss due to infertility is a lifelong process.

Infertility issues may create jealousy or anger between birth parents and adoptive parents. Adoptive mothers of newborns or toddlers may think, "How could she have a baby and give it away, and I can't have one?" The birth parent of an infant may be jealous of the adopter's ability to parent. In special needs adoptions, most often the birth parents have lost their right to parent due to abuse and neglect. The adopters of these older children often have unresolved anger toward the birth parents. "Why did she have a child if she was only going to abuse it, and I can't have one? It's not fair."

Some infertile couples choose to adopt infants out of a strong need to parent newborns, while others wish to adopt infants so they can have the biggest impact on their development. Current adoption practices in many states reflect more openness in adoption, including allowing birth parents to choose the adoptive couple from pictures and profiles written by the prospective adopter. This is accomplished via a meeting between the birth parents and the adoptive parents. Sometimes, the adoptive couple is asked by a birth family to be present at the delivery. All these events trigger multiple emotions, including the ongoing feelings of loss associated with infertility.

The infertile couple should be prepared for the possibility that the birth mother may decide to keep her baby and not pursue adoption as she originally planned. It will be an additional unresolved loss if the couple is not prepared for this possibility. Adoptive parents should also be helped to anticipate the birth parents' grief. Prospective adopters are always surprised by their own empathy toward the birth parents. Initially, some are unable to move beyond the birth parents' loss and grief at relinquishing their child, even when they know it is their gain. After a short time, they should be helped to acknowledge their joy but always remember the child's loss is to the connection to the birth family.

Prospective adopters choose international adoption for different reasons. Some couples have a strong humanitarian desire to adopt internationally. They choose this path to parenthood for social reasons. Other couples feel that domestic infant adoptions take too long and, because of their ages, pursue international adoption. Still others choose international adoption because of the negative exposure of domestic adoption. Stories of adopted children being returned to birth fathers or mothers have terrified many prospective adoptive families. Consequently, a number of adopters prefer children who have been abandoned because the likelihood of return to birth parents is greatly diminished. Couples who have experienced the many losses surrounding infertility often prefer to adopt children who have virtually no chance of being returned to birth parents. Some adoptive parents who are still in denial about their infertility believe they can eliminate the birth parents. All adopters deal with birth parent issues; for example, the fact that the birth parents are unknown or thousands of miles away does not eliminate the issue of birth parents; it may just complicate the issue.

While some couples choose older children for humanitarian reasons, others choose to adopt older children because they do not have the financial resources to pursue domestic infant or international adoption. Not only are fees greatly diminished or nonexistent for older, special needs adoptions, but there are more financial supports in the form of ongoing subsidy for families.

It is only recently that professionals have begun to acknowledge and discuss the sense of loss and grieving experienced by women and men who have fertility problems.   Fleckenstein (1991) examined the question of whether the arrival of an infant by adoption modified the emotional impact of infertility for childless couples. It did not. Both infertile couples who created a family through adoption and couples who remained childless showed improvement in depression and self-esteem over time, independent of the placement of a baby. Marital satisfaction was not found to be initially problematic and remained stable over time.

IMPLICATIONS

Adoption agencies need to explore and acknowledge infertility and its implications with both infant adopters and older child adopters. Practitioners in many clinical settings have assumed that the families who adopt older or special needs children do not have infertility problems. However, many people adopting these children have fertility issues and their feelings are no different than those of infant adopters. In addition, they sometimes have moved through a double loss, in that they will never experience parenting an infant by birth or adoption. Sometimes, adopting a special needs child is a choice over adopting an infant.

Considering the amount of loss experienced by the infertile couple, professionals should offer services that allow these clients to have as much control over their future as possible. Adoption providers should be sensitive to these issues while remaining child-focused. Ideally, child-centered practice in infant adoption means matching the needs of the child with the strengths and resources of the family; it is focused on finding a family for a child, not a child for a family. In the adoption of the older or international child, the adoptive parents are usually active participants in the matching process.

Agencies can help prospective adopters by acknowledging their losses in the initial meeting. Offering group training and education about adoption allows couples to find mutual support for their emotional losses. Asking group members about their first calls to adoption providers allows them to express their lack of control and frustration about the path to parenthood. Often this leads to a discussion about local fertility doctors and clinics, and, by the end of the first session, a sense of closeness has formed within the group.

The losses due to infertility have no identified rituals. When a child dies, the parents receive an overwhelming response to their loss. This is not true for the infertile couple even though their fantasy biological child has died. It is helpful if clinicians can develop rituals to recognize this loss. An example of this is asking the couple to each find one item that is symbolic of their fantasy child and then prepare a ceremony for burial of these items. This can help the family move through the stages of loss.

A referral to a local chapter of Resolve can be a gift to a couple who are feeling isolated and angry. Resolve is a support group that provides support, education, and referrals to couples with fertility problems.

Adoption professionals need to be knowledgeable about infertility issues and how they affect adoption and family formation. More clinical research needs to be done to identify how infertility affects the ongoing developmental issues of adoptive families. For example, according to Harper (1986), parents who have failed to recognize and work through conflicts surrounding their infertility are more likely to experience an upsurge of feelings of loss when their adopted child is an adolescent and capable of reproduction. Several authors provide a framework for understanding adoptive families, as well as specific treatment techniques for helping families uncover their grief and work through their lossess (Berman & Bufferd, 1986; Keck & Kupecky, 1995; Pinderhughes & Rosenberg, 1990; Rosenthal & Groze, 1992; Winkler, Brown, van Keppel, & Blanchard, 1988).

Another useful model for understanding loss in infertile couples is derived from the work of Kubler-Ross (1969). Kubler-Ross developed a model of the stages in dealing with loss in which people cycle through feelings of denial, anger, bargaining, depression and resolution. When this cycle is reviewed with couples, it is easy for them to identify their stage in the cycle. It also helps them normalize their own feelings and learn that other couples share their experiences.

Denial, the disavowal of reality, is usually the stage that infertile couples have passed before they make the decision to adopt. Most have accepted that pregnancy will probably not occur. However, some couples adopt with the belief that they will then conceive. This expectation puts an enormous burden on the adoptee to "cure" the infertility. When the child does not (i.e., he or she allows them to parent but they remain infertile), the parent may feel the adoption is unsatisfactory.

Anger is the second part of the cycle. Anger, or the behavior that can be engendered by anger, can destroy a family. If the family adopts a child who has unresolved anger, the child may present the family with many behavioral challenges. Some infant adoptees, as they go through adaptive grieving, may become angry and defiant. Some older adoptees enter the family angry over past abuse, moves, and disconnections. Some adoptive parents, angry at their infertility, transfer their anger to the birth parents or adopted child. This can become a difficult dynamic because the anger of the child and the anger of the parent interweave, affecting attachment of child and parent to each other. This can result in more negative outcomes for the adoptee and adoptive family.

Bargaining, or negotiating, is a stage that seems to be emphasized by the adoption process. The paperwork, classes, and home study interviews prepare people to be "approved" as a family—many adoptive families feel obligated to be "perfect." Infertile couples often have already bargained to be perfect parents who would never lose their temper, scold their children, or get tired if they could only parent. However, when parenthood becomes a reality, such as when a parent is exhausted because of the dependency and demands of a newborn or the emotional drain of an older child with special needs, the bargaining can lead to guilt or depression. This can be particularly true if parents are not supported by family, friends, or professionals. If the child has a serious problem, the family might also question whether the child is what they deserved or bargained for.

Depression is the next part of dealing with loss. Questioning the decision to adopt can result in depression. Depression can also be biologically based, as a reaction to hormones for the person undergoing infertility treatment. Depression immobilizes as well as isolates families, and interferes with spontaneity and joy.

Resolution, the last stage in which some control is achieved over feelings of loss, cycles over and over. Just when the couple feel that they are able to cope with their infertility, something occurs that triggers the cycle spinning again. These triggers can come out of nowhere, or they can be predictable, such as menopause, the anniversary of a miscarriage, or the giving away of an heirloom, because there is no one to pass it on to. Resolution is ongoing and, like all stages of loss, is never totally achieved.

It is helpful in preadoption or postlegalization work to explore how the couple is feeling about infertility at that moment. The dynamics of the family may be exposing infertility as a raw nerve and may need to be processed again. A couple still in the cycle of loss over infertility may be having a very difficult time helping a child with his losses, which all adoptees have.

REFERENCES

Begley, S. (1995, September 4). The baby myth. *Newsweek*, (126), 38–45.

Berman, L. C., & Bufferd, R. K. (1986). Family treatment to address loss in adoptive families. *Social Casework: The Journal of Contemporary Social Work, 67*(1), 3–11.

Cooper, S., & Glazer, E. (1994). *Beyond infertility: New paths to parenthood*. New York: Lexington Books.

Corson, S. L. (1990). *Conquering infertility*. New York: Prentice-Hall.

Daly, K. (1990, October). Infertility resolution and adoption readiness. *Families in Society, 71*(8), 483–492.

Daniels, K. R. (1994, January/February). Adoption and donor insemination: Factors influencing couples' choices. *Child Welfare, 73*(1), 5–14.

Davis, K. (1996, May). The agonizing price of infertility. *Kiplingers Personal Finance Magazine,* (50), 50–54.

Feigelman, W., & Silverman, A. R. (1979). Preferential adoption: A new mode of family formation. *Social Casework, 60*(5), 296–305.

Fertility clinics: What are the odds? (1996, February). *Consumer Reports,* (61), 51–54.

Fleckenstein, L. L. (1991). *Adoption: Does it modify the emotional impact of infertility?* Doctoral dissertation, Rutgers University, New Brunswick, NJ.

Fleming, J., & Burry, K. (1989). Coping with infertility. *Journal of Social Work and Human Sexuality, 6*(1), 37–41.

Greil, A. L. (1991). *Not yet pregnant: Infertile couples in contemporary America*. New Brunswick, NJ: Rutgers University Press.

Harper, J . (1986). An individual at risk? The adopted adolescent and family. *Australian Social Work, 39*(1), 9–13.

Johnston, P. I. (1994). *Taking charge of infertility*. Indianapolis, IN: Perspectives Press.

Keck, G. C., & Kupecky, R. M. (1995). *Adopting the hurt child: Hope for families with special needs kids*. Colorado Springs, CO: Pinon Press.

Kubler-Ross, E. (1969). *On death and dying*. New York: Macmillan.

Menning, B. E. (1988). *Infertility: A guide for the childless couple*. New York: Prentice-Hall.

Pinderhughes, E. E., & Rosenberg, K. (1990). Family bonding with high risk placements: A therapy model that promotes the process of becoming a family. In L. M. Glidden (Ed.), *Formed families: Adoption of children with handicaps.* New York: Haworth Press.

Rosenbaum, J. (1995, December). Beat the clock: New treatments for infertility. *American Health*, (14), 70–73.

Rosenthal, J. A., & Groze, V. G. (1992). *Special needs adoption: A study of intact families.* New York: Praeger.

Winkler, R., Brown, D., van Keppel, M., & Blanchard, A. (1988). *Clinical practice in adoption.* New York: Pergamon Press.

Wood, C., & Westmore, A. (1984). *Test-tube conception.* Englewood Cliffs, NJ: Prentice-Hall.

3

Shared Identity Issues for Adoptees

Betty Jean Lifton

In this chapter, Betty Jean Lifton, Ph.D., discusses the identity issues common to children who are placed as infants as well as when older. She adds an additional group of children who are adopted—those from other countries—in her analysis of commonalities and differences that they share. Dr. Lifton, drawing from her clinical experience, has created a theory of the "adopted self." Identity issues are explored within the context of adoptees who have grown up in the closed adoption system. Her work, which introduces concepts of dissociation and trauma, draws on Erikson's identity theory and concepts from Winnicott, Horney, and Jung.

Adopted children need to be made visible. Mental health professionals must learn to see the adopted child not only as an extension of a loving adoptive family, but as a child who has experienced disconnection and loss, which is usually unacknowledged by society. Only then can professionals help adopted children to feel validated and able to claim their real emotions as they struggle to develop a healthy sense of self.

Erikson (1958) stresses the importance of continuity with one's past in the service of the future. That is, knowing one's history serves as a foundation for the future and moving forward in the life cycle. Identity, as he defines it, is confidence in one's inner continuity amid change (Erikson, 1968). Adopted children have little continuity in their lives; for the most part, they have been cut off from, or have little knowledge of, the past. Their identities are fragile—whether they are adopted as newborns or later—and have been shaped by the trauma of separation from the birth mother, as well as by feelings of abandonment and the lack of a coherent life narrative. Such disturbances can compromise an adoptee's ability to navigate the developmental stages of the life cycle.

Erikson (1968) speaks of the psychological tasks that a young person must solve early in life, such as acquiring basic trust and trustworthiness, building self-esteem, developing a sense of right and wrong, working on independence, and taking initiative. Failure to achieve a strong sense of self by accomplishing these tasks leads to what Erikson calls identity confusion: doubt about who you are, what you want to be, and what you want to do.

All young people face these tasks, but they are particularly difficult for adoptees, who lose their basic trust when they lose their original parents for reasons that are unknown or are incomprehensible to them. According to Erikson (1968), young people who are confused about themselves have "identity hunger." I use this term to describe the starved part of the adoptee's psyche—the part that hungers for the forbidden knowledge about one's origins and the fate of one's birth family after separation from them.

It is important to recognize that a child adopted in infancy experiences the same identity hunger and trauma of separation and loss as an abused or neglected child adopted when older. The adoptee will, in most cases, attach closely, but ambivalently, to the adoptive parents. Some part of the original self, which was bonded with the birth mother in utero and immediately after birth, will stay loyal to that early bond. No matter how loving the adoptive family, the child will keep some part of the "self" separate from the adoptive parents.

Older children, who remember their birth or foster parents, struggle with divided loyalties as they try to adjust to yet another set of parents. They may become overwhelmed with grief and anger at their powerlessness to control their own destinies. Those who have experienced severe abuse and neglect may exhibit symptoms of what is known as "attachment disorder," which is the inability to love or trust. They may have fits of destructive rage, or may withdraw into themselves in order to avoid emotional involvement with their new caretakers (Magid & McKelvey, 1989).

Adoptive parents who try to live as if their adopted child was born to them—and has no other parents—fail to validate their child's reality. In effect, their denial makes the child feel unreal or invisible. On the other hand, those parents who acknowledge their children's past heritage are able to help them feel rooted in their history and recognized for their own individuality.

In the following sections, which I have organized around the issues that adoptees share, I discuss these identity concepts in more detail.

ADOPTEES SHARE GHOSTS OF WHAT MIGHT HAVE BEEN

Jung believed that among all possible ghosts that haunt us, the spirits of parents possess the greatest significance (Wickes, 1977). Having been banished from the adopted child's everyday world by the secrecy and denial in the closed adoption system, the birth parents become little more than ghosts. "Hereditary ghosts" is the term used by psychiatrist Max Frisk (1964). Unless professionals are aware of the ghosts that trail each member of the adoption triad, it will be difficult for them to understand or help adopted children, adoptive parents, or birth parents.

Who are these ghosts?

Children adopted in infancy are accompanied by the ghost of the child they might have been had they stayed with their birth mothers, and by the ghost of the fantasy biological child their adoptive parents might have had. They are also accompanied by the ghosts of their birth mothers, from whom they have never completely disconnected, and the ghosts of their birth fathers, hidden behind their birth mothers.

Older adopted children carry not only the ghosts of their birth parents, whom they may or may not remember, and the ghost of the child they might have been if they had stayed with their birth parents, but also the ghosts of the foster parents with whom they once lived. If these children are separated from birth siblings, additional ghosts may exist. The ghost sibling of the adoptee is much like the imaginary twin for whom other children yearn—a loyal friend who will be there when the child is sad and lonely. The ghost sibling connects the adoptee to the life he might have had, even as it grows up with him in his adoptive life.

Children adopted internationally carry the ghosts of the birth family left behind, the ghost of the child they might have been had they stayed in their home country, and the ghosts of the fantasy children their American parents might have had. The birth family ghosts have a different language and culture than the adoptive family, and at times may seem more real to the adoptee than the family raising them. Try as they may, adoptees can never compete with the ghost of the adoptive parent's fantasy child—in some cases, they give up before even trying.

So, too, the adoptive and birth parents are accompanied by ghosts. The adoptive parents are attended by the ghost of the fantasy biological child they never had and by the ghosts of the birth parents of their adopted child. The birth mother is accompanied by the ghost of the child she relinquished for adoption, and by the ghost of the mother she might have been, had she been able to keep her children.

All of these ghosts are members of the extended adoptive family, which includes the birth parents. Adoptees must contend with these ghosts as they struggle to put together an authentic adopted self and develop an authentic identity (Lifton, 1994). The ghosts can become powerful forces in the dynamics of the adoptees, the birth families, and the adoptive families.

ADOPTEES SHARE THE ADOPTION JOURNEY

The adoptee's journey toward selfhood, or self-concept, is much like that of the exile who becomes the eternal outsider and wanderer. It is a psychological as well as a physical journey, with mythic themes and spiritual dimensions.

The journey is physical in that adopted children are sent away by one family system and taken in by another, either in the same city or across state lines. The transracial adoptee's international journey is geographically farther, but the inner distance registers the same on the emotional scale.

The journey is psychological in that adoptees are faced, at each stage of the life cycle, with the need to solve the mystery of who they are and where they came from in order to put together a cohesive identity.

The journey is mythic in that both Eastern and Western mythological heroes were abandoned as babies. They were found and raised by kindly adoptive parents—both human and animal—and eventually went on a quest, which proved to be the quest for self-enlightenment, wholeness, and integration.

The journey is spiritual in that adopted children must, at some point in their lives, try to find meaning in and transcend their special destiny. The adoptee may ask, "Why me? Why was I chosen to be different and for what purpose? Do I have a special mission here on earth?"

ADOPTEES SHARE CUMULATIVE ADOPTION TRAUMA

Trauma is an experience that is sudden, unexpected, and abnormal; it occurs whenever an experience exceeds an individual's ability to meet its demands (Herman, 1992). It disrupts one's sense of self and identity; it threatens one's psychological core. With all the love that goes into the act of adoption, children still experience a series of traumas that I call "cumulative adoption trauma" (Lifton, 1994).

The first trauma occurs when the infant-placed adoptee is separated from the mother with whom nature intended the infant to be. During the nine months between conception and birth, the fetus is a feeling, remembering, aware being (Verny & Kelly, 1991). Deeg (1989), who is both a psychiatrist and an adoptee, speaks of the unborn child's "hidden" relationship to the mother as the origin of self. He posits that the absence of the birth mother, despite the best adoptive conditions, poses a serious threat to the baby's equilibrium. Clothier (1943) wrote, "The child who is placed with adoptive parents at or soon after birth misses the mutual and deeply satisfying mother-child relationship, the roots of which lie in that deep area of personality where the physiological and psychological are merged" (p. 223).

The second trauma occurs for the infant-placed adoptee when the child is told that she was not born to the people she calls mother and father. It is the first time the child learns that she did not come into the family the natural way, but rather through adoption. This is not to say that adopted children are irreparably damaged, as some adoptive parents fear when professionals speak of wounds or traumas. Rather, children are in need of support for the sadness and sense of loss that they feel.

Because of the secrecy and denial in the closed adoption system, children adopted at any age are usually not given a chance to grieve the loss of the birth parents, and are expected to live as if those parents do not exist. If the birth parents do not exist, then the children may feel that they do not exist, either. It is not uncommon to hear adopted people say that they feel unborn or unreal.

These traumas are further compounded when children adopted at birth realize that they are forbidden to know to whom they were born. Their birth mother and birth father, indeed, their whole clan or extended family system, have mysteriously disappeared into a void. Adopted children try to straddle their two worlds for a while. Many ask questions over and over in an attempt to make sense of what happened to them.

Older-placed children also experience the trauma of separation from their parents, as well as from siblings and foster parents. Whether neglected or abused, these children may mourn for their birth parents, siblings, and extended family members, and worry about what happened to them. They may feel guilty for the breakup of their families, or for living well while their family members may still be in turmoil.

Children adopted internationally experience the trauma of separation and disconnection when they lose their mother country as well as their birth mother and birth clan, or extended families and kinship systems. They may also experience the trauma of culture shock in their new country, and grieve for the families they left behind.

All of these children are in a survival bind. Implicit in the adoptive parents' loving message to children adopted at any age is the message "We will love you unconditionally—under the condition that you pretend that you are really our own." The children are asked to collude in the fiction that their adoptive parents are their only parents and to accept that their birth heritage is disposable.

According to Horney (1950), it is psychologically traumatic to abandon the real self. Yet this is what adopted children are expected to do—to disavow that they were once connected to another family. Instead of developing feelings of belonging, they feel isolated and helpless. In order to cope, adopted children often try to shut out the whole subject of adoption and try to live as if they were not adopted. This means that they must separate one part of the self from the rest of the self—a psychic strategy knows as dissociation, numbing, or splitting.

Both Winnicott (1965) and Laing (1965) used the terms "true self" and "false self" to describe the split in the human psyche that many children make. I believe it is more accurate to call the split in the adopted child the "artificial self" and the "forbidden self," because neither is completely true or completely false (Lifton, 1994).

The artificial self has many of the characteristics of the "good adoptee": it is almost selfless in its desire to please, but it pays the price by feeling empty and unreal. Like the adoptive family, in which it has been placed, the artificial self is artificially created. It is a social construct, an "as if" self living "as if" in a natural family. Wanting to fit in at any cost, it will deny its own needs for the sake of others. The artificial self is compliant, afraid to express its real feelings, such as sadness or anger, for fear of losing the only family it has. It cuts the birth parents off from consciousness until they are no longer available, except when they surface in daydreams or fantasies. It denies its need for origins and goes underground with its forbidden thoughts, making the adoptee feel more isolated and alone.

The forbidden self, which often acts like the "bad adoptee," is the self that might have been, had it not been separated from its mother and forced to split off from the rest of the self. The forbidden self refuses to disavow the reality that there are other parents somewhere; it goes underground for vitality and authenticity. It keeps itself hidden in order to avoid being flushed out and destroyed, or having to abandon what it feels to be its true, or potentially true, self.

Adoptees may go back and forth between the artificial self and the forbidden self at different periods in their lives. They may be compliant as children, and, then, in an adolescent struggle for authenticity, rebel against the adoptive parents whom they see as inauthentic and a barrier between them and their authentic self. Adoptees are caught between the loyalty they feel to the adoptive parents, who rescued them, and their invisible loyalty to the mothers who gave birth to them.

ADOPTEES SHARE A BROKEN NARRATIVE OF THEIR LIVES

Every family unit has its own culture and narratives, or stories, that are passed down from generation to generation. Narratives connect family members to their parents, grandparents, and great-grandparents down through the generations. They connect everyone to their ancestors and their ancestral history. They influence our identities. They tell us who we are.

Narratives can be broken by historical or personal events, such as war, divorce, immigration, death, or desertion. They can also be broken by infertility and adoption. Every member of the adoption triad (adoptee, birth parents, and adoptive parents) has a broken narrative. The adoptive parents' narrative is broken when they are unable to have a biological child to continue their family line. The birth parents' narrative is broken when they are unable to keep the child who would have continued their family line. The adopted child's narrative is broken when the child is moved out of his own genetic and historical narrative and transplanted into the narrative of the adoptive family. Whether in a closed, open, or semiopen adoption, adoptees are forced to sacrifice their own narrative in order to make the continuity of the adoptive narrative possible.

Older adoptees often feel powerless to mend their broken narratives. They may shut down as they secretly mourn the families and kin that they lost. They may resist the overtures of the families that now attempt to claim them. Until adoption professionals help them to resolve their relationships with their birth families or foster families, they will have difficulty moving on and identifying with their new parents, as well as creating a new narrative with them.

Adoptees from abroad—for example, China, Korea, South America, Eastern Europe—have an even stronger break in their narratives because their narratives are so different from those of their adoptive families. These adoptees may feel a sense of hopelessness upon realizing that they have lost the language and culture of their families and kin because of being raised as Americans. This hopelessness may infect their general attitude toward life and surface as sadness and depression. International adoptees, as well as biracial adoptees, may encounter prejudice in their communities. Although their adoptive parents may deny their differences, they eventually discover that the rest of society does not. Their task is to find out who they are in relation to their country of origin.

It is essential for adoption professionals to preserve what they can of the older adoptees' narrative and heritage, no matter how complex and traumatic, and to pass them on to the adoptive parents. The parents can help their children integrate all the parts of their lives into a cohesive whole. Professionals who treat adoptees, adopted at any age, should keep in mind that these children's life story begins before they enter the adoptive home and that these children bring with them, into the therapy, two sets of parents—one a ghostly set to which they may no longer have conscious access.

ADOPTEES SHARE A SENSE OF ABANDONMENT

Children adopted as infants often feel that they have been abandoned by their birth mother despite being told that their mother gave them up out of love. The fear of abandonment by their adoptive parents, and later by their friends and spouses, stays with them throughout their lives. "Do anything you want to me," one adopted woman told the significant people in her life, "but don't abandon me."

Many older-placed children remember being abandoned by parents who were too dysfunctional to care for them. They also lost extended families and many lost siblings as well. Having lost basic trust so early, they have trouble trusting new parents and often behave in ways to provoke abandonment and rejection.

Children of intercountry adoption often are too young to know why they were separated from their parents and sent abroad. Although they were told that their mother wanted them to have a better life than she could offer, these children still feel abandoned by that absent mother. Their attitude toward their native land, its customs and its cultures may be ambivalent. Much of the despair that these children exhibit comes from feeling that they are cut off from their origins by vast distances that seem psychologically as well as physically insurmountable. For this reason, it is crucial that adoptive parents learn as much as possible about the circumstances surrounding their adopted children's relinquishment and obtain a complete family history. Ideally, the parents should travel back to their children's country with them, so that they can feel the reality of where their children came from. By developing positive feelings about their children's country of origin, adoptive parents will help the children develop positive feelings about themselves.

Watson (1993) finds that no matter how good their adoptive families, transracial adoptees are aware that they look different, feel different, and are different. He noticed that the most rebellious adolescents come from families that are rigid, families that deny the differences in their children, and families that have unmatched expectations. Those adoptees who can speak openly with their adoptive parents, regarding their feelings and fantasies about their country of origin, feel better about themselves. Watson recalls the 14-year-old Colombian boy, adopted at 14 months, who told him, "I just want to go back for a visit. Even if I can't find my birth parents, I can see what I saw, smell what I smelled, and feel what I touched."

Abandonment and loss are primal themes in adoption and need to be acknowledged within the triad. Adoptees realize at an early age that in order to have found a family, they first must have lost one. They need to be able to acknowledge and experience the feelings associated with this realization, and to share them with their adoptive parents.

ADOPTEES SHARE THE BURDEN TO FEEL GRATEFUL

Adoptees receive spoken, or unspoken, messages that they were lucky to have been rescued by their adoptive parents. They may have been told how sickly they were as babies, and how the adoptive parents brought them back to life—as if they resurrected them.

Older children, especially those who were shunted around in numerous foster homes, are expected to consider themselves lucky to have been taken in by another family. But, these children may have too much unresolved grief for the parents they have lost to feel grateful. In fact, they may resent their replacement parents for standing between them and the missing birth parents. They may have difficulty relating to the biological children already in the family or born after their adoption.

The adoptees from abroad often were sick—infested with worms and other parasites, thinner and smaller than they should have been in their development due to lack of nutrition and stimulation. One adoptee was told by the adoptive parents, "You'd be dead if we hadn't adopted you." The child was left feeling like a throwaway who owed his life to the adoptive parents. The need to be grateful brings about guilt feelings when adoptees do not live up to the adoptive parents' expectations; the children may decide to fail rather than risk not succeeding.

It is important that adoptive parents let adoptees know that the adoptees also rescued them. Without these adopted children, they would not have been able to become parents. If the parents already have other children, they should let the adoptee know what unique things he contributes to the family. This enables adoptees to gain a sense of self-worth, in that they are giving something to, as well as receiving something from, the parents.

ADOPTEES SHARE A PREDISPOSITION TO FANTASY

Adopted children spend an exorbitant amount of time fantasizing. They may seem to be sitting quietly in their rooms or just looking out of windows, when, in actuality, they are deep in the "Ghost Kingdom" imagining scenarios that might have been or still might be in the future. The Ghost Kingdom is that awesome sphere, located in the adoptee's psychic reality, where the lost birth parents, the birth clan, and the adoptee's original self reside. The adoptee lives one life in the here-and-now in the "Adoption Kingdom" with the adoptive family, and another life in the fantasy Ghost Kingdom with the idealized, lost, denigrated birth family (Lifton, 1994).

The adoptee's fantasies—both positive and negative—are an essential part of the building blocks of the developing self, and a repository for the adoptee's inner, secret self—the part that is kept hidden from the rest of the world. Fantasizing can be seen as an attempt to repair the broken narrative. It is a form of grieving. It is a way of conjuring up the lost mother, similar to the way children grieving lost parents are known to conjure up their ghosts. In the adoptee's fantasies, the birth mother may be a movie star today and a bag lady or prostitute tomorrow. More often, adoptees suspect the latter. Some adoptees have serial fantasies, running scenarios that they add to and change over the years. It is important to recognize that most of these fantasies are not pathological, but serve a beneficial purpose for adoptees.

Children adopted as infants may fantasize about what has happened to their birth parents. They may imagine that their birth parents have been kidnapped but will return for them one day.

Older-placed adoptees may fantasize that their parents will come together again and reclaim them. These adoptees may imagine that they will be reunited with their beloved grandparents or siblings to whom they were so close.

Children from abroad, who remember the early years with their families or in orphanages, may fantasize about what their lives would have been like if they had stayed in their home countries. They might have secret fantasies about what happened to their parents, and even blame themselves for being sent away.

ADOPTEES SHARE THE CHALLENGE OF ADOLESCENCE

In adolescence, young people strive for integrity as they struggle to bring the past and the present together in order to form coherent identities. Adopted adolescents often feel stuck in the life cycle, because the beginnings of their narratives are missing, and their parents are making no attempt to help restore them. If personal narratives do not grow and develop, with concrete facts and information, there is the danger of one becoming emotionally frozen. It is difficult to make the necessary connections between the past and the future in order to grow into a cohesive self.

Powerless to master their past, many adoptees have a hard time getting through adolescence. Some try to stay securely within the confines of the artificial self, feeling safe within its constrictions, but they may pay the price with eating disorders, phobias, and an underlying depression that rises out of unresolved grief and loss. Other adoptees, courting the true self in the dark corners of the Ghost Kingdom, take an oppositional stance toward parents, teachers, or legal authorities, who try to control them. They may lie, steal, run away, drop out of school, do drugs, or become sexually promiscuous. They may become depressed and even suicidal. Their behaviors can be seen as a cry for help—as an expression of despair over being irrevocably disconnected from their origins.

Adolescence, then, is a challenging time for adoptees, who have no genetic roadmap of their past or their future. Without a continuous sense of self, the task of forming a cohesive identity is particularly difficult. Therapists should be aware that adolescence may be a more difficult stage in the life cycle for adoptees and adoptive parents than for other families.

ADOPTEES SHARE A NEED TO FORM AN AUTHENTIC SELF

Adoptees often want to know more about their origins when they reach adolescence or young adulthood. They may ask for more information about their parents or siblings, and then back away from the idea of searching as they become overwhelmed by unresolved grief, anger, divided loyalties, and fear of rejection.

Adoptees separated from their families at an older age may want to find out what became of them. They are filled with conflicting feelings of longing for their lost parents and rage at them for disappearing. If given the chance, they may experiment by moving back to their old life, only to find that they belong there no more than they fully belong in their adoptive families. They are faced with the task of forgiving their birth parents, while reconnecting, on a deeper level, to the parents who raised them.

Adoptees from abroad may have difficulty reconstructing the past, as their records often are fragmented. In recent years, some have gone on "homeland tours" sponsored by adoption agencies. But, though they may discover their motherland, they seldom recover their lost mother. They often experience a great letdown upon realizing that they will never know their family history or see their blood relatives. This may result in their returning to their homeland for a period of time, and immersing themselves in its language and culture, before they can truly claim their American heritage and their adoptive parents.

The need to form an authentic self may lead the adoptee on two different journeys. The first is an internal search, in which one sifts through the pieces of the psyche in an attempt to understand who one was so that one can have some sense of who one is and who one can become. It is a quest for all the missing pieces of the self so that one can become whole. The second is the literal search, where one sifts through records and archives for real people with real names and addresses. The search process should not be seen as problematic but as a natural endeavor for some adoptees as they form an authentic self.

THE THERAPEUTIC TASK

The adopted child or adopted teenager is often sent to therapy by the parents because of antisocial behavior or depression. It is important for the therapist to know that the child may have split off emotions related to adoption issues. The adoptee who says, "Adoption means nothing to me" is exhibiting denial of loss, grief, and anger.

Therapists must understand that adoption therapy is about repairing the split—making the unconscious conscious. They may have to do much of the talking at first, because the adoptee may have closed down and be unable or unwilling to talk. It is important that therapists try to get the adoptee's "chosen baby story" (i.e., what the adoptee was told about the circumstances of the adoption), as well as any fantasies, dreams, and fears.

The adoptee may transfer intense feelings to the therapist, as if she were the missing birth parent from the Ghost Kingdom. The therapist must help make the Ghost Kingdom a reality by giving it a foundation. This means making the birth parents real: speculating as to what they might be like and why they could not stay together and keep their child. The adoptee may feel great relief that he can speak openly and acknowledge his confused feelings and ambivalence about the birth mother and birth father.

The therapist should also help the child understand the psychology of the adoptive parents and why they wanted to adopt. Adoptive parents can sometimes seem as unreal and disconnected as the birth mother, because there is often so little open communication with their child about adoption issues.

The therapist should also educate adoptive parents about the psychological needs of their adopted child. Otherwise, parents may feel threatened by the bond the child makes with the therapist, which is much like the bond a child might have with a birth parent. Therapists should work with adoptive parents to uncover their fantasies and expectations about their adopted child.

The therapist should help adoptive parents accept that the child they are raising has a dual heritage. The parents should be encouraged to get more information about the child's past from the agency or the lawyer who arranged the adoption. It may be necessary to search for the birth mother and birth father to get updated family and medical histories. But, the search and possible reunion process should be taken at the adoptee's pace. It can be a scary venture for the child, in that it carries the threat of losing the adoptive parents as well as the only sense of self the adoptee has known.

Therapists can help adoptive parents get over their fear of losing their child should there be a reunion with the birth family. Often such a reunion relieves the adoptee of guilt and anxiety. It is empowering for the child to integrate what was, what might have been, and what is.

Adoptees usually find themselves closer to their adoptive parents once the barrier of secrecy and the mystery of their origins have been removed. They become more secure and grounded as they gradually accept their fate and the ambiguities of their dual existence.

REFERENCES

Clothier, F. (1943, April). The psychology of the adopted child. *Mental Hygiene, 27*.

Deeg, C. F. (1989). On the adoptee's cathexis of the lost object. *Psychoanalysis and Psychotherapy, 7*(2), 152–161.

Erikson, E. (1958). *Identity and the life cycle*. New York: Norton.

Erikson, E. (1968). *Identity: Youth and crisis*. New York: Norton.

Frisk, M. (1964). Identity problems and the confused conception of the generic ego in adopted children during adolescence. *Acta Paediatrica, 21*, 6–11.

Herman, J. (1992). *Trauma and recovery*. New York: Basic Books.

Horney, K. (1950). *Neurosis and human growth: The struggle toward self realization*. New York: Norton.

Laing, R. D. (1965). *The divided self: An existential study in sanity and madness.* London: Penguin Books.

Lifton, B. J. (1994). *Journey of the adopted self: A quest for wholeness.* New York: Basic Books.

Magid, K., & McKelvey, C. A. (1989). *High risk: Children without a conscience.* New York: Bantam.

Verny, T., & Kelly, J. (1991). *The secret life of the unborn child.* New York: Delta.

Watson, W. (1993). Personal communication.

Wickes, F. (1977). *The inner world of childhood.* London: Coventure.

Winnicott, D. W. (1965). *Ego distortion in terms of true and false self: The maturational process and the facilitating environment.* New York: International Universities Press.

4

Search and Reunion Issues

Jayne Schooler

In this chapter, Jayne Schooler, B.A., an adoption educator and consultant, discusses how finding a connection to the past has always been an issue for the adoptee, whether the adoptee joined the family as an infant or as an older child. This chapter examines the reasons why both populations choose to search, as well as the similarities and differences in their personal issues around adoption. It also examines the reasons why some adoptees choose not to search. Finally, the chapter outlines how to assess readiness, including expectations and possible outcomes, for the adoptee contemplating a search and/or reunion with birth family members.

In the last 25 years, American society has viewed an unexpected and unparalleled phenomenon: the reunions of thousands of adult adoptees with their birth mothers and biological families. The desire to locate their origins, once thought to be a pathological need of ungrateful adoptees, is now viewed in a more positive and understanding light. A survey conducted in the late 1980s estimated that 500,000 adult adoptees were seeking, or had found, their birth families (Stiffler, 1992). Today, thousands of adoptees continue to search for their pasts. To discuss issues in the search process, it is important to begin with a definition of the word "search."

DEFINITION OF SEARCH

When the word "search" is mentioned within the context of adoption, an image automatically emerges in one's mind. Captured within the frame of that image is a young man or woman sitting at a courthouse back-room table, pouring over dusty, yellowed files. From the person's intense facial expression, one can sense the emotional urgency to catch just a glimpse of his or her unknown past.

For an adoptee, the word "search" has multiple layers of meanings. For some, to search means to attempt to obtain information about birth parent characteristics or one's medical history. No further steps are planned. For other adoptees, the meaning and process move them profoundly deeper.

To the adoptee, the word "search" is not limited to its literal meaning of a physical effort to make a connection. The meaning expands to include all that is part of the adoptee's quest—for it is an emotional quest, a psychological quest, and a spiritual quest.

Severson (1993), in an explanation of all that resides within the concept, said the following:

Perhaps every adoptee bears within himself the imprint of a special or unique spiritual vocation. It is spiritual. It is always spiritual . . . the matter of the heart and soul. . . . The mystery of adoption is that the adoptee was truly . . . twice born . . . born first of the flesh and then again in the spirit.

If an adoptive family is anything, it is a spiritual, psychological reality whose ground is love. What's an adoptive family made of if not biology and genes? Heart and soul can be the only answer.

To be adopted, then, is to be both of the heart and born of the spirit. The life work of the adoptee, if he or she is to attain healing and wholeness, is to rejoin the heritage of the flesh and the beauties of the spirit within the secret treasuring of the heart.

Thus, the concept of the search process can be symbolic or factual. It can be a quest—a deeper exploration of the self—or a pursuit of information to fill a gap in knowledge. The meaning of the search has a relationship to the reasons for the adoptee's search.

THE REASONS ADOPTEES SEARCH: AN OVERVIEW

Adoptees search for several reasons. Early in the history of search, the prevailing beliefs, supported by research, suggested that adoptees searched either when their adoptions did not go well (Triseliotis, 1973), or when they were dissatisfied with family communication about adoption issues (Schechter & Bertocci, 1990). However, recent research and writings suggest that there are more motivating factors than initially suggested, and the motivation does not have to do with difficulties (Kaplan-Roszia, 1994; Miller-Havens, 1990), although it may be linked to unresolved feelings about loss (Reitz & Watson, 1992). The following section discusses the general reasons adoptees engage in the search process.

The Search Process as an Adventure

Anderson (1989) believes that one reason adoptees engage in the search process is because they seek adventure. Often viewed as an exciting undertaking, searching is an effort, on the part of the adoptee, to move life to a new vantage point, to fill in the missing gaps, and to clutch the time that remains with biological family members previously unknown. The search process is an effort, without contemplation, of how the reunion will alter the lives of those touched by the course of events.

Kaplan-Roszia (1994) suggests that some people, by temperament, are natural mystery solvers. Throughout their lives, they have solved problems, unraveled mysteries, and analyzed people and events. For them, the search process is yet another significant mystery to untangle. Being curious is simply a part of their nature, so searching is a natural thing for them to do.

Anderson (1989) suggests the search process can be part of a ceremony of discovery and a challenging experience, imbued at times with a fantasy of reward. She says it becomes a "drama of individuals prevailing against great odds to finally be reunited with their biological families. It can be of heroic proportion, and it may intimate that the characters should be rewarded for their efforts, perhaps by thereafter having a joyous life together" (p. 624).

The Search Process as Therapy

For most adoptees, facing the issues involved in the search process is far more than "just an adventure." It is often a frightening decision, filled with enormous physical and emotional investments. It often comes after years of pondering and waiting for the courage to begin the search process. It is a therapeutic step, in that it confronts facts, issues, people, and feelings that were once vague questions. Stiffler (1992) states that "when an adoptee says he feels incomplete as a person, and is searching to resolve this issue, the search is seen as conceptually more intricate than simply adventure. It then has a therapeutic intent, with the goal of personal change, insight, or resolution" (p. 40).

According to Stiffler (1992), there are two models of search as therapy: *medical* or *deficiency* and *psychological* or *trauma*. According to the medical (deficiency) model, two things appear to be lacking: information and experience. The cure for the adoptee occurs when the deficiency is filled, such as when iron is given for anemia. The most significant aspects of this model are the following: (a) the adoptee needs to take something into himself; (b) this something is external; (c) the process is relatively passive; and (d) resolution is complete (i.e., there is a cure).

According to the psychological (trauma) model, trauma occurs because adoptees experience something like a traumatic neurosis disorder, or posttraumatic stress disorder, presumably generated by the removal from the birth family into an adoptive home (Anderson, 1989; Stiffler, 1992). Treatment consists of recognizing and acknowledging the trauma, and then attempting to change a passive experience into an active mastery. It is thought that: (a) the adoptee suffers from a psychological trauma; (b) the problem is internal; (c) treatment is an active process; and (d) resolution is incomplete. Reunion is seen not as an end, but as a beginning step in a series of steps toward growth, development, and integration (Stiffler, 1992).

The search process brings most adoptees to some point of resolution about the complexities of growing up as adopted children. The results of the search, and the depth it carries for adoptees, spans a wide continuum. That continuum spans from satisfying their need to know by just receiving factual information to touching the deepest level of their hearts and souls with a reunion.

Understanding the broad motivation for an adoptee's need to search—either as adventure, therapy, or both—is vital information for the therapist. It is even more essential to recognize varied and specific reasons why adoptees become involved in the search process. As the reasons are acknowledged, they can provide a deeper look into the quest of adoptees to attain wholeness, completion, and resolution to psychological and emotional pain.

THE REASONS ADOPTEES, PLACED AS INFANTS, BECOME INVOLVED IN THE SEARCH PROCESS

Adoptees placed as infants have no conscious memories of their birth families, although some adoption professionals believe there are unconscious, preverbal and even prenatal memories (Verrier, 1993). The following section outlines the different reasons adoptees placed as infants become involved in the search process.

A Need to Obtain a Medical History

For many adoptees, having little or no information about their medical histories is troubling. "What is my medical background? What complications or diseases are part of my genetic makeup? What problems might I pass on to my children?" These are questions many adoptees pose, who have no knowledge of their medical backgrounds.

The tragic dilemma for many adoptees is that even when nonidentifying information is made available, valuable medical information is lacking. A brief physical description of the birth parents and a short statement about their medical histories—for example, "they are both in good health"—are often found in many adoption records of the fifties, sixties, and seventies. Because the files are sealed, they are not updated with more recent medical information.

As one adult adoptee stated:

Initially, the main reason I searched was to find my medical history. I found out about my adoption as an adult. I assumed that my [adoptive] mother's medical history was mine because of the lack of that vital information—and she had died at 42 of a heart attack. I was very concerned about my health—preoccupied is probably a better word—from the time I was first married. I wondered if I would live to see my children to adulthood. It came as a great relief to discover that my adoptive mother's medical history was *not mine*, and now I wanted to know what was mine.

Current research suggests that many health difficulties may be genetically linked, or the predisposition for certain health problems has a hereditary component. Thus, this information can help adoptees plan and proactively deal with their health. However, gaining information about one's medical history is only one reason for instituting a search by those adults who were placed as infants or toddlers. Finding a family resemblance is another.

A Need to Look like Someone

Most adoptees placed as infants or toddlers have no memory of people in their pasts. They may feel a sense of insecurity, frustration, or embarrassment because they often do not resemble anyone in their adoptive families. The need to find a genetic similarity can be the driving force that initiates the search process.

A 38-year-old adult adoptee, after getting nonidentifying information about her family, said:

For the first time in my life, I felt physically attached to someone. The information I received told me that I look like both my birth father and birth mother, suffer with her allergies, and now I understand why I have such an interest in music. My reason for the search was I just wanted to know who I looked like and who I acted like. At this point in my life, I am not ready to meet them. Maybe someday. Right now, I am able to put the compelling search effort to rest.

In many families, one of the pastimes during gatherings is to talk about how children bear resemblance to distant and current family members.   Such conversations could cause the adoptee, who doesn't resemble anyone in the adoptive family, to become alienated.

A Need for More Information

A common theme often heard from adoptees is gratitude for their adoptive parents and how they handled their adoption issues. Their parents did everything right, but it was still not enough. They want and need more information.

Sandy experienced a warm and positive home environment, yet silently struggled with an unresolved adoption question, "Why was I given away?" By age 30, her ever-present pain could no longer be hidden.

I always wanted to know facts about my adoption, but by the time I reached 30, the need was far deeper. . . . I had significant questions to ask. The ever-present one was "why was I given away?" The only way I could put the pieces of my life together was to find the pieces myself. I waited as long as I could until the anguish became unbearable. I ached inside without any answers from those who hopefully had held me, even just for a moment, before they said good-bye.

It is not unusual for adoptees to have questions they would like to have answered. In addition to the circumstances surrounding their abandonment, they may want to know if there were siblings born before or after them, how their siblings have fared, and the current life-style of their biological family members, to mention a few. The questions range from existential to practical—the adoptees are gathering information and the knowledge fills a void.

A need to obtain a medical history, a need to look like someone, and a need for more information are three critical reasons that motivate children adopted as infants or toddlers to become involved in the search process. The fourth reason is a need for continuity in the midst of life's transition.

A Need for Continuity in the Midst of Life's Transitions

There are many unique issues in the life cycle of adoptees (Rosenberg, 1992). The decision to search often emerges following a significant event, such as marriage, planning a pregnancy, pregnancy, the birth of a child, or the death of an adopted family member.

When adoptive parents die, the adoptee may suddenly feel compelled to put a name and face to the phantom "other" parents who had been companions of his/her childhood fantasies. Since the unconscious knows no time barriers, losses tend to pile up, and the most recent loss drives the adoptee to resolve the first loss, the one that remains potentially reversible (Brodzinksy, 1992).

For one young adult, this proved to be true. Dealing with adoption issues was something that 31-year-old Tina ignored throughout her life. As a young child, she pushed away thoughts and feelings about being adopted. As an adult, she found herself standing face-to-face with old feelings left over from childhood. For Tina, it was the death of her adoptive mother that brought her adoption issues to the surface.

In my heart I wanted to belong to my mom and dad. I wanted to be their biological child. I was embarrassed that I was adopted and I felt that if people knew I wasn't really a "Waler," they might think differently of me. Overnight it hit me. Somewhere out there, there is someone who looks like me. (Stevenson, 1993)

Tina's confronting the reality of her adoption is quite similar to the experience of other adult adoptees. Some adoptees face their status early and look for answers in their late teens. Still others, like Tina, do not face it until a major transition looms before them. Following the death of her adoptive mother, the reality of another person distantly tied to her life emerged. After nearly 30 years, Tina faced the reality of her adoption and its implications. She initiated a search to find out as much about her birth family as possible. Unfortunately for Tina, the need to connect was not mutual. Thus far, Tina's mother has rejected all of Tina's efforts to meet. Any attempt to locate her birth father was also blocked. Tina simply wants to more completely develop the picture that was exposed at the time of her adoptive mother's death.

Moving through life's transitions requires a connection between the past and the future. For some adoptees, the stresses of those life-cycle changes prompts them to reach back and connect with unknown people and places in an effort to alleviate confusion and pain.

A Need to Connect

Motivated by one of adoption's major issues—loss—many adopted adults initiate their search from a deep, pervasive feeling of disconnectedness; that is, they feel a piece of themselves is missing and/or incomplete. There is a compelling necessity to meet the people who brought them into the world. They long to see, touch, and talk to those people who have only been shadows in their imaginations.

For Betsie, growing up in a warm, nurturing adoptive family that gave her the message "Talking about adoption in this house is OK" still wasn't enough. The sense of disconnectedness followed at her heels. She comments about her struggle:

Where did I get my red hair? What nationality am I? These were questions I faced daily. I also knew nothing about my birth. Was it an easy or difficult labor? What time was I born? How much did I weigh? Where was I for two weeks before placement? Deeper inside me were more questions. What kind of body was I growing into? How did my birth mother feel about me—then and now? Did she think of me? Why was I given up? That was the biggest question.

In order to connect the scattered pieces of her life, Betsie decided to find her birth parents.

As I grew up I always knew I would search, but I really never pictured it as real or as potentially leading to a reunion. Adoption was steeped in unreality and disconnectedness to me—engendered by the closed system. I got the message to pretend as if this did not make a difference, that my family was like any other family. Part of me felt like an alien—alone in the world. I felt ruled by fate not knowing who I was. . . . Later I heard terms like "biological alien" and "genealogical bewilderment," which described how I felt.

To feel like a "biological alien" is to feel like a stranger in one's own family, for example, to look around at family members and not see a reflection of oneself. To sense "genealogical bewilderment" is to struggle with questions such as "Do I really belong to this family?" and "If not, where do I really belong?"

For adoptees placed as infants, issues relative to the search process are unique and emotionally packed. It is a threatening and apprehensive experience to stop one's adult life long enough to step back into an obscure past and face anonymous people with unknown reactions. However, a large majority of birth mothers, adoptive parents. and adoptees support an active search process (Sachdev, 1989). The emotional intensity of the search process is complicated by the core issues in adoption that adoptees experience (Kaplan-Roszia & Silverstein, 1995).

CORE ISSUES FOR ADOPTEES PLACED AS INFANTS

According to Yellin (1994), many adoptees struggle with integrating their intellectual understanding of the facts of their adoption with the complex feelings attached to the question "Why was I given away?" Many adoptees remain emotionally confused. In addition to feeling unwanted, they cannot comprehend how anyone could give away flesh and blood, and why no one would help their birth mothers keep their babies. They want to know what's behind the real story. Issues emerge, from these clashing thoughts and emotions, that confront adoptees throughout their lives as they attempt to put adoption within the context of their life narrative. The following discussion highlights the core issues for adoptees placed as infants (Jewett, 1982; Melina, 1986; Winkler, Brown, van Keppel, & Blanchard, 1988), many of which emerge during the search process.

Loss

Adoption is the only relationship in life where, by its very creation, everyone experiences loss. Without loss, there would be no adoption. Loss is the hub of the wheel; it is the experience that brings together birth mothers, adoptive parents, and adoptees (Kaplan-Roszia & Silverstein, 1995; Rosenberg, 1993). Every member of the adoption triad is touched by at least one life-changing loss.

For birth parents, loss begins the moment they legally finalize adoption plans. Holidays and birthdays often are painful reminders that the relationship with their birth children is gone—never to be regained again, or, at least, not until some later point in time. Also, fueling the sense of loss for birth parents is the knowledge that they will never see their children get on a school bus on the first day of kindergarten, never hear the chatter of the exuberant adolescent, never see their children graduate from high school, and never know future generations. Adoption is an experience that presents a lifetime of losses. According to Kaplan-Roszia (1994), "It is these losses and the way that they are accepted and hopefully resolved that set the tone for the lifelong process of adoption."

For many adoptive parents, loss is created by infertility, which implies loss of a birth child, loss of dreams for a family, loss of status as birth parents, and loss of providing grandparents with a birth grandchild (Schooler, 1995). Throughout the life cycle of the adoptive family, the theme of loss is revisited. On various occasions, such as Mother's Day and Father's Day, the child's birthday, when the child inquires about birth parents, or the anniversary of the adoptive placement, adoptive parents are reminded that this child is not their child by birth. When the first grandchild is born, and coupled, perhaps, with a reunion between adopted child and birth family, adoptive parents again are reminded that the child is not their child by birth. They may question where they truly fit in the life of a grandchild if birth grandparents are introduced into the family.

For the adoptee, the long list of losses also is significant. "The adoptee experiences many losses over a lifetime: loss of birth parents, loss of a biological connection to the adoptive parents, loss of status as a normal member of society with one father and one mother, loss of birth family ties, loss of cultural heritage, loss of siblings, and loss of genetic information" (Brodzinsky, 1992, p. 142).

Some adoptees encounter feelings of loss in early adolescence. By the time they enter the adolescent years, the perception of their adoption is embedded in a single word—loss. These adoptees express their inner thoughts about losing their families, heritages, and identities. Other adoptees, however, do not encounter the deeper feelings of loss until middle adulthood.

As she grew older and moved into her mid-thirties, Sue encountered, for the first time, a profound sense of loss. She now knows that, as a young person, she kept adoption issues hidden.

Before I had my daughter, much of my adoption stuff was underground for me. When she was born, I really realized that to my knowledge, she was the only connection in blood that I had. I was unprepared for the really intense feeling of loss I experienced and still do.

Challenged with new feelings and emotional experiences, Sue recognized after the birth of her daughter that she was dealing with pervasive feelings of disconnectedness in her own life. The strong bond she developed with her daughter led her to understand, for the first time, the true meaning of connectedness. Not only did Sue feel the disconnectedness as a loss, she also commented that the secrecy of her adoption left her without a history, without a life in its truest sense, which all culminates in a life without reality. Her journey is bringing resolution to these issues and feelings.

Adoptees who experience deep feelings of loss have the choice to either confront the loss directly or continue to cloak the deep-seated pain in denial. Anderson (1993) writes about loss, "Life consists of a series of losses, which by themselves do not cause psychopathology. One does better to confront a loss directly; ignoring it or wrapping it with platitudes may obviate the need for grief over the short term, but invites a problem with self-esteem over the long term" (p. 31).

Loss is at the core of issues for some adopted adults placed as infants or toddlers. The search process may be precipitated by unresolved loss or it may motivate adoptees to deal with feelings of loss. Feelings of abandonment and rejection are an outgrowth of loss.

Abandonment and Rejection

To reject means to repel, to repudiate, to throw back, or to throw out as useless or substandard. A large shadow looming over the lives of many adoptees is the feeling of being rejected. As adopted children move through their development, they acquire an understanding of the meaning of adoption. Eventually they understand more clearly the issues of abandonment and rejection.

As children, adoptees first understand adoption as gaining a family. By the time adopted children enter school, they learn that adoption is a different way to enter a family. They begin to understand that not only did they gain a family, but they lost one in the process. By early adolescence, some adoptees reach the conclusion that they not only lost a family, but were given away—they were rejected.

For some adoptees, fantasizing and replaying rejection and abandonment becomes a way of managing the pain. Feelings of rejection can override the positive and nurturing love of their adoptive parents. Their perceptions of rejection can spill over into their ability to build healthy relationships, which can result in the inability to maintain or sustain long-term friends or connections. Other adoptees develop patterns of pursuing acceptance and backing away from it when emotional intimacy appears close.

To understand the issues of abandonment and rejection, Kaplan-Roszia and Silverstein (1995) suggest some questions an adoptee can ask to sort through the pain.

• *How has rejection played a role in my life in response to loss?* This question is the first step in confronting what is happening in the emotional life of the adoptee. It encourages the adoptee to take a look at how he/she has handled friendships and relationships.

• *Have I become a people pleaser to feel accepted or am I an extremely angry and rejecting person?* The adoptee may feel a need to make and keep everyone in the world happy at a great expense to his/her own needs and sense of well-being. Other adoptees may reject people to protect themselves from intimacy.

• *Have I caused significant others to reject me over time because of those initial losses in adoption?* In asking this question, the adoptee can assess how his/her feelings of rejection have played out in setting up a recurring cycle of rejection in other relationships; for example, "I will reject you before you reject me."

• *What will I now do with this perception of rejection?* This question can help the adoptee determine the direction of his/her life and develop a plan of what he/she will do with the answers to the assessments made.

As adoptees become more in touch with feelings of loss, rejection, and abandonment, other issues may emerge, touching deep chords of self-worth as they deal with feelings of shame and guilt.

Shame and Guilt

Some adoptees experience a deep and pervasive sense of shame. Shame is the ongoing feeling that one is fundamentally bad, inadequate, defective, unworthy, or not fully valid as a human being (Smede, 1993). By its mode of creation, adoption can form this perception within a child that can translate into shame.

Feeling shame is not about what one did or did not do. It is about ourselves. It is about who we are. Shame tells us that we are unworthy. "Shame is without parallel—a sickness of the soul" (Smede, 1993, p. 7). Smede (1993) offers some suggestions about how feeling shame can make a person sick.

• *Shame exaggerates one's faults.* People who nourish unhealthy shame inside themselves are compulsive exaggerators. They have no sense of the distinction between minor misdemeanors and major felonies. A small blemish makes them feel like giant gargoyles. A petty fault feels like moral cancer.

• *Shame is chronic.* Some persons are shame-bound. They have taken out a lifelong lease on shame. Feelings are tilted toward shame. Anything can bring it on—a mild criticism of their work, a hunch that they were overlooked, a memory of a foolish remark—anything negative sets off the shame mechanism within.

• *Shame pervades one's whole being.* Unhealthy shame spills over into everything a person might attempt to do or be. Unhealthy shame has no aim or focus—it leaves one feeling undefined and undifferentiated.

For adoptees, another source of a sense of shame is the feeling that they never were what their adoptive parents had hoped for. They never measured up to the fantasy child the adoptive parents could never conceive. Shame left them with the awesome pain of never being that dreamed-of child. Shame also left them with pain in believing that they never did the right thing, which leads the adoptee to struggle with a sense of guilt.

Guilt, by definition, is the sense that one has done something wrong. For adoptees, guilt is rooted in a sense of never doing the right thing, or of never measuring up in the adoptive home. Guilt is also a feeling that the adoptee, even as an infant or small child, caused the breakup of the relationship within the birth family.

Guilt and shame are feelings that overlap. The adoptee feels guilty for something he/she has or has not done. He/she feels shame for being the type of person who would have done it. Along with the possibility of dealing with one or more of the core issues related to adoption—loss, abandonment, guilt, and shame—an adoptee may be struggling with another issue that is intricately linked with the others—identity.

Identity

Establishing an identity is not something that happens during a certain period of one's life; it is an ongoing process. Identity formation is not simple. Most people do not achieve a uniform identity; instead, they think of themselves as having different identities in different contexts. For example, someone might have an occupational identity, a religious identity, and an identity having to do with interpersonal communication or basic values. To achieve an integrated identity, an individual must blend various aspects of the self with each other over different points in time. The family plays a critical role in the development of an integrated identity. For the adoptee, there is another element to this process: adoptees have two families—the one they know, who raised them, and the one they do not know, who gave birth to them. Identity integration can be very difficult for adoptees, because they cannot gain answers when they have been separated from the people (i.e., birth family) and information that will give them those answers (Brodzinsky, 1992). Thus, adoptees struggle with identity.

Another identity development issue that adoptees experience is feeling that they are different, which can occur because of physical and racial differences. For example, Kim, a 25-year-old adoptee from Korea, encountered feelings of being different on an almost daily basis.

When we went to a restaurant, grocery store, just about anywhere, I could sense people turning their heads to look at us. I knew they were wondering where I came from. I was born in Korea and it is obvious that I'm adopted.

When Penny joined her family, she was the only child. Shortly thereafter, three children were born to her adoptive family. She grew up in a loving, nurturing family of very light-complexioned blonds. Her two sisters and brother all towered over her in height. She felt like the only "short and fat" one in the house. Her own perceptions of these major differences created a sense of confused identity.

Not only does "differentness" contribute to identity issues, but a sense that the "real" part of one's self is absent also contributes. Many adoptees, in relating what adoption feels like to them, refer to the sense of a missing piece.

People ask me, "Don't you hate your mother?" "No!" says Nanci, "How could I ever hate somebody I don't know? How could I love somebody I don't know? I just have a million questions. [For example]: Did you ever think about me? Did you ever try to find me? Were you ever curious about how I grew up? My adoptive parents are my parents—I love them to death and I don't want to hurt them. But I've always had that feeling that something was missing. I don't know how to explain it. It wasn't anything my [adoptive] parents did wrong. It's just something that's always been there." (Barieri, 1992)

Carole, an adoptee placed within weeks after her birth, experienced the same feelings.

I love my parents dearly. They raised me with good moral values, a sense of family, and a lot of love. But still, I needed to meet the woman who gave birth to me. As much of a cliché as it may seem to be, I needed to find that missing puzzle piece.

However, there is not agreement about the issues raised regarding identity development in adoptees. Benson, Sharma, and Roehlkepartain (1994), in a four-year study of adolescents adopted as infants, concluded that adoption has little impact on the identity formation process. They suggest that few adoptees think about adoption often, and, at least in the adolescent stage, report that it has made little difference in how they view themselves. Groze (1992) suggests that it is not adoption status but attachment between adoptive parent and adoptee that is most critical in shaping self-concept. Nevertheless, for at least some infant-placed adoptees, a core identity is a part of the struggle for identity. For some, this struggle leads them to search for birth family members, but for others it does not.

INFANT-PLACED ADOPTEES WHO DO NOT CHOOSE TO SEARCH

Years ago, when adoptees mentioned "the search," they were considered by some to be ungrateful, and in the worse scenario, mentally unstable. Today, the reverse is thought by strong proponents of the search process—that if adoptees do not choose to search, something must be wrong with them. Adoptees who have taken the step to search have many positive reasons for the undertaking. For those who have not, their decision needs equal validation.

Many adoptees decide not to engage in the search process. Their decisions appear to be related to a variety of reasons. In clinical narratives (Schooler, 1995), their reasons include: lack of interest, loyalty to adoptive parents, uncertainty as to the right to disrupt lives, and fear of rejection. It is not unusual for adoptees who choose not to search to base their decisions on a number of reasons, which are discussed in the following sections, with case illustrations.

Lack of Interest

Kaplan-Roszia (1994) and Benson et al. (1994) commented that some adoptees are just not interested in pursuing the search process. As Kaplan-Roszia commented, "Their lives are full and busy with families or careers. Identity is not an issue for them," she added, "and it is something they don't want to do."

June, an adoptee in her mid-thirties and also an adoption therapist, has no interest in searching for her birth parents. Married, with two children, June enjoys a close relationship with her adoptive parents, who have always left the door open for her to become involved in the search process. June stated that even as a child, she had no interest in her birth family. Now that she is an adult, she continues to have no interest in finding her birth family. "I am just not interested," she commented.

The lack of interest should not be seen as problematic. It may or may not change over time. Each adoptee's experience is unique and it is important for adoption professionals to support and validate an adoptee's decision not to pursue a search process.

Loyalty to Adoptive Parents

Loyalty can be related to how the whole issue of adoption was handled as the adoptee grew up in the adoptive family. For example, the adoptee may have received the message that it was not all right to ask adoption-related questions. It was a subject never to be mentioned. Thus, if the family dealt with adoption differences by denying them or refusing to talk about them, the adoptee may feel that he/she must be loyal to the family's denial.

A second reason is the adoptee's perception of how the adoptive parents may interpret the reason for searching. Approaching adoptive parents with the desire to search and dealing with their confusion, or hurt, are issues some adoptees choose to avoid.

At 26 years of age, Catherine doesn't plan to search right now. She feels her decision is an outgrowth of loyalty to her adoptive family that far outweighs a need for anything else. Commenting about this decision, she said:

I think the reason I am not searching at this time is that I don't think I have anything to search for. I have never felt that anything was missing from my life. I am very close to both of my parents. I would not want to do anything that would hurt them in anyway. They are both older now. Maybe my feelings will change, but for now I will leave the issue alone.

Loyalty to one's adoptive parents and extended adoptive family should not be underestimated. For some adoptees, the loyalty conflict would be more difficult to experience than their need to search.

Not Feeling It Is a Right

According to Kaplan-Roszia (1994), some adoptees are given a message from society, or from adoptive families, that asking for information about their birth families is not what they are supposed to do. They may have grown up in a family where talk about adoption was strictly avoided. They may have heard, from their adoptive parents or other relatives, just how fortunate they were to be placed in such a wonderful family. "Just think where you might have been today, if you weren't in this family" may have been a recurring theme at family gatherings.

At 27 years of age, Nancy says that her need to find out about her birth family has caused turmoil throughout her adoptive family system. This turmoil has created an emotionally complex tug-of-war. "Do I search for me . . . or do I not search for them?" she questions. "Can I handle what they will do if I do decide to search?" It is a dilemma she has yet to resolve and a dilemma that deters some adoptees from searching. Some adoptees put their own needs on hold for fear that searching for their birth families will be too disruptive to their adoptive families.

Fear of Rejection

Many adoptees placed as infants have grown up with the perception that their adoption equaled rejection. They have asked themselves a thousand times why anyone would give something of value away. Fear of rejection is a prominent concern that might deter an active search.

While growing up, Sue kept her "real" questions about her adoption put away—far from feelings and far from any conscious level. In midlife, as she faced the meaning of adoption for her—that is, she had been given away—Sue lifted those fragile feelings from the backroom closet of her heart and confronted them. As a result, she decided not to search for any family members or any information about herself. As Sue reflected on her reasons for choosing not to search, she reached deep into the hidden pain that had lain dormant for so long. For her, it is the compelling reason for leaving the issue alone.

Looking at this, I really have to say, the main reason for leaving all of this alone is the absolute fear of rejection. I am continuing to work through those feelings of rejection as the consequence of my adoption. This emotional pain has impacted me so much that to risk another is simply not worth it to me.

To chance rejection, yet another time, is clearly why some adoptees choose not to search. It is certainly taking a risk, and for some adoptees it is a risk not worth taking. The decision not to search is as complex as the decision to search. To be objective, adoption therapists need to allow each individual adoptee to stand face-to-face with the questions and risks involved in the search process, for it is their decision alone with which to grapple.

THE REASONS ADOPTEES PLACED AS OLDER CHILDREN BEGIN THE SEARCH PROCESS

Adults who entered their adoptive homes as older children usually carried with them memories of people and places. They also may have carted along a history of physical, emotional, and/or sexual abuse, and, perhaps, a history of neglect. As adults, some choose to ignore the effects of such raw life experiences. However, for most, escape is nearly impossible.

Farmer (1989), in writing about adults who were raised with abusive parents, comments:

The abuse suffered in childhood continues to substantially affect them. They long for a break from their cycles of repetitious, self-defeating patterns of behavior, yet they cling to familiar habits because they know no other way. Conflict and struggle dominate their lives as do persistent feelings of being victimized, exploited and betrayed by others. (p. 4)

Most adults who were victims of abuse carry no overt physical signs but have wounded spirits. Many have moved into adulthood under clouds of anxiety, depression, low self-esteem, and chronic loneliness. They continue to be controlled by the faint memories of a painful past, although many times they cannot acknowledge it. They are simply unaware that their present-day difficulties most likely are intricately tied to the trauma of a lost childhood.

Parker (1994) has encountered many struggling adult adoptees. "Self-doubt becomes a real issue for these young adults. Being placed for adoption and dealing with thoughts of 'what's wrong with me, why was I given up?' is compounded with feelings of knowing that one was abused or neglected as well. They think to themselves, 'It's worse than not being wanted, they hurt me besides.'"

Why do some adults, adopted as older children with backgrounds of abuse and neglect, choose to take the journey back? How do these adults move beyond the maze of emotional pain created from their abusive pasts? It is a journey not easily undertaken. The first step of the journey, beyond awareness of the pain, requires adoptees to address their own personal pasts by finding out as much factual and historical information as possible. A second step is to become aware of the silent, hidden issues created by their pasts that may have an impact on their emotional well-being. In addition to the same reasons adoptees placed as infants become involved in the search process (i.e., a need to obtain a medical history, a need to look like someone, a need for more information, a need for continuity in the midst of life's transitions, and a need to connect), two other issues influence the decision for adoptees placed when older.

Some Adoptees Go Back for Closure

Memories, created by truth or fantasy, often propel adoptees placed when older to retrace the steps of their pasts. According to Donley-Zeigler (1994), almost all adults adopted as older children have thought about piecing their lives together.

The thoughts of searching are universal. They are normal. Some think about it. Some talk about it. Others take action, pushing on in an attempt to find some resolution to their pain. I believe that for these adults, it is an issue of closure as to why they return. They are trying to figure out what happened to them and why. They have perhaps grown up with a sense that they were at fault for the abuse—that they had something to do with causing the family problem. They wonder about being defective—imperfect. Going back and finding out what happened enables many to put the adoption into the right context.

For many adoptees, facing the events of their past becomes an absolute necessity to finding emotional stability. Putting closure to haunting memories moves them to resolution. Giving facts to vague recollections help them sort out fact, fantasy, or misunderstandings. Understanding may lead to some forgiveness, even if the adoptee never forgets.

Going back for closure is one reason adults adopted as older children return to their birth families. Dealing with the disturbing rumblings of the mind is another.

Some Adoptees Feel like Walking Time Bombs

Looking into the historical context of their circumstances is part of the healing process for adults adopted as older children. For some adoptees, it helps put issues that were vague or unclear into perspective. For other adoptees, it gives them the answers they need as they struggle to deal with their emotional health and well-being. Severson (1994) says:

Many [adoptees] come to me as adults saying that they feel like a timebomb ready to go off. This happens often in those who were under the age of six when the abuse or trauma occurred. They have not seen their family of origin since that time and because of their young age, they do not have any context to relating to those persons outside the memory of the abuse.

Life is a continuum of human experience and the abusive event was so overpowering it is their only memory from which they can develop a sense of identity from a historical context. As these adults moved through adolescence and attempted to develop self image from their historical context, two issues presented themselves. First, they don't have much memory to serve them and second, what memory they do have is often traumatic and even horrifying.

Severson (1994) offers some direction to professionals working with adoptees who are older when placed and who have histories of abuse.

When I can, I work to get into the historical context of the person's memory. No one person abused a child twenty-four hours a day. I try to help this person recover any memory, however small it may be, that is positive.

Another step, in a therapeutic approach, moves the adoptee toward healing and resolution, Severson also said,

Using what I call "explaining therapy"—that is, giving them as much information as possible—is a successful tool. That information includes such things as those factors that contribute to the intergenerational patterns of abuse, social/economic influences, and the psychological make-up of the family of origin. Fifty to sixty percent of my work is explaining therapy. Going back to an agency and getting as much information as is relevant to them is essential.

According to Parker (1994), "The truth is paramount for searching adoptees, no matter what is found. Finding out answers is of immense importance because what fantasies exist for the adoptee may be far worse than the truth, which may have been magnified by secrecy."

In addition to these unique issues, many of the issues raised in the previous discussion about the reasons adoptees placed as infants engage in the search process may be relevant for adoptees placed when older. In addition to the similarities in the reasons they engage in the search process, there are similarities in the core issues for adoptees placed when older.

CORE ISSUES FOR ADOPTEES PLACED WHEN OLDER

For many adoptees placed as older children, going back into their faintly remembered past creates unexpected feelings and strong emotional responses. In addition to the core issues mentioned for adoptees placed as infants, variations of the core issues affect adoptees placed when older. These core issues include confronting survivor's guilt, dealing with an obligation to rescue, wrestling with shame, and coping with anger or rage. As with adoptees placed as infants, these issues may emerge during the search process.

Survivor's Guilt

In returning to the abusive family of origin, some adoptees discover that other siblings joined the family after they were removed, or were never removed from the family. To their horror, those siblings grew up amid abuse and/or neglect. Such a discovery may leave adoptees with the perception that they abandoned their brothers and sisters.

Diamond (1994) suggests,

One of the concerns I see these young adults carry is what I call "survivor's guilt." There is a real sense of relief that they were rescued from an injurious home environment on one hand, but guilt for leaving on the other. They asked themselves, "If I could have stayed, could I have helped them?" They feel this especially if other siblings were left at home. Some even go as far as to think that their leaving left the family in far worse shape and that they should be blamed.

These issues also may result in older-placed adoptees feeling that they didn't deserve to be rescued. In addition, some adoptees harbor anger at the child welfare system for operating inconsistently. Even though their biological families were dysfunctional, some of their biological siblings remained in the home. Closely related to survivor's guilt is another issue: it comes from a message adoptees receive, implicitly or explicitly, from birth parents—an obligation to return.

An Obligation to Return

When older children are placed in the permanent custody of an agency and prepared for adoption, part of that preparation process involves a "good-bye" visit with birth family members, whenever possible. This is a highly emotional time for parents and children, and sometimes it is during these last visits that the message "Come back and take care of me" is sent to the child. It may haunt an adoptee into adulthood.

Ward (1994) says that this farewell experience sends two profound messages to the vulnerable youngster—two messages that the youngster jams deep into the back pocket of his/her mind to retrieve at a later date. The first message that the adult adoptee retrieves from memory is that of an obligation to the birth parent to reconnect. For some, it goes beyond the faint promises made by a frightened child—it mushrooms into a driving, motivating force and a vow that cannot be broken.

The second message that emerges, encased by the feelings of unrelenting obligation, is the fantasy of rescuing the birth parents. "There is a perception that the birth parents need to be rescued. Some have created a fantasy of 'the poor people who lost their children.' These adults deny the reality of the abuse and neglect. This idealization of their birth parents propels them toward reunion" (Ward, 1994).

Survivor's guilt, a sense of obligation, and a need to rescue are issues that surface in the lives of adult adoptees dealing with a difficult abusive history. A fourth issue, a variant from the issue faced by adoptees placed as infants, strikes at the fragile nature of the human spirit—shame.

Shame within Identity Formation

Diamond (1994) reports that many adoptees, with histories of physical, emotional, or sexual abuse, carry with them a deep sense of shame. They feel embarrassed, or humiliated, by their pasts, yet they are unable to forget various events that took place. They wonder, "How far away from being like them am I really? Can I surpass them? If I want to reconnect, do I have to become what they are and not absorb the values of my adoptive parents?" For many, a wrestling match of the heart and soul takes place as they battle to define themselves. They wonder who they will become and may have some anxiety about becoming like their birth parents. The nature/nurture question nags at them and this sense of shame becomes a part of the self.

Searching for biological parents can be extremely complicated for adoptees with histories of abuse and/or neglect. Stacking the emotional shelves of life with such issues as survivor guilt, obligation to return, and shame is further complicated by feelings created by one more issue, perhaps the most controlling and destructive—anger and/or rage.

Anger and/or Rage

Abuse and neglect can leave deep emotional scars on its victims, which are often worse than physical wounds. For many adults adopted as older children, complicating the deep pain of separation from birth family members is anger and/or rage. Anger and/or rage is a product of the abuse that took place in the family of origin, as well as a way to express the bitterness resulting from forced separation.

Geta, age 33, recollects, all too well, what it felt like to hear the back door swing open and to hear the blustery, angry rantings of her violent, abusive father. She remembers the many occasions, after his fits of rage, that all members of the family had to pretend as if nothing had happened. No one could be sad. No one could be scared. And, of course, no one could be angry.

My birth father would come home from work usually drunk. It was like a tornado hit the front room. He would just blow the place apart, leaving us in the wake, physically in pain and emotionally traumatized. I learned early in life to be afraid of anger because it was so connected to violence.

I went *inside* with my anger, where it rotted over time, but never went away. As I grew older, that anger rose to the surface as depression and substance abuse. I finally went for help and learned that I could openly express the rage I had buried for so long. I want to see my birth father again; I was 10 the last time I did. But I will see him as a healthier person than I used to be. I now have found how to be liberated from the anger that so consumed me.

Some adoptees get stuck in their rage toward their birth families, agencies, and/or social workers. They continue to struggle with feelings of powerlessness and anger over the loss of control of their destinies. Emotional issues of guilt, obligation, shame, and anger, if left unattended, can sprout like weeds within the lives of adoptees with disturbing pasts, choking off growth, emotional health, and quality relationships. Choosing to rip out the festering weeds, with the help of support groups or counseling, will enable adoptees to manage whatever comes as a result of being reunited with biological families.

THOSE ADOPTEES PLACED WHEN OLDER WHO DO NOT SEARCH

Similar to adoptees placed as infants, there are a number of adoptees placed when older who do not search. However, the reasons for not searching are somewhat different. In many ways, older-child adoptions are open adoptions, although they are not planned as an open adoption. In a recent longitudinal study of older-placed and special needs adoptees, Groze (1996) found that 41% of the children had contacts with members of their birth families. Most of the contacts were with their siblings, who were not in adoptive homes, one-third had contacts with their biological mothers, and one-fifth had contacts with extended family members. These contacts, for the most part, had positive effects on the children and their adoptive families. With such an open arrangement, children do not need to search because they have the contact they need.

A second reason older children may not search is that many of them have lifebooks, medical and social service records, and memories that are sufficient to answer most of their questions. For example, many adoptees have photos of their birth parents that they can look at, so they can see someone who looks like them. Often, they have the social service records that give identifying information and health histories. So, the issues that provide impetus for adoptees placed as infants to search are often less pronounced or lacking for older-placed adoptees.

Finally, some older children have no desire to go back to the abusive or neglectful situations from which they were delivered. They avoid searching—they believe there is nothing to be gained by going back. They worry that their birth families continue to lead dysfunctional lives and that they will some day, as adults, be in a position where they may have to be responsible for them.

PRACTICE IMPLICATIONS

Assessing Readiness for the Adoptees to Search

Making the decision to initiate a search is a critical turning point in the life of an adoptee. As the adoptee journeys onto a path that may link unknown events and people from an unknown past to the events and people of the present, preparation is an absolute necessity. A multitude of concerns must be faced.

There are several factors to consider before searching. First is the readiness to begin and carry through with the process. One of the initial factors, when counseling adoptees on readiness, is to determine what steps they have taken in the search process, thus far. In particular, it is important to evaluate how adoptees have prepared themselves emotionally to begin the process. Adoptees in the midst of emotional crises probably should not engage in a search. Second, it is important to assess whether the adoptees have taken a few steps, stopped, and begun again, or whether they are impulsive and quick acting. They may need to slow down the process.

As part of the assessment, it is also important to ask questions about the future.:

- What are your concerns?

- How do you feel about those concerns and how do you think you will feel about them in six months, or next year?

- What impact do you expect a search or reunion to have on your life if you meet your family?

These questions can be addressed in therapy, or in the context of a triad support group. It is particularly helpful for adoptees who are involved in the search process to sit down with adoptees who have completed a search, to discuss the above questions.

These are important questions to filter through one's present life situation (Diamond,1994). The search-and-reunion process is one of the most powerful experiences in life. It provides opportunities for increased insight, strength, and healing and continues one's journey of self-discovery and development as an adult.

Before actually activating the search, with the primary outcome of reunion, it is important to self-assess readiness. Yellin (1994) suggests several reasons that adoptees may postpone their search until they complete further work on emotional readiness.

The first reason is searching with a planned outcome and unrealistic expectations. These searchers are not prepared for the unexpected and may be setting themselves up for more disappointments. It is a normal part of the search process to fantasize about the birth family and the outcome. A key question to ask the adoptee is "Will you be okay if it turns out differently than you had planned?"

The second reason is not being emotionally ready as a result of unmet needs in the adoptive home. Searching for a birth parent or birth family with the hope of regaining a parent-child relationship as if the adoption did not occur is unrealistic. Some grief work must be done around what was lost in the adoptive parent relationship and the birth parent relationship. It will help move one toward more readiness.

The third reason for deferring or postponing the search is that it is not motivated by the adoptee, but by others pushing the issue. It is important for the adoptee to drive the search process, not to be a passenger.

As Ken, a 33-year-old adoptee, who completed a search expressed, the search effort can be a great time of personal growth, filled with discovery, pain, fulfillment, and healing. It is something that the adoptee should only initiate himself when the time is right. It should never be another's decision.

Examining the adoptee's life experiences is also an important component to assess as part of the readiness to search. Severson (1994) commented,

One of the questions I ask myself in dealing with an adult adoptee in this circumstance is: do they have enough life experience and enough self-knowledge to forgive? If the answer is no, I am pessimistic about the reunion. If the answer if yes, I am much more optimistic.

Life experiences can create a judgmental system that can work for or against a positive reunion outcome. One of the key life experience factors I look for is: is this person a parent? If so, he/she probably knows something about parental rage.

I also look for life experiences that have created not a "black and white" judgmental perspective but more of a gray—a willingness to look at the abusive person's whole life and what it was like for them.

First, adoptees conducting a search must be prepared to encounter unexpected emotions that may propel them into confusion, anger, fear, or depression. Second, adoptees must learn to recognize unrealistic expectations within themselves and balance those expectations with probable reality. Third, adoptees must have a reasonable understanding of what circumstances they may find regarding their birth families. Finally, the adoptee must determine whether it is the right time to conduct a search and must know how to obtain support. It is a journey that must not be taken alone.

Expecting the Unexpected: Handling the Emotional Roller Coaster

When plowing new ground, the only thing for certain is that unexpected ruts, rocks, and even boulders sometimes block progress. As adoptees plow new ground, they may find themselves profoundly confused at the depth and breadth of their emotions. The following are common emotions that are part of the experience.

Anger or Rage. The search process can trigger much anger. The anger originates from and is directed at many different people.

Whatever the source, legitimate and misdirected anger or rage is something many adoptees face. What to do with it, then, becomes the issue. Although often viewed

Table 1
Most Common Questions Asked By Adoptees

Anger Aimed at:	Infant-Placed Adoptee	Older-Placed Adoptee
Birth mother	Why couldn't you keep me?	Why couldn't you get your life together? Why did you hurt me? Why couldn't you protect me?
Birth father	Why didn't you take responsibility?	Why couldn't you support your family? Why couldn't you get your life together? Why did you hurt me?
The agency	Why couldn't you help my other siblings? Why was I removed and not my siblings?	Why didn't you keep my siblings and me together? Why didn't you tell my adoptive parents the whole truth about my past?
The adoptive parents	Why didn't you talk to me more about my adoption?	Why didn't you tell me what you knew about my past? Why didn't you tell me I had brothers and sisters?

Table 1 outlines the most common questions asked, although each adoptee's situation is unique in its narrative.

as something to avoid, anger can become the ally of the adoptee. According to Lifton (1994):

We must remember that no matter how painful these waves of grief and anger are, they are part of the on-going process of mourning that comes with reclaiming one's lost emotions and integrating them into the self. Adoptees find it hard to believe at the time, but the chaos carries healing in its wake. (p. 155)

Anger experienced by adoptees as a part of healing is best encountered with help. Wentz (1994) strongly suggests that adoptees seek an open ear from a third party as the anger surfaces. "Someone outside the relationship who would not be affected by the venting of the adoptee's anger can best be that buffer. It could be a therapist or a trusted friend who understood the dynamics of the healing process." Triad support groups offer a forum for adoptees to vent their rage and gather support. In addition, using energy from rage directed toward adoption reform can be healing and empowering.

Anger is one emotion that catches the adoptee off guard. Sadness and depression are two more.

Sadness and Depression.   Some adoptees may be dealing with the losses adoption created in their lives for the first time (Norris, 1994). The sound of their birth mother's voice is enough for some to invoke the incredible sadness they kept buried within. According to Pavao (1992),

When an adoptee finds a birth parent, she is often not prepared for the depression that comes with that. The better the reunion, the harder it is sometimes. One reason is that there is a lost history. You meet the person twenty years later and you realize you missed all of his history, all of his connections. There is a real sadness about that loss.

Adoptees realize that they cannot go back in time and recapture the loss of not having grown up with their birth families, which may result in profound sadness.

Anger and sadness are just two emotions adoptees need to be prepared to face. Fear, which can be paralyzing, is another.

Fear.   As adoptees step onto the rickety bridge that connects their unknown pasts to their unknown futures, they place themselves at great peril. The perceived reality of that peril grows as adoptees confront the negative responses connected to the desire to search. Those messages—"You are ungrateful," "What's wrong with you?" or "You will just get hurt"—can stop them at the onset.

The peril broadens as the adoptee encounters losing relationships—first, the adoptive parents, and then, perhaps, the birth family. They may wonder: "If I search, will my adoptive parents reject me? If I find my birth family, will they reject me, too?"

The peril may feel overwhelming as adoptees attempt to scale the seemingly insurmountable wall of the closed adoption system. A sense of peril creates fear. Fear can be an immobilizing emotion. It can temporarily block or permanently stop adoptees' attempts to locate their birth families. Many adoptees say they fear one or more of the following may occur:

- their birth parents or adoptive parents will reject them;

- they will stir up painful memories for their birth families;

- they will ruin the lives of their birth parents by showing up;

- they will not please their birth parents;

- they will lose control over the newly created relationships; or

- they will find no answers by finding dead ends, or death.

Overwhelmed and Overloaded.   Adoptees experience a myriad of feelings during the search-and-renunion process, including being overwhelmed and overloaded. Wentz (1994), in working with all members of the triad during the search process, sees adoptees embarking on a honeymoon phase early in the reunion.

I compare the meeting of the birth parents and their child to that of young people who meet and fall in love. It is like one is on a high and can never get enough of being with that person. Acting on these feelings can do much damage to the fragile relationship without proper emotional preparation. It can become all consuming and suffocate the newly made connection.

Wentz (1994) suggests:

I recommend to those with whom I work, that there is not a face-to-face contact without laying some groundwork. That groundwork can be in the form of letters and/or phone calls. Figuring out one's boundaries prior to meeting will help keep emotionally charged plans from overwhelming either party.

In order to keep the adoptee's emotional life in balance during the search-and-reunion process, Wentz recommends the following:

• Keep the other components of one's life stable—don't make other major life changes.

• Maintain and keep healthy other relationships.

• Avoid being obsessed with being with the newfound person.

• Keep a journal of the events and feelings.

Akin to being overwhelmed by the emotional attention generated by the reunion is the feeling of being overloaded. McColm (1993) writes:

Because adoptees have lived for so many years with little or no information about their birth family, their curiosity and their need drives them to collect so much information so quickly. . . . Wanting to meet increasing numbers of birth family members, even though the original and ultimate goal was to meet her birth mother, is evidence of the depth of the adoptee's primal need to solidify her identity. . . . All this activity leads to depression and/or exhaustion. (p. 162)

Lifton (1994) encountered these same experiences during the early days of her reunion with her birth mother. She writes:

The decision for time out is not always a conscious one. In *Lost and Found* I wrote about the emotional turmoil many adoptees, including myself, experience after reunion. . . . I was so overwhelmed with anxiety and guilt after meeting my mother that I fell through the trapdoor of self, down to what felt like rock bottom. . . . For the next two months I withdrew from everything around me, staying still until I could regain the . . . energy to climb back up into the outside world again. (p.165)

Conquering the emotional roller coaster brought on by the search-and-reunion process brings many adoptees to new levels of self-awareness and understanding. Although frightening and intense, the ride is a necessary part of preparing adoptees for the reunion and the healing process. Another step of preparation is also crucial: examining expectations of what adoptees believe about the reunion relationship.

Examining Expectations

Deep longings create profound expectations. Postponed desires can inflate a person's expectations of the outcome. For the adoptee, whose innermost yearning is to reconnect to birth family members, examining his or her hopes for the reunion experience may prevent unnecessary frustration, anger, disappointment, or heartbreak.

One of the most important steps in preparing adoptees emotionally for the search process is to understand, in a general sense, what expectations other adoptees have experienced. Lifton (1992) addresses three types of expectations: instant transformation into a new person, instant emotional healing, and instant unconditional love.

Many adoptees have expectations, going into the reunion, that cannot be met. The adoptee expects to be immediately transformed and not to be the same person, but the wonderful idealized self that they might have been if they had not been adopted. They wake up the morning after the reunion and find they are still the same.

Also, some adoptees expect to be instantly healed. Like Pinocchio. He is just a piece of wood and suddenly he comes to life with all the emotions. The adoptee feels like Pinocchio and will say "I felt dead before, but now I feel." The problem is if you have never felt before, you have never really known what grief or anger is or what loss is, if you allow yourself to feel for the first time, one can be overwhelmed by the feelings.

Those feelings do not heal overnight. According to Lifton, a third expectation, which is not always met, is a surprise to many adoptees.

The adoptee is shocked to find that he may not have unconditional love from his birth mother. They think that all other people not separated from their mothers are getting unconditional love and they think that they should be getting that at the reunion.

What the adoptee finds, in some cases, is that the birth mother does not have the emotional strength to enter the relationship, or that she has constructed a life and family totally exclusive of the possibility that the birth child may someday want to reenter her life. She may not be emotionally available to the adoptee, or she may be mentally unstable, or even dead.

When these expectations are not met, the adoptee may experience profound feelings of loss, sadness, and/or depression. Being prepared for a range of outcomes can help.

Preparing for What One Might Find

In addition to being prepared for the emotional search-and-reunion expectations, adoptees must be prepared for what they might find. For some, discovery of the past brings a sense of relief and peace. For others, discovery of the truth forces further examination and resolution. Finding information that presents a dark picture of the past can be unsettling for adoptees.

Falsified Information. Sometimes the information can be false or purposely misleading.

At the age of 12, Robert found out that he was adopted. As he began to explore his background, he discovered a painful secret. He had been sold to his adoptive parents for a substantial amount of money. The doctor had falsified the original birth certificate, leaving him no clues as to his birth parents real identity. Robert was a black market baby. That meant, unless a miracle occurred, the door to his past was forever sealed.

Many adoptees feel that finding out the truth, no matter how painful, is better then secrecy and denial. In this clinical example, Robert was a young man who learned that what he thought was his identity was based on lies and falsifications. Other circumstances for adoptees have been just as traumatic.

Finding the Records Destroyed. Whether birth records were destroyed intentionally or by accident, the result is the same—there is little or nothing to go on. This dead end can leave adoptees suspended in a continuing sense of disconnectedness.

In the late fifties, a maternity home in a midwestern state placed hundreds of babies into adoptive homes. Susan, now in her late thirties, was one of those infants. However, when she began her search, she was devastated to find that the founder of the home had died and her family, seeing no need for all the clutter, destroyed the records from the maternity home. She could not talk to her adoptive parents about her need to find information and now she feels she has no way of finding out anything.

This scenario can result in deep sadness, anger, and rage. Susan will continue to fantasize about her origins, because she is unable to fill in the missing pieces of her identity with factual information.

Finding a Criminal History. When nothing is known about the birth parents, the discovery of a criminal history can shed a shameful light over the adoptee's sense of worth and value unless the adoptee is able to put the news in its proper perspective.

Once Allan discovered his birth family name, the search process went relatively quickly. His birth father had left a lasting impression upon the neighboring community, one that was not pleasant for Allan to contemplate. He was easily located because he had been incarcerated for years. Allan felt shame and embarrassment over what he had found. However, eventually, knowing the truth helped him to put his entire life into a new context.

It is often useful in a scenario such as this (finding a birth parent with a criminal history) to search further. Extended family members, including siblings, often can satisfy the need for biological connectedness.

Finding Abandonment. Adult adoptees who joined their families through international adoption often have absolutely no information about their birth families. They were literally left on park benches, in churches, or in police stations in their countries of origin. That problem exists not only overseas, but in the United States as well.

Tracy could hardly believe what her parents told her regarding her adoption. For years, she had been told her birth parents died in a car accident. Finally, she was told the truth. Tracy had been left on a park bench late one evening and discovered by a passing patrolman. No clues to her birth parents were ever found. She had not only been abandoned physically at birth, but abandoned emotionally and historically forever.

This kind of profound abandonment can be devastating for the adoptee, especially being told as a young adult, after years of forming an identity based, in part, on one's "adoption story." For international adoptees, connecting with one's original culture and language, and even visiting the "motherland" can fill the gaps. Triad support groups can be particularly helpful for transcultural adoptees to connect with other adoptees from their places of birth. Support groups are also of great importance when there is abandonment and there are no clues to finding the birth family. Adoptees can share their adoption experiences and not feel so alienated and disconnected.

Finding Death. Adoptees often enter the search process with high expectations. They have perhaps dreamed of the moments when their first contact will be made. Those expectations can be crushed in a matter of seconds when that person is not found and only a death certificate is left behind.

For Tina, the issue of the search had consumed her every waking moment. After months of waiting, a search consultant called to tell her that she had located information about her birth mother. She learned that her birth mother was dead . . . an option she had not allowed herself to consider. Recovering from the overwhelming disappointment, Tina began to search for other birth family members. Finding her parents were gone was a sad discovery, but Tina was able to find a conclusion to her search through contacts with other family members.

A situation such as this can be particularly devastating, when a birth mother keeps her child a secret from extended family members. Death of the birth mother does not stop some adoptees. They continue to search for other family members. They hear stories, see pictures, and meet extended family members and close friends who are able to share information about the birth mother. The search can still be meaningful, in that the adoptee knows much more about his/her biological family, and, therefore, can develop a clearer and stronger sense of self.

Finding difficult birth family circumstances presents adoptees with a dilemma—what do they do with what they know? For many, although the information was unpleasant or inconclusive, it provided them with a sense of completion, and a sense of connectedness to a past that, prior to the search, was nothing but a blank slate.

Listening to Advice from Those Who Have Searched

The adoptee's decision to alter relationships and events in his/her life—with birth family members, adoptive family members, and his/her own adult family—is an important one. Juggling the emotions, facing the fears, weighing the overload, confronting people and issues—what a task for any one person to handle! Listening to advice in the early stages can bolster the adoptee's courage to do what must be done. The following comments from adoptees who have made the search-and-reunion journey can help lead the way for those who follow.

Although I am an advocate for feeling emotions strongly and deeply, I advise keeping the expectations in perspective. Do not allow fantasies to cloud realities. I would change nothing and do nothing differently. I try to allow things to just happen. I was fortunate—our reunion could not have happened any more beautifully than it did. (Carol, age 26)

Never give up searching, but have a strong faith in God and in yourself to accept whatever you find. Then go on with life. Make sure you have a good network of support to guide you and help you make wise decisions. (Tammy, age 38)

I think the first thing I try to get across, to those I help in searches, is that unless they are comfortable with their own feelings and willing to accept the bad as well as the good, then they are probably not ready to search. The one thing that tips me that they are ready is their concern for "not" making waves in their birth parents' lives. (Kathy, age 45)

I also tell them, don't give up. Sometimes you need to step back and go at the search from a different angle . . . but just don't stop. Take a vacation. Go to the beach or mountains. Come back renewed and start again. You are healing while you seek those lost loved ones and the missing pieces of your own story. (Susan, age 43)

I would advise others involved in the search process to always keep a positive attitude in dealing with their expectations. Searches very often take a long time and are very taxing on your emotions. Get involved in a good support group. Look at your search from every angle . . . see how it affects you as well as others who will sooner or later become involved. But the main thing is keeping a positive attitude . . . one day you will find. (Shelly, age 32)

Every experience involving the search process is unique. Outcomes depend a great deal on the original reasons for the search and the level of expectation considered. Lifton (1994) considers the search process as a kind of mythic quest. A search for the lost mother is really a search for the lost self, enabling feelings of wholeness and completeness.

Attending Support Groups

The intensity of search-and-reunion issues for infant-placed and older-placed adoptees creates the need for a support system, during and after the search. It is a journey that should not be taken alone.

Norris (1994) explains:

Our society has supported a huge amount of denial regarding some of the realities of adoption. In my search I had to acknowledge that there had indeed been a loss. Before joining a support group of adoptees and birth parents, everyone I knew had only emphasized what I had gained from adoption. I felt alone in realizing that there was a lot more to it than that. What a relief it was when I found others who were speaking honestly and openly about the realities I knew, but had never even dared put into words.

As my search progressed, I was open in talking with my friends and family about what I was doing. Many were very supportive. However, it was only the other searching adoptees that I knew who I felt truly understood what was actually driving me to search.

It was a very emotional time for me with many ups and downs. I can't imagine having gone through that time thinking that I was alone in this need, without a supportive community behind me.

Since my reunion, being involved in an adoption group has remained an important part of my life for several reasons. Along with my own personal benefit, I feel committed to helping the system change to better meet triad members' needs, and to being there for others so they do not have to go through all of this alone.

For all those touched by it—the adoptee, the birth family, the adoptive family, and the extended family—adoption is a lifelong process. Research in the past 20 years has helped us to understand how each member of the adoption triad deals with the issues of loss, rejection, guilt/shame, and identity (Kaplan-Roszia, 1994; Lifton, 1992; Rosenberg, 1992). It also helps us to understand how the issues affect the ability to proceed in a healthy and productive way in search and reunion.

There is, within every person, a hunger to know who he/she is, who he/she is connected to, and where he/she has come from. There is a hunger to know the truth. When that knowledge is lacking, there is a deep yearning, an unsettleness that cries out from loneliness and emptiness. The search-and-reunion journey—whether it leads to a fulfilling adult relationship, simply answers questions, or results in the discovery of a painful reality—leads to somewhere and that somewhere is to the truth.

REFERENCES

Anderson, R. (1989). The nature of the adoptee search: Adventure, cure or growth. *Child Welfare, 68*(6), 624–632.

Anderson, R. (1993). *Second choices: Growing up adopted.* Chesterfield, MO: Badger Press.

Barieri, S. (1992, March 23). Adoptees try to fill in the blanks: A half million Americans are looking for answers they can only get by finding their biological parents. *Orlando Sentinel Tribune,* D1.

Benson, P. L., Sharma, A. R., & Roehlkepartain, E. C. (1994). *Growing up adopted: A portrait of adolescents and their families.* Minneapolis, MN: Search Institute.

Brodzinsky, D. (1992). *Being adopted: Lifelong search for self.* New York: Doubleday.

Diamond, R. (1994). Personal phone interview.

Donley-Zeigler, K., trainer/consultant for National Resource Center for Special Needs Adoption, Chelsea, MI. Personal interview, 1994.

Farmer, S. (1989). *Adult children of abusive parents: A healing program for those who have been physically, sexually or emotionally abused.* New York: Ballantine Books.

Groze, V. (1992). Adoption, attachment and self-concept. *Child and Adolescent Social Work Journal, 9*(2), 169–191.

Groze, V. (1996). *Successful adoptive families: A longitudinal study of special needs adoption.* Westport, CT: Greenwood Publishing.

Jewett, C. L. (1982). *Helping children cope with separation and loss.* Boston: The Harvard Common Press.

Kaplan-Roszia, S. (1994). Personal phone interview.

Kaplan-Roszia, S., & Silverstein, D. (1995). *Intergenerational issues of adoption.* Presented to Adoptive Families of America Professional's Day Conference, Dallas, TX, June 29–30.

Lifton, B. (1992). *Healing the cumulative trauma.* Presented to the American Adoption Congress, Philadelphia, March 19–22.

Lifton, B. (1994). *Journey of the adopted self: A quest for wholeness.* New York: Basic Books.

McColm, M. (1993). *Adoption reunions: A book for adoptees, birth parents and adoptive families.* Ontario: Story Book Press.

Melina, L. R. (1986). *Raising adopted children: A manual for adoptive parents.* New York: Harper & Row.

Miller-Havens, S. (1990). *Connections and disconnections: The birth origin fantasies of adopted women and search.* Unpublished doctoral dissertation, Harvard University.

Norris, B. (1994). Personal interview.

Parker, M. (1994). Personal phone interview.

Pavao, J. (1992) *Counseling the adoptee: Postsearch.* Presented to the American Adoption Congress, Philadelphia, March 19–22.

Reitz, M., & Watson, K. W. (1992). *Adoption and the family system.* New York: The Guilford Press.

Rosenberg, E. B. (1992). *The adoption life cycle: The children and their families through the years.* New York: The Free Press.

Rosenberg, K. (1993). Healing our losses. *Adoption Therapist, 4*(2), 4–9.

Sachdev, P. (1989). *Unlocking the adoption files.* Lexington, MA: Lexington Books.

Schecter, M., & Bertocci, D. (1990). The meaning of search. In D. Brodzinsky & M. Schecter (Eds.), *The psychology of adoption* (pp. 62–90). New York: Oxford University Press.

Schooler, J. (1995). *Searching for a past.* Colorado Springs, CO: Pinon Press.

Severson, R. (1993). *Transformation.* Presented to the American Adoption Congress, Cleveland, April 1–4.

Severson, R. (1994). Personal phone interview.

Smede, L. (1993). *Shame and grace: Healing the shame we don't deserve.* San Francisco: Harper & Row.

Stevenson, T. (1993, November/December). Growing up adopted—what it feels like as an adult. *Family Ties Newsletter.*

Stiffler, L. (1992). *Synchronicity and reunion.* Hobe Sound, FL: FEA Publishing.

Triseliotis, J. (1973). *In search of origins: The experience of adopted people.* Boston: Beacon Press.

Verrier, N. (1993). *The primal wound: Understanding the adopted child.* Baltimore: Gateway Press.

Ward, N. (1994). Personal phone interview.

Wentz, B. (1994). Personal interview.

Winkler, R. C., Brown, D. W., van Keppel, M., & Blanchard, A. (1988). *Clinical practice in adoption.* New York: Pergamon Press.

Yellin, L. (1994). Personal phone interview.

5

The History, Elements, and Ongoing Need for Adoption Support

Rita Laws

In this chapter, Rita Laws, Ph.D., gives a historical perspective on adoption support for older children and infants. Drawing from Native American traditions, her extensive involvement in adoption support, and a triad perspective, Dr. Laws offers some unique ideas on adoption support for both populations.

Jamal read in a magazine that tens of thousands of U.S. children are waiting to be adopted. He would like to adopt a child or two but has no idea where to start. Marie and Dave want to make an open adoption plan for their expected infant, but don't know who to call. Pete was adopted as an infant, and has recently been diagnosed with a rare genetic disorder and needs detailed family medical records. All of these people are in need of adoption support—the bridge between adoption the concept and adoption the reality.

Studies show that adoptees, birth parents, and adoptive parents benefit from support services before, during, and after infant and older child adoptions (Babb & Laws, 1997; Barth & Berry, 1988; Brodzinsky & Schechter, 1990; Rosenthal & Groze, 1992). Yet, other studies have shown that adoption support services have been waning, sporadic, inadequate, and difficult to locate, access, and keep (Barth & Berry, 1988; Cohen & Westhues, 1990; Groze, Young, & Corcran-Rumppe, 1991; North American Council on Adoptable Children [NACAC], 1989; Nelson, 1985).

The first step in the provision of adoption support services is to understand the history of adoption support in this country. The second step is to identify and describe the elements that make up adoption support services. In the last step, adoption professionals and volunteers must commit to making support services readily available to all who need them.

THE HISTORY OF ADOPTION SUPPORT

Pre-Columbus Tribal Communities and Adoption

Researchers agree that current adoption practices have their roots in English law (Adamec & Pierce, 1991; Cole & Donley, 1990; Nelson, 1985). However, the United States is a relatively young country, just a little over 200 years old. This land also has a history with adoption prior to the European immigration, even though books about adoption rarely mention it.

Adoption existed among American Indians. While individual tribal practices did not have the impact on modern U.S. adoption that the English system had, white adoption practices were exposed to Indian adoption practices and were affected by them.

While pre-Columbus American Indian adoption practices differed among the many tribes, in general, tribes saw their children as a valuable resource and viewed adoption as one way to safeguard that resource. An example of adoption practice among ancient American Indians is illustrated by the tradition of the Blackfoot tribe. Orphans were given to elderly widows and grandmothers to be adopted (Hungry Wolf, 1982). This was good for the child because he or she now had experienced parents. This was good for the women because the children could help them in their old age. Thus, adoption was viewed as having mutual benefits for both adoptees and the adoptive parents.

The Blackfoot tribal society was supportive of adoptive mothers because these mothers were raising children who otherwise might have perished. The adoptive mothers were also given a specific type of adoption support by other mothers in the tribe. Hungry Wolf (1982) offered an example of this help when she described the adoption of her grandfather; his mother had died while giving birth to him, so he was adopted by his grandmother. Since it takes time for a mother's milk to be reestablished, the adoptive mother would take the baby to other nursing mothers within the tribe to be fed. The infant was also allowed to suckle at his new mother's dry breasts until her milk supply gradually returned and she was able to breast-feed the infant.

Another example of the ancient Indian attitude toward adoption is found among the Choctaws of Oklahoma and Mississippi. Adoption was an everyday fact of life among the Choctaws (Oklahoma Choctaw Council [OCC], 1983). This was especially true after European diseases, new to the Native Americans, killed many people and created an even larger number of orphans.

Claiborne (OCC, 1983), a nineteenth-century explorer, commented on Choctaw adoption customs in his writings. He wrote that the adoption of orphans was common, even among families that already had children. Further, adopted children shared equally in any inheritance, and were sometimes allotted the best share.

The Choctaw attitude toward the *alla toba*, or adopted child, mirrored the tribe's attitude toward family ties. Children were cherished and encouraged to play instead of work (OCC, 1983). The tribe was not seen as a collection of families, but as one large family system living in many different homes. In the Choctaw culture, all men were uncles and all women were aunts to all children. Therefore, even adoption by a stranger was, culturally, an adoption by close relatives or kin. Children without parents were immediately placed within the tribal family. This attitude of community as family, and of adoption as a culturally normal response to a parentless child, defines adoption support at its best.

Adoption support helps create and keep families together and functioning well. Full cultural acceptance is a type of silent, but highly effective, adoption support. When adoption is a cultural norm, families feel supported because of the widespread acceptance. When adoption is seen as an unusual or inferior way to build a family, it is more difficult for the adoptive family to function optimally within a society.

From Colonial Times to the Twentieth Century

For most of our nation's early history, adoptions in the United States were informal. That is, adoptions did not require court intervention or legal action. This informal approach to adoption, among both American Indians and other races living in America, continued into the mid-nineteenth century (Cole & Donley, 1990).

However, there were differences in philosophy between the native groups and other groups. Whereas American Indians saw adoption as preserving a tribal resource (the children), the early American colonists tended to adopt for practical reasons. If a family needed an heir, or additional members to share in the workload, adoption was one way to meet that need.

Adoption became formalized in colonial times when the Massachusetts legislature was asked to pass a special bill granting legal adoption status to a particular child. The Governor of Massachusetts, Sir William Phips, was the first adoptive parent on record in the 13 original colonies. He adopted a son and legally changed the boy's name to the Phips name (Adamec & Pierce, 1991).

American adoption was eventually affected by the industrial revolution and the new attitudes it spawned during the eighteenth and early nineteenth centuries. Early in the industrial revolution, orphaned children were indentured to work in factories and, sometimes, adopted to work in families. During the latter part of the industrial revolution, the practice of indenturing orphaned children to put them to work fell out of favor (Cole & Donley, 1990). Of course, this practice was for older children who were old enough to work. Besides, infant mortality rates were very high for children residing in institutions at the turn of the century—as high as 100% in some institutions (Chapin, 1911, 1917)—so it was often the older children who were placed with families. In 1836, Massachusetts passed the first child labor law prohibiting the exploitation of children for labor. By 1851, the United States had its first adoption statute, "an Act to Provide for the Adoption of Children." Coincidentally, this law was also passed in Massachusetts. For the first time, the courts affirmed that adoption law was designed to promote the welfare of children. In 1891, Michigan passed a statute that was the grandparent of today's home study.

The statute called for an investigation of adoptive parents in order to protect adopted children (Adamec & Pierce, 1991).

At the same time that there was a movement to legislate the welfare of children, there was a movement to develop other forms of care for children besides orphanages and institutions. In the mid-1800s, most orphans were living in almshouses and in mental institutions with adults; foster family care was only an occasional experiment. Charles Loring Brace, the founder of the New York Children's Aid Society, began the "orphan train movement" in response to this problem. Orphans in large numbers were sent by train to mostly western states to be instantly adopted by rural families who met the trains. The orphan trains went from town to town until every child had departed.

Brace believed it was better for children to be adopted/fostered and taught how to earn a living on farms than to grow up in asylums alongside mentally ill adults. By 1859, 24,000 children had been placed in adoptive and foster homes as a result of the orphan train movement (Cole & Donley, 1990). When the movement ended in 1929, the total number of children placed exceeded 150,000 (Adamec & Pierce, 1991). Tragically, the families in which these children were placed were not investigated prior to these train platform placements. Some of the children were overworked and ill treated by their new families. Most of these children were older.

In essence, two forces shaped adoption during this period. One force was the utilitarian nature of adoption to create inheritance, or for labor supply in rural areas or factories. The second force was the gradual shift from children as commodities to children as entities with special rights, needs, and values.

Adoption in the Early to Mid-twentieth Century: Emphasis on Infants

As the value of children in America was enhanced, formalized adoption became a normative practice. The first of two trends that contributed to a new attitude toward children involved the proliferation of child labor laws restricting the use of children in the labor market. Congress passed the first federal child labor law in 1916 (some state laws had been in existence for 75 years prior to that time). By the 1930s, it was no longer considered acceptable to adopt children simply to put them to work in factories or on farms (Adamec & Pierce, 1991). The second trend was brought about by psychologists. Beginning in the early 1900s psychology turned its attention to the study of children. G. Stanley Hall (1844–1924) was the first psychologist to study children in a laboratory setting. His work generated a great deal of interest in the field of child psychology, a discipline that matured shortly after World War II (Adamec & Pierce, 1991; Elkind, 1981).

The more children were studied and written about, the more the public thought about the welfare of children. The new revelations and attention to children spurred debate about proper adoption practices. Also, since children were no longer of value as a work commodity, the public had to accept the inherent value of children, particularly those who were orphaned or abandoned. As care for children improved and infant mortality in orphanages and institutions decreased, alternatives to institutionalization were created, including the growing practice of placing infants for adoption. Even with the enhancement in the value of children in America during the first part of this century, adoption agencies had to push for adoption acceptance by mainstream American society. The public was not enthusiatic about infant adoptions for two reasons: the "illegitimacy" of many of the children available for adoption, and the idea of bringing a nonblood relative into the family (Nelson, 1985). The European custom of attaching importance to the marital status of a child's parents migrated to the United States with the first colonists, and took firm root. To this day, the word "bastard" is considered a grievous insult in America.

Edna Gladney, who founded an adoption agency in Texas more than 100 years ago, worked hard to eliminate the stigma attached to children born out of wedlock. She believed that children should not suffer for the choices of their parents. She said that it is not the children who are illegitimate, but their parents. In 1933, she persuaded the state of Texas to remove references to illegitimacy on birth certificates (Adamec & Pierce, 1991).

The second main objection to adoption by the American public involved the idea of bringing nonrelative children into the family. At the turn of the century, many people worried that children who were nonblood relatives might have "bad blood" or be conceived of as "bad seeds." Prejudice fueled this fear. Prospective adopters often wanted assurances that the child they were going to adopt had no minority ties, such as Irish ancestry (Cole & Donley 1990).

Infant adoptions increased briefly after World War I. However, the adoption practices of today had most of their roots in the post-World War II adoption boom. By 1950, adoption practice consisted primarily of healthy infant adoptions. The adoption of older children became a rarity; the adoption of children with special needs virtually never occurred. Infant adoptions, older child adoptions, and special needs adoptions changed dramatically beginning in the 1960s.

MODERN-DAY ADOPTION

Birth Parents: An Emerging Force in the 1960s

Adoption support for birth parents and concepts such as birth parent rights, open adoption, and open records had their genesis in the 1960s. Before this time, birth parents kept a low or nonexistent profile since out-of-wedlock birth was closely associated with mental illness, moral depravity, and personality disorders (Brodzinsky, 1990a). After 1960, the social stigma associated with such births diminished. Between 1960 and 1976, the percentage of babies born to unmarried parents increased from 5% to 24%, while the percentage of infants placed for adoption decreased from 80% in 1970 to 4% in 1983 (Brodzinsky, 1990a). Some birth parents, mainly mothers, formed support and advocacy groups to find their voice and to share their experiences, feelings of grief, and sense of loss. Groups like Concerned United Birth parents (CUB), Adoptees' Liberty Movement Association (ALMA), and American Adoption Congress (AAC), made up primarily of birth parents and adult adoptees, formed to offer support services and to contribute to adoption reform. These groups have been successful, on a state-by-state basis, in developing new legislation to deal with issues such as the legal rights of birth fathers, the opening of sealed records, developing an array of options for openness in adoptive placements, and developing adoption registries for adoptees and birth parents.

Focus on Older and Special Needs Children

Even before the 1970s, there was a shortage in some parts of the country of healthy white infants to adopt , as more poor parents and single parents decided not to surrender their children for adoption. Since fewer infants were available, older children and children who were formerly considered unadoptable (such as minority children, children with histories of physical or sexual abuse, children with developmental disabilities and handicaps, and children who were part of sibling groups) became a priority for adoptive placement. These children became more valued for their own uniqueness and the emphasis in adoption practice shifted from finding children for parents to finding parents for children.

Older child and special needs adoption practices can be traced to events that started with the first professional adoption conference, the National Conference on Adoption. This conference was sponsored by the Child Welfare League of America (CWLA) in 1955. The entire adoption field was slated for a reform that was centered around a concept called "the best interests of the child." Social services casework policy and practice underwent a revolution over the next 20 years; the special needs adoption movement was an outgrowth of this conference (Cole & Donley, 1990).

Massachusetts, the first state to institute child labor and adoption statutes, provided some of the first innovations for promoting the adoption of older and special needs children. It was the first state to publish a photo listing book—a book with pictures and short biographies of children needing families—to serve the new and growing movement to adopt older and special needs children. The Massachusetts Adoption Resource Exchange (MARE)—which begain in 1950 and is still in existence—photographed and created biographies of the state's waiting children. The majority of these children were older or hard to place because they were special needs children. MARE then used the waiting-child catalogs to recruit adoptive families for these children.

Photo listing is a popular and important recruiting tool in contemporary adoption practice for matching waiting children and prospective families. Electronic photo listings of waiting children are also available on the Internet. The age of paperless matching of children with families is a concept of the 1990s.

Special needs adoptive parent support groups began appearing in the 1970s. These groups demanded the deinstitutionalization of all waiting children and permanency planning for children who were adrift in the foster care system. Many of these children were inappropriately placed in restrictive settings such as residential treatment facilities and group homes. This initiative became known as the permanency planning movement, a cause involving thousands of social workers and volunteers (Nelson, 1985). In 1978, special needs adoption advocates brought about a revolutionary new federal law called the Adoption Opportunities Act (Public Law 95-266). This act sought to remove obstacles to adoption, provide a means to match waiting children to families, and establish regional adoption resource centers. For the first time, the U.S. Congress sent a clear message that waiting children were a valuable resource in this society. In 1980, the Adoption Assistance and Child Welfare Act (Public Law 92-272) was passed making it financially possible for adoptive parents to afford to adopt older and special needs children. This law did, on a federal level, what most states had already done on a much smaller level: it provided financial and medical subsidies to make the adoption of children who had special needs for special services affordable. It was a big boost for special needs adoption because it removed many financial barriers (NACAC, 1989).

Several additional factors have contributed to the increase in the number of special needs adoptions since the 1970s. One factor is the easing of eligibility requirements for adoptive parents. Race, disability, marital status, income, home ownership, gender, and religion no longer keep Americans from adopting children. Age is usually not a factor unless the youngest parent in a couple would be older than 65 by the time the adopted child turned 18 (Nelson, 1985). In some states, older adults can adopt who meet this age restriction as long as there is a notarized plan on file of who will raise the child in the event that the parent does not live long enough for the child to reach majority age. Adoption agencies are working more with people interested in transracial adoption as well as with single people and gay and lesbian singles or couples who want to adopt children with special needs.

A second factor that influenced the special needs adoption movement was the proliferation of special needs adoption agencies and adoption support groups, such as Adoptive Families of America (AFA) and Adopt a Special Kid (ASK), during the sixties and seventies. These activities increased the number of placements during the seventies and eighties. For example, NACAC is an umbrella organization that represents 600 special needs adoption support groups in North America. Many of the small agencies devoted primarily to placing older and special needs children were founded by adoptive parents who used support group advocacy as a stepping stone to starting an agency (NACAC, 1989).

THE MAIN ELEMENTS OF ADOPTION SUPPORT

Adoption support for birth parents, adoptive parents, and adoptees is just one type of social support network. A social support network is defined as a set of interconnected relationships that provide durable patterns of interaction, interpersonal relations, nurturing, and reinforcements for coping with daily life

(Garbarino, 1983).   Support for adoptive families has been described more specifically as the provision of any item or service that helps adoptive families to form, function effectively, and stay together (Laws, 1995).   Support group participants glean much the same resources found in any social support network—a sense of self, encouragement, protection from stress, knowledge and resources, and socialization opportunities—regardless of who they are in the adoption triad—birth parent, adoptee, or adoptive parent (Maguire, 1991).

Adoption support consists of various elements that can be broken down into three categories: support *before* the adoptive placement, *during* the adoptive placement, and *after* the adoption is legalized (post adoption). While the various services can overlap the various periods of placement, in a general sense, there are specific components of support needed at each phase of the adoption process (Laws, 1995). These support services are consistent with the philosophy that adoption is a life-long process and not just a one-time legal event. Not every family will need support during each phase, but all birth parents, adoptive parents, and adoptees will require support at some phase, whether the adoption involves infants or older children.

Support Before Adoptive Placement

Birth Parents. For birth parents, the before period, or preplacement phase, is the time extending from the initial discovery of pregnancy and the decision to make an adoption plan, to the actual legal relinquishment of the child. During this phase, birth parents need legal and practical information about: (a) alternatives to adoption, (b) adoption's short-term and long-term psychological effects, (c) open adoption, and (d) their rights and the rights of their children.

This crucial information usually comes from birth parent support groups and the adoption agency, the attorney, or the intermediary with whom the birth parent(s) choose to work. These resources are needed to deal with the stress of making an adoption plan and with the subsequent grief and sense of loss that accompany both the decision and implementation of the plan.

In the computer age, a growing number of birth parent support groups and informational resources can be found on the Internet at news groups and at various online services. The anonymity of these online support groups can be very helpful for birth parents who have doubts, questions, and concerns, but are hesitant to raise them with people they know. A limitation of online support is that it is usually not geographically specific. That is, a local support group will know more about local laws than a national or international online group, and can, therefore, answer more questions with greater accuracy that deal with local regulations.

In the last two decades, there has been an explosion of books about, by, and for birth parents, especially birth mothers. A trip to the local library or bookstore is definitely recommended for all prospective birth parents who are thinking about their options during this phase.

In the case of adoptions that involve nonvoluntary surrender due to neglect or abuse, which is often the case with older children, the before or preplacement period begins with the state's direct involvement in the child's care, and ends with the cessation of parental rights. For children placed when older, most birth parents have been forced to surrender—the placement is not voluntary. These birth parents may be so incapacitated by mental, physical, or emotional problems that they cannot parent. Rarely are they agreeable to the relinquishment. In some cases, women may relinquish the child under pressure from a boyfriend or new husband who does not want the child; however, this is a rarity. Voluntary relinquishment occurs when the birth parents recognize that they were not meant to parent, or when their health may be slowly failing, such as in the case of cancer or AIDS. In these cases a parent makes an adoption plan.

Support services for birth parents relinquishing older children should include mental heath services, marital counseling, grief and loss counseling, and concrete assistance such as job training, medical care, and legal aid. These services may have been mandated and, in contrast to birth parents surrendering infants, are usually not provided through support groups but from public and private social service agencies and typically as part of a court order.

Adoptive Parents. For prospective adoptive parents, the before period, or preplacement phase, is the time extending from the application for adoption to the actual physical placement of the child. The shortest period for this phase is 40 days and the longest period is several years. Nine to 24 months is the average waiting period. For adoptees, this phase begins with the match-up between a child waiting for an adoptive placement and adoptive family, and ends with the entry into the adoptive home. This phase is concerned with supporting the family as it is formed or enlarged through adoption.

The preplacement preparation of the child and family by the agency contains the same elements described for birth parents: support groups, one-to-one support, reading materials, and factual information. This preparation is the foundation upon which the placement will build.

For families with older-placed children, the buddy family, a type of one-to-one support found in support groups, is a concept invented by NACAC (Possin, Hocking, & NACAC, 1989). A prospective adoptive parent, or couple, is matched to another parent, or couple, who is experienced in adoption. Ideally the match is a close one. For instance, if a prospective adopter is interested in adopting a sibling group of three children, the support group running the Buddy Family matching service finds an adoptive parent who has already adopted a sibling group of three children. This mentoring is supportive of both families because they share a unique experience, in this case, sibling group adoption. Some buddy pairs end up as lifelong friends.

Assigned reading, or bibliotherapy, is the next element of support. Adoption agencies assign reading lists (AASK, 1993) to prospective adopters to either supplement their adoption issues or make up the bulk of it. Books are the most common items on these lists, but government publications and periodicals are listed, also.

Laws (1995) found that the articles in adoption periodicals do not usually encompass the elements of adoption support in a balanced way. Such articles focus too much on media-sensationalized adoption cases, preparation, and nature/nurture studies, and not enough on all elements of adoption support. However, the imbalance is not severe enough to make adoption periodicals a poor choice. In fact, parents who subscribe to adoption magazines and newsletters, especially in their early stages of the adoption, should find a good deal of important and helpful information.

The factual information should cover the following: adoption in general, a brief history of adoption, some statistics, and adoption studies and issues, such as studies about transracial placements, adoptee issues, search and reunion, open adoption, and the media portrayal of adoption. A discussion of this information would lead into an overview of special needs adoption and a list of the most common special needs found among waiting children, such as emotional problems, learning disabilities, attachment disorders, and attention deficit hyperactivity disorder (Brodzinsky, 1990b).

Adoptees. The preplacement phase for the adoptee begins with news of a prospective family and ends with the actual move into the new home. For infants, they are often moved with little regard to having familiar objects, smells, or sounds accompany them. However, infants need time to prepare for a move. As part of preplacement, the adoptive parents can make visits to the infant's foster home to take over more of the baby's care (i.e., feeding, bathing, changing diapers, rocking, etc.) to prepare for the move. In this way, the baby becomes accustomed to the sight, smell, sound, and touch of the new parents, while still enjoying the security and familiarity of the foster parents. Also, adoptive parents can come to understand the child's routine and integrate that routine to ease the transition from one placement to the other.

Older children are often shown a "lifebook" prepared by the adoptive family. Lifebooks contain photographs, or a video, of the new family, pets, the home, church, school, and community. The lifebook helps prepare the older child for the next step, the visit with the family. The lifebook is the child's concrete link to his or her future.

During the early preplacement phase, older children need and want assurance that there will be ongoing contact with their friends and foster family after their adoptive placement. By knowing that their past is secure, they can look to the future with more ease. After their new family is identified, older children need access to their social workers to have their numerous questions answered. Younger children also need a concrete way to count the days between visits and until placement.

It helps if adoptees in preplacement have access to other children who have recently been adopted and who can offer support, information, and reassurance. Some children want immediate access to their future family. As they wait for the date of the first visit, they want to write letters or talk on the phone to their new family.

Whether the child is six days or 16 years old, adoptive parents should continually ask themselves, "What would I want or need if I were going to a new home at this age?" Each child is unique and will have different concerns, but preplacement is a time of conflicting and ambivalent emotions: excitement, anticipation, joy, grief, loss, and mourning.

Special Issues for Adoptive Parents to Consider During Preplacement

False Abuse Allegations. Educating adoptive applicants about false abuse allegations may frighten them initially, but it is a topic of growing importance. Even though adoptive parents are one-third as likely to be abusive as other types of parents (Barth & Berry, 1988), they are much more likely to be falsely accused of abuse by their adopted children when those children have emotional problems at placement (Cline, 1992). An emotionally disturbed child's description of abuse can be chillingly realistic when it is based on actual abuse suffered prior to adoption. Adoptive parents need to know how to prepare for the possibility of false abuse allegations by protecting themselves from possible legal repercussions. One strategy involves obtaining a letter from the child's therapist, or the child's placement agency, stating the child's history of abuse and neglect, and mentioning the possibility that false abuse allegations could be made by the child in the future to "punish" the parents for any number of reasons.

Disruption Prevention. Preventing adoption disruption, the removal of the child from an adoptive placement prior to legalization, begins with a good match. A good match between child and family involves making sure the "fit" is best for everyone. Parents should be warned not to "stretch" too much the type of child they feel they can manage (Nelson, 1985), or to allow themselves to be stretched by others. This means that they should know what characteristics of a child they can parent.

Educating adoptive parents includes providing them with correct and complete information about the child or sibling group (Barth & Berry, 1988; Groze, 1986; Nelson, 1985). Full disclosure of all the child's difficulties is crucial if the adoptive parents are to be prepared to help the child, and to integrate the adoptee into the family. Less than full disclosure greatly increases the risk of adoption failure or disruption. Parents can usually manage if the information is given to them beforehand; it is not having the information that causes the greatest difficulty.

Full disclosure is no less important for those who adopt infants than for those who adopt older children with complicated placement and abuse histories. There are many physical and mental disorders that do not show up in infancy but for which children may be at-risk (i.e., learning disabilities, developmental delays, substance abuse, "attention deficit disorder," various psychiatric disorders, mild cerebral palsy, and asthma). While prenatal and birth records are important for all adopted children, these records are of greater value to those parents adopting infants because the records represent the child's recent history. The adoptive family should request an information release form from the hospital where the adopted child was born. The child's records, which are most easily "deciphered" by a medical professional, will have the name and address of the birth parents deleted, but will be intact otherwise.

The medical records of the birth parents and the birth records of the adopted child can be of great help to the family physician in diagnosing and treating health problems, as well as in understanding developmental lags. Adoptive parents have discovered previously unknown information, such as the existence of maternal alcohol and tobacco usage, how much prenatal care was received, brief periods of infant oxygen deprivation, and what the newborn's Apgar scores were. All of this information is helpful in developing early intervention plans for the adopted child. It may also help prevent adoption dissolutions, which is the process of legally terminating the adoptive parents' rights, after legalization.

Just as pregnant women do not want to think about the possibility of miscarriage, prospective adoptive parents often resist any discussion of adoption disruption or dissolution. However, since the overall disruption rate for special needs children has been measured as high as 10% and dissolutions may be as high as 2% of all adoptions, it is essential that adoptive parents learn about risk factors for disruption and dissolution (Barth & Berry, 1988; Donley, 1981).

Attachment Disorders. An attachment disorder (AD) is a serious disorder that is common among older adopted children who survived bonding breaks, abuse, or neglect during the first one and a half to two years of life (also known as the attachment years). AD is characterized by an inability to trust and severe behavioral problems that tend to worsen with age. These problems are also resistant to many forms of traditional professional treatment.

Attachment is a process during infancy whereby the baby becomes attached to the caregiver through the need-resolved need cycle—that is, every time a baby cries or expresses a need for food, warmth, or love, and that need is met, the baby learns to trust the caregiver. Once the child attaches to the parent, the child can attach again to other caregivers such as the adoptive parent. The baby or toddler who never experienced secure attachment, whether because of abuse, neglect, institutionalization, or multiple caregivers, will probably always be insecurely attached, or have trouble attaching to and trusting future caregivers and significant others.

Adoptive parents quickly learn that the inability to give and receive trust affects all aspects of the child's behavior. Attachment-disordered children do not obey or mind consistently. Children with AD must be supervised constantly so that they do not act out, take dangerous risks, or victimize others. These children seem to have little or no conscience and may abuse pets, steal, horde food, and deceive their parents in countless ways.

Adoptive parents who have adopted children with attachment disorders are likely to believe that only parents who have similar children can truly understand the difficulties they face every day. Agencies may view the problem as adjustment-related. Many therapists are too often taken in by the young "trust bandits" and may blame the adoptive parents for the child's difficulties. In many cases, only the compassion and concrete suggestions of support groups keep a placement with a child with an attachment disorder from disrupting.

Since attachment disorders develop from experiences in infancy, usually before the age of 18 months, adoptive parents of older babies and toddlers may also have to deal with the problem, especially those who adopt children from institutions or orphanages overseas. When a child who was adopted at an older age acts out, the family and the community are more likely to blame the problems on the child's preadoption experiences. However, if the child was adopted as an older baby or toddler, the community is more likely to blame the adoptive family for the behavior problems, and the adoptive family is more likely to blame themselves, also. This is tragic, because blaming causes stress for all involved and it may stop the adoptive family from opening its home to an adoptee.

Support groups, in which some of the members have experience with children with attachment disorders, can help the newer families find effective therapists, respite care, and be there when the frustrated parents need a sympathetic ear. They can show adoptive families how to negotiate a "safety net" (Babb & Laws, 1997) into the adoption assistance contract that will guarantee help from the state should their adopted child ever need residential treatment or other specialized services. For those families who wish to adopt again, and to avoid attachment disorders, support groups can help them sort through photo listings and find a child who is at lower risk.

Support During the Adoptive Placement

Birth Parents. For birth parents, this phase of the adoption process lasts from the moment of legal relinquishment to the moment when relinquishment is final. In some parts of the United States, birth parents can legally stop the adoption of their children for seven days after signing relinquishment papers. In other parts of the United States, the waiting period is 30 days, which is just one of the many ways in which adoption laws vary from state to state, and even from county to county within the same state.

Because adoption laws are not uniform in America, it is crucial that birth parents and their immediate family be well informed of their rights during the waiting period after relinquishment. Grandparents also have rights they need to know about. In the case of American Indians, federal law requires that agencies first notify the tribe and attempt to place children with members of extended families. For most people, continuing with the same agency and support groups they began working with in the preadoptive phase is the right choice. However, birth parents who feels uneasy about their choices during this time should seek independent legal and professional help. Therapists and lawyers who are not affiliated with adoption agencies can be neutral in advising birth parents.

Open adoption is a relatively new option for birth parents. An open adoption is one in which there is some type of ongoing contact between the birth and adoptive families. This type of adoption, while rare in international and special needs placements, is growing in popularity among infant adoptions. Open adoptions can be loosely structured, that is, based on a verbal agreement between parties, or highly structured, as in signed and legally binding agreements. Some birth parent support groups recommend highly structured agreements to protect birth parents from losing contact with their children in the future.

International adoption is rarely open from the start, and more difficult to open later, than any other type of adoption. Some internationally adopted children are foundlings, meaning that birth parents were never seen or identified; others are orphans. In many cultures, especially Asian, open adoption is not a socially accepted idea. In spite of these problems, however, some American adoptive parents have been successful in opening international adoptions after legalization. In most cases, the families lose nothing by trying, and the adoptees may gain a better sense of self and cultural identity.

Special needs adoptions are not very likely to start out as open placements since most of the children were forcibly removed from their birth parents due to neglect or abuse. In those rare cases when special needs children are surrendered voluntarily, they will probably not be open because almost all occur through state agencies, which do not like open adoptions. However, special needs adoptions may enjoy some level of openness later as contact is made between the adoptees and other members of the extended birth family, such as siblings, aunts, uncles, cousins, and grandparents.

Opening an adoption months or years after the legalization requires much thoughtfulness and a delicate touch. The process of finding the adoptee's relatives is usually the easy part. Making initial contact and building a relationship of trust between the birth and adoptive families is not as simple. Adoption triad support groups are ideal in such situations because one or more families have been through a similar process already—with either grown or minor children.

Adoptive Parents. For adoptive parents, the "during phase" is the postplacement and prelegalization/prefinalization phase when the child is in the home but the adoption has not yet been legally finalized. This period of time is usually mandated by policy or law to last no less than six months, and no more than two years. Support areas in this phase center on helping the family function well and integrating the adoptee into the family.

The first element of support deals with money, including subsidies (Adoption Assistance Payments, AAP), subsidy advocacy, tax information, and other financial assistance (Anderson, 1990; Bussiere, 1990; NACAC, 1989). If a child is federally eligible for a subsidy according to law and has a special need, the family can apply for financial help until the child reaches the age of majority. These subsidies have been proven to reduce disruption rates significantly, but many families are unaware that these subsidies exists or do not know how to negotiate subsidy rates (Barth & Berry, 1988).

Parents who adopt infants may assume that an adoption subsidy is not needed, but agencies should encourage all families to apply. A large number of infants who demonstrate no special needs at placement may develop needs for special services later. An adoption subsidy can become very important. It is much easier to cancel a subsidy if it is not needed than to apply for it after an adoption has been legalized. Some states have recently developed postadoption subsidies, which families can apply for if there is a need later in the child's life for therapy or other specialized services.

Families need to learn how to write, negotiate, and renegotiate a subsidy contract, how to apply for subsidies and subsidy increases, how to obtain Medicaid or extra medical services as needed, and how to apply for other financial aid programs, such as the nonrecurring adoption expenses reimbursement.

Finally, families using subsidies need to be educated about tax laws. Subsidies are not normally taxable as income, but may affect taxes in other ways.

Also important, in this phase of adoption support, is training in behavior management methods that have been proven effective with emotionally and behaviorally challenged adopted children (Barth & Berry, 1988; Cline, 1992), with an emphasis on dealing with sexual acting out (Le Pere et al., 1986), lying (Ekman, 1989), stealing, violence, and attachment problems (Barth & Berry, 1988). Such training should not be delayed until it is deemed necessary. If the child being adopted is suspected of having emotional or behavioral problems, the entire family should be fully prepared to deal with those difficulties as soon after placement as possible.

Support groups are helpful for adoptive parents. Support groups for families who adopt infants often focus on such topics as the core issues in adoption, adoption issues throughout the life cycle, and other developmental tasks of adoptees and adoptive families. For families of older-placed children, support groups offer social support, respite care, warmlines (phone support services), and other direct support services (Possin, Hocking, & NACAC, 1989; Tremitiere, 1992). Support groups and social support focus on introducing the adoptive families to other similar families in social as well as educational settings. Respite care is specialized child care for children with special needs. Warmlines offer worried parents a sympathetic ear on the telephone at all hours.

Support groups may well be the best recognized and most important element of special needs adoption support. Support groups can be highly organized with a board of directors, regular meetings, and newsletters, or loosely structured with infrequent gatherings, or an emphasis on telephone support (warmlines) alone.

Most repeat adopters give credit to their support groups when they adopt a second or third time. Long after the adoption agency is out of the picture, support groups continue to be a source of understanding and help.

The adoptive family in this phase also requires help advocating for the child in the school or day care center environment (Hensley, 1989; Magid & McKelvey, 1988), and negotiating adoption preservation services as needed (Barth & Berry, 1988; Bourguignon & Watson, 1987). Educational advocacy is a learned skill. Parents whose child is at risk of learning or behavioral problems in school need to be taught how to advocate for the best possible school environment and program.

Adoption family preservation services, such as frequent prolonged visitation by the social worker and concentrated mental health services, have been effective in saving some troubled placements (Barth & Berry, 1988). Parents of adopted children who have severe behavioral and emotional difficulties must be made aware of the availability of adoption preservation services.

Adoptees. For the adoptee, the "during phase" begins when the adoption is legalized or disrupted. For older children, this is both an exciting and anxious time; although their dream of having a "real family" again is coming true, they may be worried about the possibility of disruption. Some professionals call this the "honeymoon" phase because everyone in the family is likely to be on their best behavior. Adoption support services can relieve some of this anxiety.

Adopted children, especially those who came up through the foster care system and were adopted at older ages, are no strangers to separation and loss. They have said good-bye to their birth families, extended families, one or more foster families, and case workers.

Although adoption has a highly celebrated positive side, the process is also built on losses for all three sides of the adoption triad (Babb & Laws, 1997). The birth family loses a child, the adoptive parents (in cases of infertility) lose the dream of having a biological child, and the adoptee loses his or her biological parents. Children adopted as infants may not feel a sense of loss for many years, but they are not, as a group, immune to such feelings.

Dealing with separation and loss is not something an adoptee can do in a specified period of time; it is a long-term or lifelong process. The support group is an ideal setting for adoptees (as well as for birth and adoptive parents) to discuss these important issues.

Because separation and loss is one of adoption's significant themes, and because it is difficult for some people to express their feelings without fear of hurting the feelings of someone else in the triad, these issues are well suited for online support groups. Online adoption support groups, unlike traditional adoptive family support groups, are usually made up of all three sides of the adoption triad. In fact, birth parents are usually the most vocal, and separation and loss are likely to be major topics of discussion.

Adoptive parents may find that in these discussion groups they will be expected to know how to post with online etiquette (also known as "netiquette"), and what to post, before having the experience to know such things. There is surprisingly little patience in any online forum for "newbies," as new people are called. People new to the online work may be surprised or shocked by the passion of the discussions. They may find themselves in heated arguments over issues such as reunions, open adoption, attachment disorders, and adoption disruption.

For the first few days online, newbies may want to only read the discussion and not reply. By reading, you can become familiar with the issues and the proper vocabulary. Learning the proper vocabulary is an important initial step in joining any online group. For example, a bpar (pronounced bee-par), or birth parent, is not one who has produced a biological child but one who has relinquished a biological child. If apars, or adoptive parents, are not aware of the issues faced by birth parents and adult adoptees before coming online, they are quickly educated. They learn that many birth parents who relinquished their infants because of the stigma of unwed motherhood are unhappy with America's closed system of adoption. They find solace and healing in their online forums.

Adult adoptees are frank about the tug-of-war that is often played out by their feelings. On one side is a deep love for their adoptive families, coupled with a desire not to hurt their adoptive mothers or fathers. On the other side is a need or a desire to find and know their birth families, and to have a familiar-looking face explain to them why they were relinquished for adoption in the first place. Because discussions by personal computer and modem are anonymous and national or international in scope, people are more likely to express their feelings openly, and to express their opinions forcefully. All triad members should be aware that online discussions sometimes turn to heated arguments known as "flames."

Currently, most people who go online for support use chat rooms, a type of instant forum. Instead of leaving typed messages via E-mail and coming back later to read posted replies, those who use chat rooms have an instantaneous dialogue that is typed directly onto the screen by everyone in attendance in the virtual chat room at that moment. Chats are simply live conference calls where the dialogue is typed instead of spoken; they can be very intense but also very helpful.

Support After the Legalization of the Adoption (Postadoption)

Birth Parents. Even when birth parents are well prepared and fully informed during the preadoptive phase, and during the adoption itself, grief and loss can be a significant problem in the postadoption phase. Ongoing, even lifelong, professional and support group help can make a big difference to birth parents (Brodzinsky, 1990a).

For birth parents who did not experience open adoption, search and reunion may someday become a personal goal. This is an easier process than it once was in the United States. The laws that keep all records closed are being challenged, and in a few states they have been overturned or amended. In states where open records are not a reality, there are often adoption registries where birth parents and adoptees can find each other again. There are also privately run registries and reunion services. Some of these are free and run by volunteers, while others charge fees. Libraries and bookstores stock an ever-growing number of books dedicated to search-and-reunion techniques. Finally, adoption forums and chat areas via the Internet can be invaluable resources for people involved in search and reunion. On rare occasions, adoptees and their birth family members actually "meet" online.

Adoptive Parents. The period after legal finalization, the post-adoption phase, is concerned with helping the new family stay strong and grow together. Since people touched by adoption never stop needing support services entirely, there is no limit on this time period. Most families have little need for formal services. However, for a significant portion of families, the postadoption period support services include: subsidy continuation and expansion (Barth & Berry, 1988), ongoing support and contact with the placement social worker, intensive adoption preservation services (Festinger, 1990), crisis intervention (Barth & Berry, 1988), and help with dealing with the mental health system, juvenile justice system, or residential treatment.

Traditionally, the emphasis in the postadoption phases has been on those families who adopt older children. However, families who adopt infants need these services as well. Infant adopters may want help and information about medical problems and learning disabilities that may reveal themselves as the child ages. They may want to know how to discuss adoption with their child and how to help the child understand what adoption means at different developmental stages. They may also want some advice about how to deal with intrusive questions of strangers.

Families who adopt infants whose disabilities are already known should make sure that all available services have been explained to them and offered to their child. Sometimes, parents fail to think ahead to how expensive the special needs may become as the child grows. Consequently, they do not seek out all the information they need or insist on their rights at the time of placement.

If contact with the social worker is ongoing, it is easier to facilitate long-term special needs adoption support such as renegotiating a subsidy contract or obtaining crisis intervention services. Too often, adoptive families want to put their relationships with their social workers behind them when the adoption becomes legal. However, ongoing contact with social workers has been shown to be one of the most important elements of long-term adoption success (Barth & Berry, 1988; Festinger, 1990).

Since many older-adopted children have emotional problems, adoptive parents need to be aware that these problems could worsen in adolescence. Delinquent behavior demands preparedness on the part of the adoptive family (Cline, 1992). Part of being prepared is becoming familiar with the services and policies of the local mental health system and the local juvenile justice system.

During the postadoption phase, some families require out-of-home care, such as residential treatment services, for the child (Goodrich et al., 1990; Nelson, 1985). Residential treatment centers may be for-profit or nonprofit, and public, private, or church affiliated. They may accept youth referrals locally, regionally, or nationally. Families may need assistance in securing residential care for their child, although, clearly, most families never use this service.

Parents also need help emancipating adult children, and support services geared toward adoptive grandparenting. When a troubled teen becomes a parent, the adoptive parents, now grandparents, often find they must also parent the grandchild. The cycle of support services begins anew.

Adoptees. One of the most important advantages of belonging to a support group, for both infant-placed and older-placed adoptees, is the way in which the group assists children with adoption-related issues, specifically identity and, when appropriate, racial and cultural identity issues. Social events, sponsored by the support group, bring together children from all economic, religious, and racial backgrounds, yet they all share one thing in common—they are adoptees. They have all contemplated these questions: Who am I? Why was I adopted? And they have shared the same self-doubts: Why did my birth parents not keep me? Am I lovable?

Transracially adopted children welcome the opportunity to meet and socialize with other same-race adoptees. Other adoptees provide not only same-race mentors, but same-race friendship, cultural interaction, and companionship. Adoptees placed transracially as infants need this opportunity to socialize with same race adoptees even more than other children. Older-adopted children have memories of living in same-race homes and communities, and may feel more comfortable among people of both races, whereas the child transracially adopted in infancy may not have had many opportunities to interact with people of his or her own race.

RECOMMENDATIONS—THE ONGOING NEED FOR ADOPTION SUPPORT

Birth Parents

Birth parents, once almost invisible in our society, are now organized, vocal, and involved in all aspects of adoption reform. Birth parent support groups are important resources for people who are in the process of making adoption plans, and people who have already done so. These support groups, whether local, national, or online, offer helpful information, moral support, and concrete assistance in sorting through the emotional issues of adoption as well as issues regarding the search-and-reunion process. Adoption agencies, lawyers, intermediaries, and adoptive parent support groups can assist birth parents, in any stage of the adoption process, by encouraging them to avail themselves of the services offered by birth parent support groups.

Adoptive Parents

Whether the placements are infant or older children, open or closed, and international or domestic, adoptive parents are becoming increasingly aware that ongoing adoption support services are needed by the adoptive family. Adoption-related issues and challenges do not simply fade away after a court finalizes the placement; special needs remain and demand attention. Most adoptive parents find that they must become educational and medical advocates for their children, a role that requires adoption support services.

In the case of special needs adoption, drugs, poverty, crime, AIDS, neglect, child abuse, teenage pregnancy, and the disintegration of the family have all combined to create a crisis in America's child welfare system. Hundreds of thousands of American children are in foster care (Petit & Curtis, 1997). Complicating the crisis is the fact that social services budgets throughout the country are inadequate (Cohen & Westhues, 1990).   Some families simply do not turn to adoption agencies because help is too difficult to obtain (Barth & Berry, 1988; NACAC, 1989) or because they do not know that such services exist.

Adoption support services must be available to adoptive families at all times and these families must have no trouble accessing services as needed. To do less is to risk more adoption disruption or dissolution and to discourage these and other families from attempting adoption in the future.

Adoptees

An adoptee posting on an online forum once asked the age-old humorous question "How many adoptees does it take to change a lightbulb?" Her answer was "None. It doesn't get changed because we're used to being kept in the dark." Adoptees can feel powerless due to laws that keep them from having access to their original birth certificates.

Adoptees can also experience ongoing feelings of loss, grief, and isolation. Adult adoptees may struggle with issues of identity, and may need assistance and emotional support should they decide to search for their birth families. For these reasons and others, adoptees need ongoing support. Triad support groups, as well as adoptee groups, have much to offer adoptees of all ages, whether adopted as infants or adopted as older children.

Making adoption support services available to adoptees gives them the option of using these services. This, in turn, empowers adoptees by giving them additional control over their lives.

Adoption Support for Those Who Wait

Adoption is often described in terms of a triad that includes birth parents, adoptees, and adoptive parents. However, in reality, it is a quadripartite—shared by four parties. The fourth side is no small group—it is the waiting children of America, the possible adoptees of the future living in foster care's limbo, some of whom will age-out of the system before being matched to a permanent family.

More than 400,000 U.S. children were in foster care in 1994 (Kroll, 1994); 15% to 25% of these children cannot return to their birth parents and need adoptive placements. Estimates of the number of children in the United Stataes who wait to be adopted range from 60,000 to 100,000 (Kroll, 1994). The federal government has long promised exact figures but these have yet to materialize. The Christian Children's Fund of Virginia estimates the worldwide number of orphans, many living on the streets, to be about 80 million.

Sadly, some infants and children in America never make it to foster care, much less to adoptive homes. They die abandoned. The United Way reported that in 1993, 73 infants were abandoned in the city of San Francisco. There were, no doubt, infants in other cities who had been abandoned, died, and their remains were never discovered. Multiply this figure nationwide and the statistics are horrifying.

Since waiting children are truly "society's children," society is their advocate. This particularly applies to those children who have been touched by adoption. The other three sides of the quadripartite owe it to those who wait to make sure that these children are adopted, and that their families will receive the support services necessary to maintain the placements. We owe it to birth parents everywhere to make sure that we make it possible for those who want to keep their children to do so, and for those who want to make an adoption plan, to do so without undue stress that would encourage abandonment.

When adoption support services of all types are available for and fully utilized by all who need them, more of our nation's waiting children will not only find permanent homes, they will be more likely to remain in those homes permanently.

REFERENCES

Adamec, C., & Pierce, W. L. (1991). *The encyclopedia of adoption.* New York: Facts on File.

Adopt a Special Kid (AASK) America. (1993). *AASK AMERICA* suggested book list. San Francisco: Author.

Anderson, J. (1990). Changing needs, challenging children. In North American Council on Adoptable Children, *The Adoption Assistance and Child Welfare Act of 1980 (Public Law 96-272): The first ten years* (pp. 41–50). St. Paul, MN: North American Council on Adoptable Children.

Babb, L. A. & Laws, R. (1997). *Adopting and advocating for special needs children.* Westport, CT: Bergin & Garvey.

Barreiro, J. E. (1993). Taino. The journal of Diego Colon, Indian adopted son of Christopher Columbus, admiral of the ocean sea: An historical reconstruction (Doctoral dissertation, State University of New York at Buffalo, 1992). *Dissertation Abstracts International, 53,* 3232A.

Barth, R. P. & Berry, M. (1988). *Adoption and disruption: Rates, risks and responses.* New York: Aldine de Gruyter.

Bourguignon, J. P. & Watson, K. W. (1987). *After adoption: A manual for professionals working with adoptive families.* Springfield, IL: Illinois Department of Children and Family Services.

Brodzinsky, A. B. (1990a). Surrendering an infant for adoption: The birth mother experience. In D. M. Brodzinsky, & M. D. Schecter (Eds.), *The psychology of adoption* (pp. 295–315). New York: Oxford University Press.

Brodzinsky, D. M. (1990b). A stress and coping model of adoption adjustment. In D. M. Brodzinsky, & M. D. Schechter (Eds.), *The psychology of adoption* (pp. 3–24). New York: Oxford University Press.

Brodzinsky, D. M., & Schechter, M. D. (Eds.) (1990). *The psychology of adoption.* New York: Oxford University Press.

Bussierre, A. (1990). Implementation of p.l. 96-272: Adoption assistance. In North American Council on Adoptable Children, *The Adoption Assistance and Child Welfare Act of 1980 (Public Law 96-272): The first ten years* (pp. 75–86). St. Paul, MN: North American Council on Adoptable Children.

Chapin, H. D. (1911). The proper management of foundlings and neglected infants. *Medical Record, 79,* 283–288.

Chapin, H. D. (1917). Systematized boarding out vs. institutional care for infants and young children. *New York Medical Journal, 105,* 1009–1011.

Cline, F. W. (1992). *Hope for high risk and rage filled children: Reactive attachment disorder.* Evergreen, CO: E. C. Publications.

Cohen, J. S., & Westhues, A. (1990). *Well-functioning families for adoptive and foster children.* Toronto: University of Toronto Press.

Cole, E. S., & Donley, K. S. (1990). History, values, and placement policy issues in adoption. In D. M. Brodzinsky & M. D. Schechter (Eds.), *The psychology of adoption* (pp. 273–294). New York: Oxford University Press.

Donley, K. S. (1981). Observations on disruption. In U.S. Department of Health and Human Services, Office of Human Development Services, Youth and Families Children's Bureau, *Adoption disruptions* (pp. 5–14). U.S. Department of Health and Human Services publication no. (OHDS) 81-30319. Washington, DC: Child Welfare League of America.

Ekman, P. (1989). *Why kids lie.* New York: Charles Scribner's Sons.

Elkind, D. (1981). *The hurried child: Growing up too fast too soon.* Menlo Park, CA: Addison-Wesley.

Festinger, T. (1990). Adoption disruption: Rates and correlates. In D. M. Brodzinsky, & M. D. Schecter (Eds.), *The psychology of adoption* (pp. 201–220). New York: Oxford University Press.

Garbarino, J. (1983). Social support networks: Rx for the healing professions. In J. K. Whittaker & J. Garbarino (Eds.), *Social support networks: Informal helping in the human services* (pp. 3–28). New York: Aldine de Bruyter.

Goodrich, W., Fullerton, C. S., Yates, B. T., & Berman, L. B. (1990). The residential treatment of severely disturbed adolescent adoptees. In D. M. Brodzinsky & M. D. Schechter (Eds.), *The psychology of adoption* (pp. 253–269). New York: Oxford University Press.

Groze, V. (1986). Special needs adoption. *Children and Youth Services Review, 8,* 81–91.

Groze, V., Young, J., & Corcran-Rumppe, K. (1991). *Post adoption resources for training, networking and evaluation services (PARTNERS): Working with special needs adoptive families in stress.* Prepared with Four Oaks, Inc., Cedar Rapids, IA for the Department of Health and Human Services, Adoption Opportunities, Washington, DC.

Hensley, J. L. (1989). Children's rights to special education. In North American Council on Adoptable Children, *Parent group manual* (pp. 4.21–4.27). St. Paul, MN: North American Council on Adoptable Children.

Hungry Wolf, B. (1982). *The ways of my grandmothers.* New York: Quill.

Kroll, J. (1994, April 26). Letter to state and provincial representatives of the North American Council on Adoptable Children, North American Council on Adoptable Children, St. Paul, MN.

Laws, R. (1995). Special needs adoption support and periodicals: A study of parent-written and adoption professional-written articles (Doctoral dissertation, California Coast University, 1995). *Research Abstracts International, 20*(05), LD-03161.

Le Pere, D. W., Davis, L. E., Couve, J., & McDonald, M. (1986). *Large sibling groups: Adoption experiences.* Washington, DC: Child Welfare League of America.

Magid, K., & McKelvey, C. A. (1988). *High-risk: Children without a conscience.* Lakewood, CO: CDR Distributors.

Maguire, L. (1991). *Social support systems in practice.* Silver Springs, MD: National Association of Social Workers Press.

Massachusetts Adoption Resource Exchange (1993). Annual report 1993, n.p.: Author.

Nelson, K. A. (1985). *On the frontier of adoption: A study of special needs adoptive families.* New York: Child Welfare League of America.

North American Council on Adoptable Children. (1989). *Parent group manual: Resources and ideas for adoptive parent support groups.* St. Paul, MN: Author.

Oklahoma Choctaw Council. (1983). *Choctaw social and ceremonial life.* Oklahoma City, OK: Oklahoma Choctaw Council.

Petit, M. R., & Curtis, P. A. (1997). *Child abuse and neglect: A look at the states, 1997 CWLA stat book.* Washington, DC: Child Welfare League of America.

Possin, C., Hocking, N., & North American Council on Adoptable Children. (1989). Basic organization of parent groups. In North American Council on Adoptable Children, *Parent group manual* (pp. 2.1–2.11). St. Paul, MN: North American Council on Adoptable Children.

Rosenthal, J., & Groze, V. (1992). *Special needs adoption.* New York: Praeger.

Tremitiere, B. A. (1992). The large adoptive family: A special kind of normal (Doctoral dissertation, Union Institute, 1991). *Dissertation Abstracts International, 52,* 4094A.

6

Ethics in Contemporary American Adoption Practice

L. Anne Babb

In this chapter, L. Anne Babb, Ph.D., discusses the values, ethics, and standards in contemporary American adoption practice that affect infant, older-child, and international adoptions. She begins with the historical antecedents of current values in adoption and the standards that currently exist. She then includes a research study on ethical codes of conduct that influence adoption practice. Dr. Babb concludes with a recommended model for ethical standards in adoption practice, policy, and service delivery for adoption triad members.

Benet (1976) wrote that "the moral views of every society have influenced its practice of adoption more heavily than have pragmatic considerations" (p. 13). Certainly this is true of American adoption practice, supported by societal values of providing permanent families for children deprived of them and the protection of abused, neglected, or abandoned children. Coexisting with these values, and not always peacefully, are the values of blood relatedness and the preservation and support of the biological family, along with the values of identity, self-determination, and of knowing as much about one's own history as others know. In writing about value issues in contemporary adoption, Dukette observed that "values often clash with personal interests or with other values, and adoption is full of conflicting values" (1984, p. 234). How are adoption professionals, agencies, and the recipients of adoption services to understand and make ethical decisions in such a complex area, especially when the interests of those involved may be at odds? The answer lies in defining the values undergirding adoption practice and identifying the ethical codes and standards that embody them.

Dolgoff and Skolnik (1992) defined ethics as "values in operation, the guidelines for transforming values into action" (p. 100). For the purposes of this chapter, I define values as those ideals regarded as desirable in adoption practice, and ethics as the formal, professional rules of right and wrong conduct. Values might thus be seen as the skeletal system supporting the flesh and blood of our ethical codes. Standards are commonly accepted rules of right and wrong conduct in a field that are not necessarily formally, or professionally, adopted.

Adoption professionals have been unable to translate ethical principles into behavior, a failure at the root of many of the problems with adoption services in the United States (Conrad & Joseph, 1991). This chapter examines the historical antecedents of current adoption values, the standards that currently exist, and the research on ethics in adoption practice. It begins with a review of the social and psychological literature on values and ethics in child welfare and adoption, then assesses current practices and existing standards in adoption practice, considering the ethical dilemmas and the attendant research. The chapter concludes by offering recommendations for practice, policy, and service delivery for each person who is party to an adoption.

HISTORICAL ANTECEDENTS OF CURRENT VALUES IN ADOPTION

The view that values are of fundamental importance in adoption was established in the earliest literature regarding adoption. Some of the earliest values supporting the nurturing and care of orphaned children include preventing and punishing child abuse and neglect and providing permanent families for children who had been orphaned or abandoned (Doxiadis, 1989). Maintaining familial ties, providing heirs, and regarding the state as the protector of society also provided a framework for the treatment of children.

Ancient historical and philosophical works refer to the obligations of society toward children, particularly to those who, deprived of parental care, needed the protection of the state. Plato urged the guardians of orphans to regard them as a supreme and sacred trust, requiring individuals who defrauded orphans to pay damages twice as high as those normally paid to children with living parents. Aristotle later wrote that, since infanticide was forbidden by ordinance, birth control should be practiced by all citizens, and if a child was conceived in spite of contraception, an abortion "should be procured before the embryo has acquired life and sensation" (Sinclair, 1951). Aristotle also wrote that "no cripple shall be reared," recommending instead that deformed or handicapped children should be abandoned. The values underlying the approach of the Greek city-state to children in special circumstances was clearly that the needs of families and individuals were secondary to the mandates of the state. Should the citizens become too numerous or, due to incapacity, require resources of the state without showing any promise of contributing to their own keep, their numbers should be reduced. Thus, although children had some sentimental value and healthy children were regarded as the future of the citizen-state, the Greece of Plato and Aristotle subjected the value of the individual child to the value of maintaining a well-functioning state.

In the first century A.D. in Rome, the Emperor Narva established colonies for poor families to abate the drowning and abandonment of infants, largely due to the value the state put on its youngest citizens. The increase of the Roman empire required an ever-growing supply of soldiers and pioneers, resulting in the utilitarian value of children "not for their own sake or for any moral reason, but again for the interests of the state" (Doxiadis, 1989, p. 14).

The origination and expansion of Christianity had a profound effect on the values related to the treatment of orphans. The interests of the state became subject to the interests of the individual human being, created in the image of God. Children came to be regarded as valuable for their own sake, perhaps based on biblical admonitions such as that of the Apostle James: "This is pure and undefiled religion in the sight of our God and father, to visit orphans . . . in their distress" (James 1:27, New American Standard Bible).

In A.D. 452, the Synod of Arles provided for the shelter of abandoned infants in any church for a minimum of 10 days while officials searched for the biological parents; such laws respected both the value of caring for children deprived of parental care and the value of blood ties. During the fifth century in the Byzantine Empire, Saint Basil founded the first orphan asylum for abandoned infants; historical works were replete with references to numerous foundling asylums established for the care of abandoned children during that time. In the West, Archbishop Datheus established the first foundling asylum in A.D. 787. Nurses at the orphanage breast-fed infants and children were fed and clothed until they were eight years old.

The value of protecting orphaned children deprived of parental care continued to find expression across political boundaries and through subsequent centuries. In the sixteenth and seventeenth centuries, acts of parliament in France demanded that nobles who found abandoned infants on their property be required to raise the children as their own, but few complied (Doxiadis, 1989). Napoleonic codes defined standards for adoptive parents and supported the termination of parental rights and permanency of adoptive ties, upholding the value of providing permanent families for children whose parents could not raise them (Cole & Donley, 1990).

In 1741, charitable workers in London, England established the country's first foundling home for the many foundlings who were abandoned daily in the streets. Children were valued as heirs or as workers and contributors to the family's upkeep, and though abandoned or abused children came to be protected, English common law did not provide for adoption. Adoption was created by a 1926 statute in that country. Even then, the laws did little to define adoption-specific values. To the contrary, the history of adoption before colonial times demonstrates an overriding concern for the needs and interests of adults rather than children. Any benefit to children "was a secondary gain" (Cole & Donley, 1990, p. 274).

As in England, adoption in the United States was a statutory creation. Massachusetts enacted America's first adoption laws in 1851. Until then, adoptions had been undertaken informally, established by special legislative acts, or through the filing of a deed to the child in much the same way that property was acquired. Usually, the purpose of adoption was to provide an heir to a family, rather than providing families for children who needed them.

During the mid-1800s, humane societies serving both animals and children developed nationally, promoting values that were hotly debated at annual conferences and in the literature (Anderson, 1989). Reforms of the time concentrated on the removal of children from adult institutions such as jails but also focused on children remanded to almshouses, where orphans as well as the indigent, the insane, the elderly, and petty criminals were housed (Sutton, 1990; Weisman, 1994). The fact that humane societies of the time served both animals and children demonstrates the relative value of children.

In 1851 Massachusetts established the first statute designed to safeguard the rights of children, a law that included the control of adoption. The protection of abandoned children fell largely upon private charitable organizations during this time. One such organization was the New York Children's Aid Society, founded by Charles Loring Brace. This organization sent needy children to rural Midwest "free family homes" on what became known as "orphan trains" for foster care beginning in 1854. By 1859, 20,000 to 24,000 children had been placed throughout the Midwest in this manner (Cole & Donley, 1990). Such arrangements had no written contracts. Philanthropists and opportunists alike removed orphaned and needy children from urban areas to the countryside to teach them agricultural skills, to reform those in need of reform, and to provide inexpensive farm hands for rural families (Platt, 1969). Over time and with the rise of industrialization, the countryside remained a common site for children's placements in America, and in other countries as well (Kristinsdottir, 1991). The children who were removed usually came from orphanages or almshouses, were poor, were between 12 and 14 years of age, and often were moved without consent or through force. Some have suggested that the goal of these removals was evident: to clear the cities of the poorest children for the comfort of the upper class and emerging middle class (Zelizer, 1985).

Rapid industrialization after the 1860s provided new occupations for poor children. By 1870 approximately one out of every eight children was employed (Zelizer, 1985). There is no record of any significant demand for adoptable infants in the late 1870s and 1880s, and unwanted babies were more likely to die than be adopted. The infant mortality rate in foundling asylums was between 85% and 90% (Zelizer, 1985). The only profitable undertaking involving infants was the "business of getting rid of other people's [unwelcome] babies" (Zelizer, 1985, p. 170). Individuals who came to be known as "baby farmers" agreed to board unwanted, and usually illegitimate, children for around $10.00 a month. The only children in great demand by adoptive or foster parents during this period were typically older than 10 and male, with three times more boys placed than girls (Rosenberg, 1992). The citizenry of the time, much like the Greeks and Romans, showed more concern for the needs and interests of adults rather than children. Though orphans and poor children were sheltered, fed, and, hopefully, emotionally nurtured by foster and adoptive families, this benefit was secondary to providing useful children for families who needed them.

The National Conference of Charities and Correction passed a resolution in 1876 calling for the withdrawal of children from almshouses. By the turn of the century, 12 states had enacted legislation mandating such removals. Because the states did not provide for the establishment of alternatives to the almshouses, however, removed children were usually sent to other public or private institutions, including independent baby farms (Sutton, 1990; Zelizer, 1985).

At the 1915 National Conference of Charities and Correction, Carl Carstens, the general agent of the Massachusetts Society for the Prevention of Cruelty to Children, called for the development of public programs of child welfare. He also asked for cooperation among progressive children's societies with one goal being the development of standards addressing child placement. A few years later, during the 1919 White House Conference on Child Welfare Standards, the Committee on Cooperation for Child-Helping Organizations established the Bureau for the Exchange of Information among Child-Helping Agencies, which became the Child Welfare League of America (CWLA) in 1921. Carstens, the first executive director of the CWLA, "considered the league a professional federation and insisted upon qualifying standards for membership" (Anderson, 1989, p. 227).

The Child Welfare League developed standards for child welfare service and child protection before it developed adoption standards. While statutes governing the adoption of children were still evolving, foster care, indentured servanthood, and apprenticeship models of caring for children deprived of parental care, based on the labor value of children, had been established for over a century. The separate functions of child welfare services—child protection, foster care, and adoption—fragmented the practice of child welfare in the United States and made establishing nationally uniform standards much more difficult (Anderson, 1989). Societies such as the American Humane Association and the Child Welfare League of America "jockeyed for ascendancy as the standard-setting federation in child protection," competing, too, with private organizations such as Catholic Charities USA and the Florence Crittenton Association in establishing such standards (Anderson, 1989, p. 240; Sutton, 1990).

The process of developing standards regarding the treatment of children in the labor force, foster care, and adoption resulted in conflict between professionals who specialized in child placement and those, such as doctors and attorneys, who did not (Cole & Donley, 1990; Solinger, 1992). The practice among some doctors and attorneys of selling children subverted professional adoption practice and conflicted with the evolving ideal of sentimental adoption. At loggerheads were the values of providing children for families who wanted or needed them (children as chattel, utilitarian adoption based on adult needs) and that of providing permanent, qualified families for children whose parents could not raise them (adoption in consideration of the child's best interests).

Although public regulation of adoption increased and licensing standards for foster homes and adoption agencies were developed, baby brokering did not stop. Studies of the time showed that the majority of children adopted in the 1920s were adopted without assistance from social agencies (Zelizer, 1985). Such independent adoptions were often arranged informally by nonprofit adoption facilitators. But in many cases, intermediaries, often doctors or attorneys, built a profitable business by selling babies in the black or gray market that thrived in the 1930s and 1940s.

In the private sector, many maternity homes of the time failed to offer social work services to unmarried mothers, and in most areas the available services were "spotty and not professionalized" (Solinger, 1992, p. 131). Adoption agencies did not offer posttermination services for birth mothers and expected mothers who relinquished children to go on with their lives without benefit of grief counseling or an understanding of the long-term effects of surrendering a child (Brodzinsky, 1990). By the end of the 1950s, however, most private maternity homes provided casework services through professionals such as psychiatrists, clinical psychologists, and social workers (Solinger, 1992). Many such professionals expressed discomfort at the separation of mothers and infants through adoption, when mothers had historically been designated as those who were best-equipped to care for their own children, whether they were married or not (Solinger, 1992). Most professionals, however, did not even begin to discuss their ethical responsibilities to apply the values of the larger society to child welfare concerns until after World War II (Doxiadis, 1989).

By the mid-1950s, 90,000 children per year were being placed for adoption, an 80% increase since 1944 (Solinger, 1992). There was still no federal law prohibiting commercial placement or independent adoption of a child across state lines, and 34 states had no laws against selling children within the state.

The CWLA sponsored a national conference on adoption in 1955 that set the stage for reforms in practice that reflected a growing concern with the needs of children rather than adults (Cole & Donley, 1990). At the same time, Senator Estes Kafauver, chair of the Subcommittee to Investigate Juvenile Delinquency, was enjoined by the federal government to investigate black market interstate baby selling, along with other matters. One of the goals of the subcommittee was to propose federal legislation that would control or eliminate the black market in adoption. The federal government and the CWLA, with its member agencies, thus worked concurrently to define ethical and practice standards in adoption through legislative and professional means as a way of supporting the transition from a market economy in children, based on adult needs, to one that valued children based on their needs. The CWLA developed its first standards for adoption practice in 1959 (CWLA, 1959). The concept of the best interests of the child as a primary value in child welfare was more fully defined some 20 years later, when Goldstein, Freud, Solnit, and Goldstein (1973) published their seminal work on this subject.

Other adoption and child welfare agencies also began to develop standards of practice in child placement during the 1960s and 1970s for the purpose of providing services based on increased knowledge and professionalization in the adoption field (Catholic Charities USA, 1989; CWLA, 1959, 1960, 1971, 1973, 1976; National Association of Social Workers, 1979, 1987). Kadushin (1984) summarized these practice guidelines but characterized them as resulting from practice wisdom, social values and philosophy, and "a modest amount of empirical research" (p. 4).

The U.S. Children's Bureau also proposed standards of care and service to children in the United States, particularly those who were dependent, neglected, or deprived (Sorosky et al., 1989). The National Council for Adoption Ad Hoc Committee on Ethical Standards in Adoption established principles of practice in infant adoptions, commenting that "many in the field are concerned about the unprofessional and unethical practices in both [independent and agency] systems and have expressed a desire to set basic standards for good adoption practices to protect the parties in an adoption" (NCFA, 1991, p. 1).

CURRENT STANDARDS IN CONTEMPORARY CHILD WELFARE AND ADOPTION

A number of authors have identified foundational values in child welfare and adoption, or means of making values-based decisions in social work, which is one of the professions most commonly involved in adoption. Sachdev (1984) identified the following guidelines for adoption practice as set forth by various national and international organizations such as the CWLA and the United Nations:

1. Adoption is always a substitution for the biological home and should not be considered as an option until it becomes clear that the child's own family will not be able to raise the child; the best place for the child is with his own family, in his own community, and in his own country. The value of blood ties or blood relatedness underlies this standard.

2. If a child's family cannot raise him or her, the first efforts should be made to find an adoptive home in the child's own racial, national, ethnic, and religious community, underscoring what Dukette (1984) called the "value of identity." Closely tied to the value of blood relatedness, such an approach esteems the adoptee's racial, cultural, and national origins.

3. The primary purpose of adoption is to provide a permanent family for the child, and the child's welfare, needs, and interests are the basic antecedents of good adoption practice—*the best interest of the child* standard, based upon the belief that all human beings, including children, have innate worth and dignity.

4. When a child cannot be raised in his or her own family, adoption is the best alternative, an expression of the value of providing permanent families for children whose parents cannot raise them (also an expression of the value people place on families, as compared with that of institutions).

5. Every child who needs adoption should receive the service as soon as possible.

6. Everyone who is party to an adoption should be given the opportunity to make informed, thoughtful decisions regarding the alternatives to adoption and help in

implementing the alternative of choice. If adoption is chosen, assistance should be provided in understanding the implications of adoption, the anticipated problems, and the necessary preparation. The values of integrity and respect are fundamental to this standard: integrity, in facilitating adoptions and offering assistance with a commitment to presenting information both positive and negative about adoption, which provides an accurate picture of the service and its alternatives; respect, in recognizing each person's right to what social work calls the ethic of self-determination—to autonomous decision making.

7. Some delays—between the decision to surrender the child and the actual legal surrender, and between the placement of the child for adoption and the legal finalization, of the adoption—should be introduced so as to allow for informed, thoughtful decision making. Again Sachdev (1984) emphasizes the primary value of exercising professional authority ethically in adoption by providing clients with the information and time they need to consider their options and make informed decisions.

8. Adoption severs the relationship between the biological parents and the adoptee, and that confidentiality regarding the identities of the biological parents and the adoptive parents should be safeguarded. Implicit to this guideline are the values of confidentiality and privacy.

9. Adoption is a lifelong process, not a one-time event. Dukette (1984), commenting on traditional American adoption practice, which forces a complete break with the adoptee's genetic past, wrote that adoption triad members "are striving to complete a broken circle, a completion that does not deny adoptive ties but weaves them into a complete life experience, with a beginning as well as a future" (p. 242). Viewing adoption as a lifelong process respects the value of blood ties and identity, but also recognizes the rights of others to self-determination, autonomy, and tolerance. A system based on respect would acknowledge the adopted child's need for protection and security, and the adoptive family's desire for cohesion, at the same time making allowances for the needs of adult adoptees to know their identities, and of relatives separated by adoption to locate and establish relationships with one another if they choose to do so.

10. The community has a concern in adoption: the right to intervene in family life in order to protect children who are abused, neglected, or otherwise deprived of adequate parental care.

11. In implementing "this concern [of the community in adoption], some attention needs to be given to developing a trained professional cadre of social workers with a specialized knowledge of and skill in adoption practice" (Sachdev, 1984, p. 6), again reflecting the value of protecting children, as well as the value of professional integrity.

Among postindustrialized nations, only the United States and some provinces of Canada uphold the eighth principle, that of confidentiality, by judicially sealing identifying information about the adoptee's birth parents and original family identity (Babb, 1996). Other countries observe confidentiality by allowing the adult adoptee, and sometimes birth and adoptive parents, access to the identifying information (sometimes referred to as open records), while not making the same information available to the general public (Sorosky, Baran, & Pannor, 1989). In this way, confidentiality of adoption records is respected in much the same way that medical records are safeguarded in the United States. Such records can be released to and by those to whom it belongs, thus supporting the ethic of confidentiality while also respecting that of client self-determination.

Vitillo (1991) also identified some of the foundational values in child welfare and adoption by examining the adoption standards embraced by the United Nations Convention on the Rights of the Child in its 1985 Declaration on Social and Legal Principles relating to the Protection and Welfare of Children, with Special Reference to Foster Placement and Adoption Nationally and Internationally. The standards, adopted by the U.N. General Assembly on December 3, 1986, are:

1. Priority should be given for a child to be cared for by his or her own parents and support for the family should be provided by governments.
2. Intercountry adoption should be considered only when adoption in the child's own country fails.
3. Biological parents and the child should be involved in the decision to place internationally.
4. Children in intercountry placements should receive special protections.
5. Countries should enact measures to combat child abduction and illicit placement.
6. Placements resulting in "improper financial gain for those involved" should be condemned.

Sachdev (1984) and Vitillo (1991), in recounting the standards established by American and international child welfare organizations and the United Nations, underscored the values from which such standards arise. As Doxiadis wrote, "Each culture is sensitive to the special needs of children" (1989, p. 13). The standards identified by Vitillo, like those enumerated by Sachdev, spring from the following values:

- the value of protecting children who are abused, neglected, or abandoned because of the innate worth and dignity of human beings, including children
- the value of blood ties and identity; the latter includes knowing as much about one's own past as others know, respecting and maintaining when possible a person's racial, cultural, national, and religious identity
- the value of family, expressed by providing permanent families for children whose original parents cannot raise them
- the value of professional integrity, including honesty, loyalty, and trustworthiness
- the value of respect of humanity, including recognition of each person's right to autonomy, self-determination, privacy, and tolerance
- the value of citizenship, including upholding laws that give responsibility to professionals and institutions to act as agents of society, punishing those who mistreat children (including those who use children for personal or financial gain), and respecting the legal processes of nations

Some of these same values can be seen in Cole and Donley's (1990) list of standards underlying adoption practice. These include raising children in nurturing families, the family of origin when possible; providing an adoptive family in a timely manner when birth parents cannot raise a child; regarding adoption as a lifelong process; enabling birth and adoptive parents to choose the type and extent of pre- and post-adoption contact; giving adoptees all the information about their birth, original families, genetic and social histories, placements, and reasons for being adopted, even if adoptive parents disagree with disclosure; making the same information available to the adoptive parents of infants and young children; and preparing adoptive parents for competent parenthood rather than scrutinizing them.

THE VALUES UNDERLYING AMERICAN ADOPTION PRACTICE

The Value of Helping the Helpless

We have seen that, from antiquity, the nurture and care of orphaned children has been valued in all societies worldwide. Plato and Artistotle considered orphans worthy of special care and protection. Particularly in Greek and Roman times, the state was seen as the protector of society. As such, the state had an interest in the protection of orphans. Early societies recognized that orphans had been deprived of humankind's most important natural protection, that provided by parents. This value has continued to be fundamental in adoption and child placement up to modern times. Much evidence of humankind's continuing concern for the helpless can be seen in the laws and social programs of all countries, particularly those related to adoption. The value of protecting children who are abused, neglected, or abandoned is expressed through the power of states to intervene in family life, the responsibility of helping professions to act as agents of society, and the punishment of parents (and others) who abandon or mistreat children.

The Value of Human Relatedness in the Context of Families

The value of human relatedness in the context of families includes the value of blood ties and that of providing permanent families for children whose parents cannot raise them. Early societies valued maintaining family ties, and considered the provision of heirs through adoption as one means of underscoring the value of families. From early times tribes, governments, and nations have provided permanent families for children whose parents cannot raise them. The gain of providing children for families who want them has come to be regarded as only secondary (Dukette, 1984). Adages such as "blood is thicker than water" and "the hand that rocks the cradle rules the world" are common expressions of the value placed on the family, and especially of blood ties. Dukette (1984) called this the value of identity, expressed through standards of giving birth parents every chance to raise their own children and of providing timely and permanent adoptive placements for the children of those parents who cannot raise them. Dukette (1984) also pointed out that the value of families has been expressed in traditional American adoption by the erroneous establishment in practice, as well as in law, of adoptive parents as the only parents, which has led to the secrecy and judicially sealed adoption records that continue to be part of our standard adoption practice.

Development and passage of legislation encouraging the adoption of waiting children, such as the Adoption Assistance and Child Welfare Act of 1980 (P.L. 96-272), or the more recent Multi-Ethnic Placement Act, uphold the value of finding permanent families for children and continue to influence child welfare practice.

The Value of Human Beings, Including Children, as Having Innate Worth and Dignity

Values arising out of this primary one include the recognition of each person's right to autonomy, self-determination, privacy, and tolerance, the respect for the uniqueness of each person, and the consideration of humans as alive and growing toward increasing levels of satisfaction in life. Other beliefs related to this value are that all people, regardless of their situation in life, have common needs (food, shelter, safety, education, health care, and recreation) and mutual responsibilities to one another and to their society (Poppendieck, 1992).

With the rise of Christianity came an increased conviction of the worth of children among Christian nations. Rather than being viewed merely as the building-blocks of the family or society (i.e., valuable only insofar as they served a purpose), children more and more often came to be viewed as inherently valuable, even if not particularly useful. The care of the early churches for orphans through orphan asylums in Eastern and Western Christendom illustrated the growing concern of societies for children. This concern continued to manifest itself through the ongoing improvement of institutional care for needy children, bringing us into the modern era.

Christianity, of course, did not provide the only basis for the belief that children have innate worth and dignity. All of the world's religions share values of helping the helpless, particularly children, and of regarding people as having innate worth. Politically, the spread of Christianity had a larger impact on Western culture and, thus, our practice of adoption than did other religions.

The Value of Protecting the Powerless

Child protection can be seen as the earliest form of child welfare. Even the earliest societies valued protecting children who were abused, neglected, or abandoned by their parents. Governments have typically given themselves and their agents, including professionals, the right to intervene in family life when the good of society was threatened. In modern times, the state has a right to intervene in family life whenever the good of any individual, regardless of age, circumstance, or personal characteristic, is threatened. Such protections express the belief that human beings have innate worth and dignity and have shared needs and responsibilities for one another and society.

In America, reforms in child welfare during the mid-1800s focused on removing children from adult institutions and placing them in environments more suitable to children. While the interests of adults continued to be served at the expense of children, the consideration of the best interests of the child, who was powerless and dependent on adults for protection, began to emerge in policy and practice in the late 1900s, continuing to contemporary times. United Nations declarations, such as the 1985 Convention on the Rights of the Child or the 1995 U. N. Convention on the Rights of the Child, are illustrative of these shared values.

The Value of Expertise and Science, as Expressed Through Professional Behavior

Societies governing child welfare services and child protection also emerged in the United States during the early 1900s. More and more, child welfare, child protection, and adoption became the concern of people with experience in these areas, for example, experts or professionals. Ideas about professional behavior and preferred approaches to dealing with people provided the impetus for the growing professionalization of child welfare. The values included client self-determination (whenever possible), integrity among professionals, and the improvement of professional competence in child protection and adoption. These values are expressed in modern social work's principles of propriety (high standards of personal conduct as a social worker), competence and professional development, service to others, integrity, and scholarship and research (NASW, 1990).

The expressed concern about professional behavior and establishment of the helping professions, other than medicine, as bona fide professions was preceded by the commitment of child protection workers to achieving desired outcomes for children. Workers and societies first sought to meet the basic needs of children for food, shelter, safety, education, health care, and recreation. The development of helping professions such as social work came later, once child advocates saw that they had made some headway in protecting children and serving them according to their needs. Poppendieck (1992) noted that social work has always been more successful at achieving desired outcomes for people than it has been at achieving social justice or broad-based recognition of the discipline as a profession.

The development of child placement standards by various societies in the 1960s and 1970s underscored the confidence of professionals and society that their services were valuable. By 1973, Goldstein, Freud, and Solnit had developed their work on the best interests of the child, firmly establishing the value of providing child-centered, informed services for children. Much of this work has focused on rectifying some of the power imbalances experienced by children in societies governed by adults.

ETHICAL CHALLENGES IN PSYCHOLOGY AND SOCIAL WORK

The following sections identify the conflicting values and ethical challenges faced by adoption professionals. The desire to create an ethical discourse in any field of practice has been seen as a sign of the professional's desire to better serve the interests of clients (Kristinsdottir, 1991; Pine, 1987). Adoption of and adherence to a code of ethics is the cornerstone of a profession and differentiates between professional and quasi- or semi-professional practice (Etzioni, 1969; Greenwood, 1957; Poppendieck, 1992). Among the professions, ethics are the formal, professional rules of right and wrong conduct.

Ethical inquiry has only been reflected in the professional literature of psychology and social work for a scant 20 years. In addition, there has been a great deal of debate and disagreement regarding ethics in the practice of child welfare in general, and adoption in particular. The professions have no clear criteria or means of applying ethical decision making in cases of child abuse, bioethical situations, or adoption, nor any way of determining when an action promotes or detracts from the best interest of the child (Amadio, 1991; Fein & Maluccio, 1992; Melton & Flood, 1994; Pine, 1987; Sachdev, 1992; Walden, Wolock, & Demone, 1990).

Some of the areas that have proved to be challenging for professionals at best, and problematic at worst, are conflict of interest, identifying the client, disclosure of information, responsibility to clients, and maintaining and improving professional competence. These areas are examined in the following sections.

Conflict of Interest

A number of researchers identified conflict of interest as particularly problematic in planned infant adoptions when professionals or agencies served more than one party to an adoption (Valentine, Conway, & Randolph, 1988; Voss, 1985). Legal professionals have considered the issue of possible conflicts of interest as they serve both birth and adoptive parents in independent infant adoptions (Amlung, 1990; Silverman, 1989). Social workers and psychologists who specialize in adoption have also examined conflict of interest (Amadio, 1991; Babb, 1996; Dukette, 1984; Sachdev, 1992).

Professionals who practice adoption are not the only parties susceptible to conflicting interests or values. The needs of waiting adoptive parents who want to adopt healthy infants and toddlers conflict with the needs of waiting children who have special needs, and combine with a market economy in children to produce situations in which agencies and adoption facilitators can "sell" the waiting child to naïve and desperate adoptive parents (Babb & Laws, 1997; Valentine, Conway & Randolph, 1988).

Identifying the Client

Professionals could not agree about whether the birth mother, the birth father, the adoptee, the adoptive parents, or a combination of these were the client(s) in an adoption, particularly in infant adoptions (Babb, 1996). Valentine et al. (1988) found that professionals saw themselves as child advocates rather than advocates for either set of parents, a view that obscured the "potentially devastating consequences for adoptive parents and families" of adoption disruption (p. 136). Voss (1985), writing for Catholic Charities agencies in the United States, considered the unborn child of the pregnant woman the client, calling unborn children "the most oppressed sub-group in contemporary American society" (p. 40). Dukette (1984) likewise, having found adoption to be full of conflicting values and interests, settled upon the best interests of the child as the guiding principle in adoption because the child is the "most dependent party" (p. 234).

Disclosure of Information

In international adoptions, the duty of adoption agencies to disclose medical information has been discussed (Campbell, 1988; Hostetter et al., 1989), as have the ethical problems of kidnapping, child selling, coercion of birth parents, and abusive adoptive parents in unregulated international adoptions (Fieweger, 1991; Vitillo, 1991). The need for full disclosure of background and medical information has likewise been described as it relates to domestic adoption of infants and older children (Feigelman & Silverman, 1986; Rosenthal & Groze, 1992).

Attorneys have examined their roles in nonagency infant adoptions (Davie, 1984; Silverman, 1989), and a new tort of "wrongful adoption" has been established (Amadio, 1989). Courts have begun to recognize that adoption agencies have a duty to obtain and disclose health and background information about children placed for adoption, and adoption agencies have been ordered to pay monetary damages for failing to carry out this duty (DeWoody, 1993). Failure to accurately or fully disclose background, health, and behavioral information about adoptable children has been particularly problematic in special needs and older child adoptions (Babb, 1996; Rosenthal & Groze, 1992).

DeWoody (1993) identified four areas in which an adoption agency could be legally liable for monetary damages: (1) intentional misrepresentation of the health or background of the adoptee; (2) deliberate concealment of health or background information; (3) negligent disclosure of information, or giving information that later proves to be inaccurate; (4) negligent withholding of information, or sharing information, but failing to disclose some information so that adoptive parents are misled.

Another aspect of disclosure is the common American practice of judicially sealing the adoptee's original birth certificate and adoption file and allowing their disclosure to the adoptee only by court order. The issue of adoptee-accessible adoption records versus sealed adoption records is rife with ethical and theoretical conflicts (Cole & Donley, 1990; Gonyo & Watson, 1988; Rompf, 1993). The development and perpetuation of judicially sealed adoption records in the United States was said by some to result from myths and tradition more than from ethical principles or sound professional practice (Baran & Pannor, 1990; Feigelman & Silverman, 1986; Watson, 1992). Dukette (1984) pointed out that the freedom of information movement during the U.S. civil rights era was initiated by people who considered their civil rights violated when others had information they themselves were barred from having. The issue of unsealing the original birth certificate and some adoption records for adult adoptees has been seen as an ethical one, since giving adoptees equal access to their birth records relieves power imbalances, allowing adult adoptees to more equally share power in society with birth and adoptive parents (Babb, 1996; Dukette, 1984).

Researchers urged agencies to revise policies and practices to reflect current social changes and research findings in adoption (Gonyo & Watson, 1988; Sachdev, 1992). Sachdev (1992) contended that agencies promoted sealed adoption records in adoption based on the assumption that it provides safeguards against unwanted intrusion by the triad members, and that contacts between them would be problematic. He challenged these claims by showing that secrecy in adoption "hardly serves the interest of the participants in adoption; instead it promotes fears and misconceptions about each others' motives" (Sachdev, 1992, p. 66). A few authors noted that adoption agencies are often ignorant regarding the laws surrounding confidentiality and disclosure of adoption information (DeWoody, 1993; Gonyo & Watson, 1988).

Responsibility to Clients

The needs of each party to an adoption to receive professional services, including postplacement and postadoption services, have been established (Blanton & Deschner, 1990; Deykin, Patti, & Ryan, 1988; Rosenthal & Groze, 1992; Watson, 1992). In their study of failed adoptions, Valentine, Conway, and Randolph (1988) found that the overwhelming majority of adoptive families whose adoptions failed were not offered and did not receive any postdisruption contact or counseling from either their adoption agencies or their adoption workers to help them with the loss of their adopted children and the accompanying grief. The authors found that professionals "stretched" families too far in placing children with special needs and in giving the adoptive parents children with characteristics that the adoptive parents had stated they could not accept.

Adoptive families in the study had been given inaccurate or incomplete information upon which they based their adoption decisions. Many families felt social workers "sold" them children and that they were persuaded by professionals to take these children against their better judgment. Few of the families studied were prepared for special needs adoptions, and nearly all felt that the adoption professionals' involvement in their placements only intensified the stresses of adoption. The authors concluded that adoption professionals and adoption agencies should develop empathy with adoptive parents and become family advocates rather than being child advocates alone (Valentine et al., 1988).

While some studies showed how professionals "sell" children to prospective adoptive parents (Babb & Laws, 1997; Valentine et al., 1988), other research demonstrated how professionals sold adoption to expectant mothers by telling them that "their baby would be better off with people who [could] take 'proper' care of a child and that the best thing for them to do would be to place their child for adoption and go on with their lives" (Brodzinsky, 1990, p. 309). In infant adoptions, relinquishing mothers in particular have suffered as a result of inadequate (or nonexistent) pre- and postsurrender counseling. Brodzinsky (1990) noted that "when counseling does occur, it is often compromised by conflicts of interest, limited understanding, and lingering social stigmata associated with out-of-wedlock pregnancy" (p. 309).

Schechter and Bertocci (1990) wrote about the dearth of postplacement services and professional support for adult adoptees originally placed through independent means or agency adoptions, particularly through public agencies. They concluded that "the need for these services beyond the placement should compel the provision of adequate legislation, funding, and staffing, with expansion of research efforts at all levels" (p. 87).

Spencer (1987) proposed a model for a postadoption service center where the professional staff would: (1) keep up with social changes as they apply to adoption; (2) share background information with parties to an adoption; (3) offer intermediary services for the exchange of nonidentifying information; (4) assist with searches; (5) offer counseling for individuals and families; (6) offer illustrations and explanations of functional family relationships; (7) give transracial and transcultural adoptive families an understanding of the culture or ethnic group from which the adoptee came; (8) assist transracial adoptive families with coping as a mixed family; (9) help children understand why adoption was planned for them; (10) assist transracially adopted individuals with identity issues related to transracial adoption and adoption; (11) provide for more openness; (12) offer counseling to those in private adoptions or relative adoptions.

Other researchers also urged adoption agencies to establish and adhere to professional standards of conduct in their child placement practices (Dukette, 1984; Gonyo & Watson, 1988; Sachdev, 1992).

Maintaining and Improving Professional Competence

Researchers have recognized the value of obtaining, maintaining, and improving professional competence in adoption practice. Sachdev (1984) called for the development of a core group of professionally trained social workers who possess a "specialized knowledge of and skill in adoption practice" (p. 6). In addition to calling for professional education in ethics, researchers recommended mastery among practitioners, expertise from the normative specialties of moral philosophy, theology, and law, and proficiency from the social sciences of psychology, sociology, and social work (Conrad & Joseph, 1991; Kugelman, 1992; Rest, 1988).

In their research on certification for child protective workers in Texas, Birmingham, Berry, and Bussey (1996) found that "over the past decade the number of trained social workers involved in child welfare services has fallen while the need for trained, highly specialized staff members has risen" (p. 728). They wrote that only 28% of American child welfare workers in 1987 had undergraduate or graduate social work degrees, and that many states hire workers with degrees in other disciplines and some require no degrees at all. They concluded that "the child welfare service system has been deprofessionalized," but found that most Texas child welfare supervisors supported efforts to professionalize child welfare services through certification (p. 728).

Ethical (In)Competencies

A handful of researchers have studied ethical problem solving in various social work settings, including those involving adoption, and discovered that ethical dilemmas are common (Conrad & Joseph, 1991; Dolgoff & Skolnik, 1992; Kugelman, 1992; Poppendieck, 1992). Researchers also found that social workers, including those handling adoption-related dilemmas, rely upon rules more readily than principles, fail to systematically use the NASW Code of Ethics, are usually unable to define ethical dilemmas in "value and ethical terms," and tend to have a nontheoretical, lay perspective with regard to ethics (Conrad & Joseph, 1991, p. 12; Kugelman, 1992). Silverman and Weitzman (1986) wrote that adoption, involving some of the most sensitive, fragile, and complex aspects of all human services, has historically "been more completely in the hands of lay persons than any other area of social welfare" (p. 2).

Moreover, Conrad and Joseph (1991) studied master's-level social workers who were field instructors in the discipline and learned that only 2% could identify the central ethical dilemmas in their case studies. Likewise, only 2% of the social workers based their interventions on ethical issues that had been correctly defined. Instead, they resolved ethical dilemmas using lay philosophies, technical practice methods or techniques, organizational rules, administrative power, or personal experiences, a finding supported by other research (Conrad & Joseph, 1991; Kugelman, 1992; Thomasma & Pisaneschi, 1977).

Joseph (1983) found that ethical competencies can improve social work practice and strengthen client confidence. Kugelman (1992) found that those social workers who were motivated by ethical principles persevered in advocating for the best interests of the client, whereas the majority of the social workers who were not informed by ethics failed to fully advocate for the client. The author concluded that the lack of ethical decision making had "clearly negative" consequences "in respect to quality of services delivered in the field" (Kugelman, 1992, p. 76).

Pine (1987) identified ethical issues as "inherent in all aspects of child welfare practice," but noted that they are "rarely sorted out and dealt with systematically" (p. 315) and that, in child welfare practice, decisions were often made without regard to ethical concerns. Rest (1988) concurred, finding that education in ethics was poorly delivered and received in American professional schools. Researchers stated that ethical functioning in professional situations required special education and preparation, but found that this rarely occurred (Dukette, 1984; Pine, 1987; Rest, 1988). The reasons for this educational failure included lack of institutional time, training, and supports; the concept that competent practice is based on clinical, not ethical, competence; an overemphasis on the need for value-free practice; and the idea that ethics is the purview of the philosopher, not the practitioner.

The literature reflected a paucity of models and standards for ethical decision making and professional competence in the field of child welfare. One report characterized the failure of child welfare to develop and apply scientific and ethical knowledge as system-wide, writing that:

The field needs scholars who are committed to work in the area, knowledgeable about previous findings (including relevant research in other disciplines), thoughtful and creative in developing theories and hypotheses, and expert in overcoming the various legal, ethical, and methodological hurdles that they face. (Melton & Flood, 1994, p. 21)

ETHICAL CODES OF CONDUCT INFLUENCING ADOPTION PRACTICE: A RESEARCH STUDY

This section is an overview of research that has been described in more detail elsewhere, studying the procedures established by licensed adoption agencies and adoption-related organizations in the implementation and application of professional ethics in adoption practice (Babb, 1996). This survey analyzed adoption practice standards for licensed child-placing agencies and the codes of ethics, values, or standards adopted by professional, child welfare, and adoption-related organizations in the practice of adoption. The 50 state licensors of adoption agencies and 23 professional and child welfare associations and adoption-related organizations were surveyed.

Methodology

In her research of the ethical codes of the professions, Schmeiser (1992) identified 13 major areas of ethical conduct: the professional's role in society; integrity; client-employee relations; objectivity and independence; diligence and due care; confidentiality; fees; form of practice; advertising and solicitation; consulting, advising, and evaluation; contractual relationships; communication; and supervision. Her research found a high degree of commonality among the ethical codes of the professions and a popular operational definition of ethics that promoted "the same type of ethical standards" although they were applied to "very different types of work" (Schmeiser, 1992, p. 7).

Schmeiser studied the codes of ethics of the professions of accounting, advertising, architecture, banking, engineering, financial planning, human resource management, insurance, journalism, real estate, dentistry, medicine, mental health, nursing, social work, and law. Of these, the professions most often involved with adoption were social work, law, medicine, nursing, and mental health, including psychology, counseling, and marriage and family therapy (Babb, 1996). These five professions shared the following ethical standards:

1. The professional's role in society (uphold law, maintain professionalism, improve profession, assure product safety and quality; maintain public interest)
2. Client/employee relations (responsibility to client, type of client, no discrimination)
3. Integrity (unfair tactics, undue influence, violations of law, fraudulent practice, honesty/fairness, misconduct, misrepresentation)
4. Diligence/due care (competence, improvement of knowledge, impairment, obligations, maintenance of competence)
5. Confidentiality (authorized disclosures)
6. Communication (warning of adverse consequences, disclosures)

Of the five professions commonly involved in adoption (social work, mental health, nursing, law, and medicine), all but one shared these additional ethical standards:

1. Objectivity/independence (conflict of interest, adverse positions), except medicine
2. Fees (type of fee, commissions, maintaining client property), except nursing
3. Consulting services/advising/evaluating (opinion founded on adequate knowledge, objective and truthful reports, not financed by interested parties, referrals, expert testimony), except nursing
4. Contractual relationships (professional should represent the client's interest), except nursing

Adoption-specific items reflecting the ethical standards of these 10 categories were included in the instrument used in this research. The respondents were asked to complete a 53-item questionnaire of adoption-specific items corresponding to Schmeiser's (1992) 10 ethical categories common to the professions most often involved with adoption, and return it within two weeks. A follow-up questionnaire was mailed if the completed questionnaire had not been received. Respondents were asked to return the second questionnaire within one week.

Sample

The National Council for Adoption (NCFA) declined participation in the research and stated that the NCFA had no positions on the ethical standards asked about in the survey and would not respond unless guaranteed confidentiality. The Institute for Black Parenting failed to return the survey after a second contact and two telephone calls. Of the 75 organizations surveyed, 73 returned completed questionnaires for a return rate of 97%.

The final population consisted of the 50 state licensors of adoption agenciesand 22 professional, adoption-related, or child welfare associations. The 22 associations and organizations surveyed were: Academy of Adoption Professionals, Adopt a Special Kid (AASK America), Adoption ExchangeAssociation, Adoptive Families of America, American Academy of Adoption Attorneys, American Academy of Pediatrics, American Adoption Congress, American Association of Open Adoption Agencies, Catholic Charities USA, Children Awaiting Parents, Child Welfare League of America, Concerned United Birthparents, Council for Equal Rights in Adoption, International Concerns Committee for Children, National Adoption Center, National Association of Black Social Workers, National Association of Social Workers, National Resource Center for Special Needs Adoption, North American Council on Adoptable Children, National Council of Juvenile and Family Court Judges, Native American Child and Family Resource Center, and Rocky Mountain Adoption Exchange. Surveys for the Academy of Adoption Professionals were completed by separate individuals representing different constituencies for a total of 23 respondents.

Preliminary Analysis

Once the frequency data had been tabulated, a second level of data analysis was undertaken in which the chi-square statistic was used to identify patterns of significant differences between groups. To this end, the population was further divided into the following categories: state licensors, groups with over 50% birth parent members, groups with over 50% adoptive parent members, groups with over 50% professional members, groups with membership divided among the triad, associations of private adoption agencies, special needs adoption groups, ethnic minority advocacy or service groups, legal professional associations, medical associations.

Frequency data were tabulated for various items and summarized through the use of frequency tables. The data were then analyzed using the chi-square statistic, allowing any patterns of ethical behavior or standards established to be identified through the analysis. Main effects and interactions between independent variables were identified and described through factorial analyses, which were used to explore the effects of particular variables. Complete results are available through University Microfilms International (Babb, 1996).

Major Findings: Shared Themes

The research results showed that shared standards for ethical adoption practice could be identified and categorized. Shared standards were found in areas of the adoption professional's role in society, client-employee relations, non-discrimination, diligence and due care, communication, objectivity/independence, fees, what constitutes the best interest of the child, contractual relationships, and some aspects of confidentiality. The shared standards are described in more detail in the following sections.

The Adoption Professional's Role in Society. This common ethical standard describes the professional's duty to uphold the law, maintain professionalism, improve the profession, assure product (or service delivery) safety and quality, and maintain public interest. Respondents said that adoption practice specifically should be based upon common values or a code of ethics, professional practice principles, and research and clinical findings in adoption.

Client-Employee Relations. This ethic speaks to the professional's responsibility to the client and the professional's duty to avoid discrimination in any form. Respondents said that adoption professionals should always inform birth mothers of their rights to reclaim their surrendered children and that adoptive parents should always receive nonidentifying information about birth families and children's histories prior to finalization of adoptions. They said that birth parents and adoptees should be given nonidentifying social, educational, and medical history information prior to the finalization of adoptions. After adoptions are finalized, adoptees, adoptive parents, and birth parents should be given nonidentifying information about each other.

Although the respondents underscored the adoption professional's duty to observe nondiscrimination, the findings showed that the mentally ill, gay men, and lesbians were more likely to be discriminated against in adoption placement practice.

Diligence and Due Care. This ethical standard speaks to the professional's competence, improvement of knowledge, impairment, obligations, and maintenance of competence. The majority of respondents said that adoption-specific training or education should be required of professionals working in adoption. Most responded that competence in adoption work could be vouchsafed through generalized education in a helping profession, in-service training, and on-the-job training or experience.

Communication. This standard requires professionals to warn clients of adverse consequences of actions or services offered and asks professionals to tell clients about their rights, risks, opportunities, and obligations associated with professional service to them. There was universal agreement that adoption clients should receive accurate and complete disclosure of information about adoption and the adverse consequences of adoption.

Objectivity/Independence. Conflict of interest and adverse positions are addressed by this ethic, which asks professionals to avoid relationships that can impair the professional's objectivity or ability to serve the client well. Respondents agreed that adoption professionals should define who the client is in an adoption (for their own benefit and that of the client) and what relationship the professional will have with each person involved in an adoption. Birth and prospective adoptive parents who are party to the same adoption should have separate adoption workers and nearly always have separate legal counsel.

Best Interest of the Child Standard. One ethical standard identified by the research that is unique to work with children is the "best interest of the child" standard. The other professions agree that professionals should serve the client and consider the welfare of the client as of paramount importance. The research showed that consideration of the best interest of any child involved in an adoption was a primary concern of those surveyed.

The three most important factors in determining the best interest of the child were the desire and ability of birth family members to raise the child, the potential or actual parenting ability of those parents, and the option of being raised with biological relatives. The findings supported Dukette's (1984) conclusion that birth parents should be given every opportunity and support to raise their own children, a valuation of biological relatedness shared by the respondents to this survey.

A possible conflict between the value of supporting client self-determination and that of serving the best interests of the child thus exists in adoption. In infant adoptions where an agency or professional may serve the expectant parents, prospective adoptive parents, and child, the professional may be unable to identify only one client. In addition, the needs of one client, such as the child, may be perceived by the professional to conflict with the needs of another client, such as the expectant or birth parent. The increased value conflicts in adoption result in a similarly increased need for professional watchfulness, self-analysis, and peer review, lest personal bias or discrimination occur in adoption practice delivery in spite of the professional's best intentions.

Contractual Relationships and Fees. This ethic speaks to types of fees, commissions, and maintenance of client property. Most respondents agreed that adoption service fees should not be charged. Children needing the service of adoption should be considered the responsibility of the local, state, and federal governments and service fees for their care and placements charged to the appropriate governmental agencies. If service fees are charged, they should be disclosed to the person responsible for paying them prior to an adoptive placement and should be based on the client's ability to pay. Any fees charged for special needs adoptions should be lower than those for the adoptions of children without special needs. Fees for search or nonidentifying information should not be charged by agencies.

The market economy in children coexisting in the United States with a child-centered, service model of adoption conflicts in the area of fees. Public and private agencies compete for the same moneys funding special needs adoptions, while independent practitioners and private agencies compete for a dwindling supply of healthy adoptable infants in a society with ever-increasing demands. When the demand for the product (the child) drives the entire system, professionals, too, succumb to the market economy, either as they work for agencies whose continued existence depends upon completed adoptions, or as they work independently to achieve the same end.

Some respondents commented that though they believed that special needs adoptions, in particular, should be accomplished either with no fees or at substantially reduced rates, they also recognized that special needs adoptions were more labor-intensive for professionals and required much more ongoing postlegal support than healthy infant adoptions. Still, as public and private agencies compete for dwindling government funding, professionals who work in special needs adoption and those who specialize in infant adoption face the same conflicts: a professional obligation to serve clients to the best of their abilities, and a responsibility to serve the organizations within which they work, which are largely supported by financial means and fees. Watson (1994) was one of few professionals who had concrete suggestions regarding the philosophy behind charging fees in adoption and a plan for abolishing adoption fees. The data supported Watson's contention that agencies should find other ways besides charging fees to finance adoption services.

Contractual Relationships. This ethic says that the professional should represent the client's interest first and foremost at all times. Participants responding to questions in this area believed that professionals or others outside the organization should be consulted when it is in the best interest of the client, and adoption clients should be allowed or encouraged to seek advice, information, or support from other groups even when the philosophy of the group differs from those providing the primary services.

Confidentiality. Confidentiality requires authorized disclosures, professional respect of the client's privacy, and a mandate to hold in confidence all information obtained in the course of professional service. There was complete agreement that birth and adoptive parents should be told, prior to an adoption, that the adoptee may conduct a search for the birth parents in the future. The majority (62%) said that adult adoptees should be given access to their original birth certificates, supporting the idea that the ethics of confidentiality and client self-determination can be observed without conflict in adoption practice. The value of supporting client self-determination (in the case of the adult adoptee wanting his original birth certificate) and that of observing confidentiality (of the birth parents) are interpreted as conflicting only in the United States and some provinces of Canada, which continue to support the sealed record as one aspect of confidentiality. Other nations do not operationalize the confidentiality ethic similarly. The findings of the research showed that agency licensors, professional groups, child welfare, and adoption organizations in the majority agreed.

Second Level of Analysis: How Issues Affect Members of the Adoption Triad

Ethical areas that adoption agency licensors and organizations could not agree on were aspects of *objectivity and independence* (including conflicts of interest and defining and serving the client), *integrity* (honesty, disclosure, misrepresentation), and *confidentiality* (access to adoption records). In each area, the disagreement involved direct service to the client, that is, whether that service involved actually defining who the client was, or the release of accurate (or any) information to adoption service recipients. The following sections provide a description of some of these specific ethical values, and how the lack of clear values and resulting practice standards affects members of the adoption triad and the professionals and agencies serving them.

Defining the Client. Most adoption groups were interested in the ethical practice of adoption and chose values-based adoption over any other basis of practice. They said that the primary client in an adoption should be identified clearly, for both the client and the professional. Groups disagreed, however, about who the client is in an adoption, a finding supported by other research (Dukette, 1984; Valentine, Conway, & Randolph, 1988; Voss, 1985).

Some respondents considered an unborn child in a proposed infant adoption the client, while others considered the expectant mother the client. Still others considered the mother and the child the clients, while 45% considered the expectant parents, the unborn child, and the prospective adoptive parents the clients. Considering more than one party to an adoption as the client, especially when only one adoption professional serves those clients, presents many opportunities for conflicting interests and values. If an unborn child is seen as the client, by what standard does the adoption professional serve the child? What values guide the professional? Does the professional compare the resources of the birth and adoptive families, and choose to advocate for the unborn child in whichever direction best serves the child, in his or her opinion? Because the unborn child has no voice and does not even exist as a person legally, the professional cannot apply general professional ethics established for work with adult clients. The danger that subjective standards, driven by something other than ethical codes, will be used in serving the (unborn) client is thus great.

Adoptees placed as older children fare differently as clients. State agency licensors tended to see the child as the client (instead of the birth or adoptive parents), possibly because child welfare adoption specialists in state agencies more often serve older children awaiting adoption as their primary clients. Special needs adoption groups tended to see either the birth parents, the child, or all three parties to an adoption as the clients, rather than seeing adoptive parents as the primary clients. When older adoptable children are the primary clients and are identified as such, less confusion exists and the means of serving the child through casework services become more simple. If one client, and one client alone (the child), is being served, then the professional can identify the child's needs and work to find ways of meeting those needs (photo listing, fost-adopt, adoption, group care).

Expectant and birth parents have not fared as well as clients. When they enter an adoption counselor's office, expectant parents considering adoption generally consider themselves to be the clients (Babb, 1996). If such clients knew that nearly one-fourth of adoption organizations or professionals might consider their unborn child the client, they might be surprised. Does the adoption professional tell the expectant parent(s) that he or she considers their unborn child the client, and is ethically bound to serve the unborn child's best interests, rather than the best interests of the expectant parents, if those interests conflict? Young, single mothers are most at-risk of suffering the adverse consequences when professionals do not clearly define, and serve, the expectant mother as the client. Of such women, Jones writes, "Most young, single women with modest incomes and average educations are destined to remain among the least powerful people in our society. It is no coincidence that this is the group which most frequently relinquishes children for adoption" (1993, p. 13).

Respondents agreed that adoption professionals should define who the client is in an adoption and what relationship the professional will have with each person involved. The majority of respondents also agreed that separate social workers and attorneys should be provided to birth and adoptive parents who are party to the same adoption when the legal processes for both sets of parents are concurrent. These findings concurred with other research that showed that adoption is replete with conflicts of interest, which can in part be avoided through providing birth and adoptive parents with separate adoption and legal workers.

Integrity. The results supported a need for honest disclosure of background and medical information in domestic and international adoptions and particularly in special needs adoptions. The majority of respondents (77%) had received complaints about unethical behavior among professionals, and most of the complaints involved the failure to offer or release accurate information, or the withholding of critical information during the adoption process. Adoptive parents most often complained about the disclosure of the adoptee's complete history. Special needs adoption groups in particular reported that adoptive parents often expressed discontent over critical information being withheld by professionals simply being unavailable, a finding echoed by other research. Rosenthal and Groze (1992) wrote that "the desire of many special-needs parents . . . for more depth in background information seems to us to parallel the search that many adopted at infancy undertake to learn about or make contact with their birth families. Neither adoptive parent nor child desires that the child exist without a past. Instead, knowledge of the past strengthens the adoptive family system" (p. 208).

The lack of information is not only harmful to adoptees and adoptive parents: birth parents also complained about the failure of adoption professionals or agencies to disclose information to them, particularly about adoption alternatives or the psychological and emotional consequences of surrendering a child, which supported the findings of others that birth parents have not been well served in this and other areas of adoption counseling (Brodzinsky, 1990; Jones, 1993).

Confidentiality. The area of confidentiality describes authorized disclosures, including what kinds of information may be disclosed, to whom, and under what circumstances. Groups agreed that confidentiality as a value should be upheld, but disagreed about what is meant by the term in adoption work. All agreed that birth and adoptive parents should be told that the adoptee may search for the birth family in the future. The majority also said that adult adoptees should be given access to their original birth certificates. This supported the idea that sealing of adoption records results from myths and tradition more than from ethical principles or sound professional practice (Baran & Pannor, 1990; Feigelman & Silverman, 1986;

Watson, 1992). Adoption and helping professionals, legal professionals, and medical professionals tended to favor more, rather than less, openness in responding to the question regarding adult adoptees' access to their original birth certificates, whereas state licensors, charged with upholding the laws of the 50 states, tended to support the sealed record.

The finding that the majority of respondents supported open access of adult adoptees to their records supplemented previous research that showed that many adoptees have a normative desire to have identifying information regarding their biological parents. Adoptees placed as infants and those placed when older express similar desires to have information to which others are already entitled (Sorosky, Baran, & Pannor, 1989).

Perhaps the most controversial area involving confidentiality is the conflict between the assumed need of birth parents to have their identities kept secret and the needs of adult adoptees to know their identities at birth and to have access to their original birth records. Some professionals and many detractors of open records say that birth mothers and fathers were given an implied promise of ongoing confidentiality that cannot be violated simply to satisfy the adoptee's desire to know his or her identity at birth. Instead, they say that such records only should be accessible to the adoptee due to compelling need (NCFA, 1996). Birth parents, and birth mothers in particular, argue that they not only were never promised perpetual confidentiality of identity, but that they never wanted it (Jones, 1993; Sorosky, Baran, & Pannor, 1989). Maintaining secrecy (complete confidentiality) past the time when it has served a useful purpose has been experienced, by many birth parents, as destructive (Brodzinsky, 1990).

The issue of confidentiality and how to apply it to adoption clients is clearly a challenge to adoption professionals and the agencies employing them. Professionals must seek to balance the rights and responsibilities of clients, accounting not only for present circumstances, but also for what may happen in the future. The challenge to professionals and agencies is great, underscoring the need for ethical competencies and the availability of professional services throughout the life span of an adoption.

Diligence and Due Care. Respondents favored three primary means of ensuring competence among adoption agency workers: generalized education in a helping profession, in-service training, and on-the-job training or experience. The literature, however, showed that only 2% of master's-level social workers who were field instructors in the discipline could identify ethical dilemmas in their case studies or based their interventions on ethical issues that had been correctly defined (Conrad & Joseph, 1991). The literature also indicated that the lack of ethical decision making had negative consequences in terms of service delivery to clients, and that professionals need special education and preparation in the area of application of ethical standards, since these are rarely taught or mastered (Dukette, 1984; Kugelman, 1992; Pine, 1987; Rest, 1988).

Most respondents (80%) agreed that adoption-specific training should be required of those working in adoption, and all agreed that such professionals should receive continuing education in adoption. There was disagreement as to how and when such training should be undertaken and by what means, which supported previous findings. Fewer respondents considered adoption conference attendance, a child welfare course with an adoption unit, or work with lay search and support groups as valuable to the adoption worker, although all of the latter means of education are adoption-specific.

Summary

The literature reflected professional thought and recommendations regarding professional adoption practice but provided little research or commentary regarding ethical standards for adoption; only one study offered data regarding what constitutes ethical adoption practice in the United States. The literature did not provide clear criteria for applying ethical decision making in adoption or any way of determining when an action promotes or detracts from the best interest of a child or any adoption client. The data gave scarce attention to how the adoption professional may identify or ethically serve his or her client(s), and presented a dearth of adoption-specific ethical standards or ethical decision-making models.

Professionals who must operationalize the best interests of the child and "communicate . . . about ethical adoption practice" need a standard against which they can measure their behavior (Hughes, 1993). If left without clear guidelines and models for such decision making, practitioners will fail to utilize ethical analysis (Joseph, 1983; Pine, 1987). In the absence of ethical standards and models, adoption workers exert a power that is without professional authority (Severson, 1994). Severson (1994) explains:

Under normal circumstances when such power is wielded, it is done so only within a context of multiple checks and controls. This is simply not so in adoption social work. . . . Power corrupts and absolute power corrupts absolutely, so runs the old truism. Over the last century, adoption work has become corrupt in all too many cases. Unfortunately, the corruption is not flamboyant or excessive in ways that would make it easily identifiable. Rather it is the more pernicious form of laziness, inertia, institutional smugness, mediocrity, poor and undemanding preparation of the professional, hypocrisy and complacency, and widespread polite collusion in platitudes and cliches. . . . It is the corruption that weeps with sentimentality but remains dry-eyed when the suffering is real. (p. 212)

RECOMMENDED MODEL FOR ETHICAL STANDARDS IN ADOPTION

Professionals who practice adoption have long been considered to be the most competent among adoption practitioners due to their professional and child welfare training and experience, and the most principled due to their adherence to a professional code of ethics (Barth, 1987; Child Welfare League of America, 1976; NASW, 1990, 1996; Sachdev, 1989; U.S. Children's Bureau, 1961; Walden, Wolock, & Demone, 1990).

Among professionally trained adoption workers, however, there has been a problem of persisting lay attitudes, positions based on cultural values and personal experience rather than professional knowledge, ethical values, or research (Cole & Donley, 1990). In addition, professional adoption workers bring with them, into their adoption work, a profusion of personal beliefs and common knowledge about what children need and what types of parents will act in the best interests of their children. It is such personal beliefs and knowledge "which they, as adults moved by an urge to 'rescue' children, are tempted to impose. The risk that actions and decisions in child placement will rest on personal values presented in the guise of professional knowledge is therefore great" (Goldstein, et al., 1973, pp. 16–17).

Adoption practice has increasingly come under scrutiny and attack by recipients of adoption services, including birth parents, adoptees, and adoptive parents, for actions that adoption service recipients say run counter to their best interests (Babb, 1996; Cameron, 1989; Gonyo & Watson, 1988; Sorich & Siebert, 1982). Throughout the industrialized world, the practice of adoption as a specialty of child welfare has been reformed in law and social policy as a result of pressure brought to bear by social changes and by the dissatisfied recipients of past adoption services (Cole & Donley, 1990; Sachdev, 1992; Sorosky, Baran, & Pannor, 1989).

The reform of adoption in other countries and an increased scrutiny and criticism of adoption practice in the United States have caused several U.S. professional organizations to establish or revise standards for adoption practice as well as to call for the professionalization of adoption as a specialized human service. Another result of the increased scrutiny of adoption practice has been that organizations concerned with professional adoption practice have uniformly opposed the facilitation of adoptions through intermediaries such as medical doctors and attorneys who are neither trained nor licensed to provide child-placing services (Babb, 1994; Barth, 1987; Child Welfare League of America, 1976; NASW, 1990, 1996; Sachdev, 1989; U.S. Children's Bureau, 1961).

Although the majority of state licensors of adoption agencies and professional and adoption-related groups say that a code of ethics should underlie adoption practice, there is no uniform code of ethics in adoption (Babb, 1996). Most organizations base their adoption practices on general professional ethics, which are, according to research, ill-understood and poorly applied by professionals. The value of establishing an adoption-specific professional code of ethics can be seen. The second most-embraced foundation of adoption practice, professional practice principles, are so ill-defined as to be nearly useless to any adoption professional grappling with questions about who the client is in an adoption, for whom the worker should advocate, to whom, why, and how adoption information should be disclosed, or how the best interests of a child can be served in complex human situations.

Professionals, though bidden by their respective codes of ethics to base their practice on research and clinical findings, had problems in this foundational area as well. The professional organizations and their various directorates neither publish adoption-specific journals nor host adoption-specific conferences. Indeed, only about one-third of adoption licensors, groups, and professional organizations considered adoption conferences in their current form—hosted by grassroots, lay, or state organizations—to be of any value in educating adoption professionals in spite of the inclusion of workshops and research-oriented meetings for professionals at most such conferences (Babb, 1996; Severson, 1994).

Adoption professionals have only general means by which to exchange information specific to adoption, participate in dialogue concerning adoption standards, or obtain a comprehensive picture of what is happening in adoption today. To this end, the establishment of an association for adoption professionals could be helpful. Such an organization might consider the certification of adoption professionals in order to ensure adoption-specific training and competencies. Starting in fall 1997, a journal for adoption professionals was initiated.

Professionals tend to favor generalized education in a profession and state that such preparation is sufficient to ensure competence in adoption work; lay adoption groups, who are the recipients of professional adoption services, disagree (Babb, 1996; Severson, 1994). Professionals who seek to better serve their clients would do well to heed what adoption triad members have to say about competence in adoption work. The literature showed that professionals are, in general, ill-prepared in the area of ethics, and that ethical complaints are common. If adoption-specific standards and education were developed, perhaps we would find that birth parents, adoptive parents, adoptees, and children needing the service of adoption would all be better served. To that end, that of truly serving our clients, and based on the history, literature, and research, the following standards for serving the adoption triad (birth parents, adoptive parents, and adoptees) are proposed. The standards are divided according to the ethical value invoked.

Principle 1: Responsibility to Clients

The first ethical area to be considered is that of client-professional relations, or the professional's responsibility to the client. Responsibility is an ethical concept embodying the values of accountability, self-restraint, and pursuit of excellence. Professional behavior as it relates to responsibility to clients includes several of Levy's (1973) preferred instrumentalities in dealing with people, such as respecting client self-determination, autonomy, and dignity and relieving power imbalances, including those inherent in the professional-client relationship or those between the client and the agency. How the responsibility to clients should influence services to adoption triad members is described below.

Birth Parents. Adoption professionals have ethical obligations to expectant parents considering adoption for born and unborn children, to birth parents who voluntarily surrender their rights to parent their children, and to those whose parental rights are terminated by the states.

Nondiscrimination.   Nondiscrimination should be observed in counseling expectant and birth parents. The professional should not discriminate against the adoption client or condone such discrimination on the basis of any personal characteristic of the client, including age, race, color, sex, marital status, sexual orientation, mental or physical handicap, national origin, or any other basis or condition. If adoption professionals apply the same standards of service to all clients, regardless of the social mores or personal beliefs of the professional, those professionals have achieved the goal of nondiscrimination.

Foster client self-determination. The adoption professional should foster maximum client self-determination.

Preserve the birth family whenever possible. Adoption professionals should take care to explore and offer adoption alternatives to expectant parents considering adoption. Parents should be taught about the worth they have to their children and helped to understand practical aid available to help them raise their children. Every attempt should be made to preserve the family of origin.

When offering adoption alternatives to parents experiencing crises, adoption professionals should educate parents about how they may receive help to raise their own children. The education process may be accomplished through the use of orientation classes, recommended readings, video lending libraries, support through online computer resources, free newsletters, organizational membership, local support and parent assistance groups, parenting classes, and treatment programs.

The availability of financial aid should be discussed and printed information given to clients about Aid to Families with Dependent Children (AFDC), Medicaid, local social service organizations, church programs, other community supports, community mental health programs, General Education Diploma (GED) and other educational programs, and assistance for secondary education available through government grants and loans, financial aid, and need- and achievement-based scholarships. The adoption professional should also give birth parents written information about and referrals to other professionals and agencies regarding job training programs, unemployment benefits, Social Security Income (SSI) for children with special needs, food stamps, and subsidized housing.

Value birth fathers and treat them with respect. In our society birth fathers have often been regarded as unnecessary or even as threats to the adoption process. The adoption professional should consider fathers as important and treat the birth father with respect, considering him to be of vital importance to the child whose family is in crisis. The adoption professional should serve birth fathers by offering written information specific to fathers and parenting (articles, magazines, books, pamphlets), access to discussion and support groups, dad-only groups, men's groups and organizations both locally and nationally. Expectant fathers and fathers of born children should be fully considered in service delivery and their rights supported and protected. Birth fathers should be taught about the worth they have to their children and should be helped to understand how they can raise their children.

Value parents as parents. Adoption professionals should value the birth parents as parents. With regard to pregnancy, becoming a family, childbirth and child rearing, parents should be educated about the development and needs of unborn and born children. Expectant mothers should be taught about the changes pregnancy brings to one's body and emotions, and the considerable body of research regarding the lives of unborn children and their prenatal attachment to their mothers as well as their dependence upon the mother for nutrition. Both parents should be given information about childbirth, infant and child care, and referred to other agencies and professionals as needed.

Respect the client's beliefs. If a client is religious, the professional should be respectful of the client's religious beliefs without exploiting the beliefs or using them to support either relinquishment of a child or preservation of the birth family. The duty of the professional is to support the client in making his or her own decisions, not to influence the client in implementing the decision that the professional or any other person believes is best.

Inform the client about legal rights. The adoption professional should encourage birth parents to obtain legal counsel independent of the adoption agency or adoption professional and give birth parents written information about their legal rights in the state of relinquishment and that of placement of a child.

Adoption professionals should also inform birth parents of their legal rights, if any, to reclaim their surrendered children, the legal procedures for doing so, and the time frame in which reclamation must occur. In states imposing a best interest of the child standard upon contested adoptions, birth parents should be notified in writing of their legal rights, and of the possibility that an attempt to reclaim their children may pit them against agencies, professionals, or adoptive parents in a contest of fitness.

Finally, the adoption professional should also advise birth parents of their right to have copies of all legal documents related to their children's births, the consent to adopt, court proceedings, and termination of parental rights, including the right to have their children's original birth certificates.

The right to openness in adoption. The adoption professional should educate all parties to the adoption regarding research results in open adoption, the need of adoptees to know their biological histories, name at birth, and identities of their birth parents, and the risks and benefits of ongoing contact. Clients should be informed of the availability of open adoption as a possibility for birth and adoptive parents in infant and older child adoptions.

When birth and adoptive parents have established or seek to establish ongoing contact in an adoption while the adoptee is still a minor, the adoption professional should make every effort to help establish, support, and maintain such contact and to communicate the desire for such contact as expressed by any party to the adoption.

The adoption professional should provide ongoing support and professional counseling to adoptive and birth parents in open adoptions as requested.

Right to information about adoptee and adoptive parents. Birth parents should be given accurate and complete nonidentifying information about the adoptive parents prior to finalization of an adoption and ongoing nonidentifying information about the adoptive parents and adoptee after an adoption has been finalized when requested. The information should comprise social, psychological, medical, educational, and emotional content.

Continue to serve the client. The adoption professional or agency serving birth parents should not abandon or neglect birth parents after an adoption has been finalized. Ongoing programs of support, counseling, and education should be provided to birth parents, as well as programs offering support during search and reunion when requested by the birth parent. Postrelinquishment support to birth parents can include referral to support or grief groups for birth parents, and provision of grief counseling, reading materials, and information about organizations serving birth parents and other adoption triad members after an adoption has been finalized.

Adoptive Parents. In support of the ethical guidelines governing client-employee relations and the responsibility to clients, the following standards are suggested for adoptive parents:

Nondiscrimination. Nondiscrimination should be observed in serving prospective adoptive parents and adoptive parents. The adoption professional should take special care to be nondiscriminatory in working with prospective or other adoptive parents who do not fit the traditional model for adoptive parents (those who are single, older, gay or lesbian, etc.). Placement decisions should be based on research and sound practice principles.

Foster client self-determination. The adoption professional should foster maximum client self-determination.

Prepare adoptive parents. Adoptive parents should be taught about the adoption process, prepared to live with the differences between the adoptive and biological family, and prepared to deal with adoption-related grief, loss, and other adoption issues as part of the adoption process for themselves and the adoptee. Prior to and during an adoption placement, the professional should serve adoptive parents with consistent devotion and the maximum application of professional skill and competence.

Respect the client's beliefs. If a client is religious, the adoption professional should be respectful of the client's beliefs without exploiting the beliefs or using them to support adoption in general or the adoption of certain children. The duty of the professional is to support the client in making his or her own decisions and determining his or her own limits when adopting a child or children.

Inform the client about legal rights. The adoption professional should encourage adoptive parents to obtain legal counsel independent of the adoption agency or adoption professional and should inform adoptive parents about their legal rights. When the parental rights of one or both birth parents have not been terminated and a child is placed with a prospective adoptive family, the adoption professional should apprise the adoptive parents of their rights and the legal and emotional risks inherent in such a placement.

Finally, the adoption professional should advise adoptive parents of their rights to have copies of all legal documents related to a child's postsurrender care, the petition to adopt, the final adoption decree, and the original birth certificate.

Child-parent matching. The adoption professional should take great care to base placement decisions on research and clinical findings related to infant and older child adoptions; measures of temperament, ability, and fit for both prospective adoptive parents and prospective adoptees; the desires, wishes, and needs of both the prospective adoptive parents and the prospective adoptees; and the wishes of families of origin.

Full disclosure of adoptee history. Adoption professionals, workers, and agencies should disclose all known background information concerning prospective adoptees to adoptive parents prior to placement. The adoptees' histories should include complete and accurate social, psychological, medical, educational, and emotional facts as well as information about and access to all former caretakers and the birth families, including birth parents and grandparents.

Provision of postplacement services and information. The adoption professional should be able to provide adoption-aware and family-oriented postplacement counseling and support to the adoptive family, or be able to refer the adoptive family to such professionals locally. Such services should include, but not be limited to, respite care, access to support groups, reading materials (books, newsletters, magazines), parent training, conference information, training on behavior management with difficult children, basic child care appropriate to the age of the child, child development, ongoing counseling and support in open adoptions, and counseling and support during the adoptee's search and reunion, or when adoptive parents seek to open an adoption or increase contact with the birth family.

After an adoption is finalized, adoptive parents should be given nonidentifying information about birth parents as available and identifying information as allowed by the birth parent(s) prior to the adoptee reaching the age of majority.

The right to openness in adoption. The adoption professional should educate all parties to adoption regarding research results in open adoption, the need of adoptees to know their biological histories, name at birth, and identities of their birth parents, and the risks and benefits of ongoing contact. Clients should be informed of the availability of open adoption as a possibility for birth and adoptive parents in infant and older child adoptions.

When birth and adoptive parents have established or seek to establish ongoing contact in an adoption while the adoptee is still a minor, the adoption professional should make every effort to help establish, support, and maintain such contact and to communicate the desire for such contact as expressed by any party to the adoption. The adoption professional should provide ongoing support and professional counseling to adoptive and birth parents in open adoptions as requested.

The adoption professional should not abandon or neglect adoptive parents after an adoption has been finalized. The adoption professional should be available for ongoing counseling and consultation as described above and should inform adoptive parents about ongoing professional services and support. The need of adoptive families for professional support, information, and education does not end with the finalization of the adoption: adoption professionals should thus make themselves accessible to adoptive families long after the adoption has become legal.

Adoptees. In support of the ethical guidelines governing client-employee relations and the responsibility to clients, the following standards are suggested:

The adoption professional should regard adoption as a service to children who need permanent families.

Nondiscrimination. Nondiscrimination should be observed in counseling adoptees and in the adoptive placement of children needing the service. The adoption professional should neither practice nor condone discrimination on the basis of race, gender, sexual orientation, age, religion, national origin, mental or physical handicap, or any other preferential or personal characteristic of children entering into the adoption process, except insofar as such qualities can be demonstrated to have a negative impact on a particular proposed or actual adoptive placement and with regard to a specific child. The adoption professional should not allow any such characteristic to unreasonably postpone or prevent the permanent adoptive placement of a child needing the service of adoption.

Protect the child's right to grow up in his or her family of origin. The adoption professional should, to the best of his or her ability, see to it that children can be cared for by their own parents, or, in the case of failing parental care, by a member of the extended family.

Protect the child's right to grow up in his or her own community. The adoption professional should safeguard the child's right to grow up in his or her own community, culture, race, nation, and religion and support intercountry adoption only when adoption within the child's own community is unavailable.

Oppose black and gray market adoptions. The adoption professional should not participate in adoptions in which illegal, illicit, or unethical behavior occurs among adoption facilitators, whether those facilitators are professionals or not. The professional should not condone the behavior or policies of others, including agencies and attorneys, who treat adoption service as an industry and adoptees as property or objects.

Provide age-appropriate adoption counseling. The adoption professional should explain the adoption process to the child needing the service in an age-appropriate way through the use of words, pictures, videotapes, the life book, play, and any other means available to him or her.

Allow for the child's consent to adoption when possible. When a child cannot remain with his or her birth parents, the adoption professional should consider the child's wishes and opinions and encourage him or her to participate in the adoption process and give consent to being adopted verbally and in writing, as appropriate to the child's age, circumstances, emotional health, cognitive abilities, and development.

Facilitate grieving. When a child older than infancy leaves his or her birth family, the adoption professional should give the child the opportunity to say good-bye to his or her parents, siblings, pets, neighbors and friends, and other loved ones and help the child through counseling for grief, separation, and loss.

The adoption professional should be prepared to address the adoptee's developmental needs to recycle through the grief process throughout the life span.

Right to information about oneself. The adoption professional recognizes and supports the right of the minor adoptee, with the permission of the adoptive parents, to have information about him or herself, including his or her name at birth; social, medical, psychological, educational, cultural, and racial background; birth parents' history, and reason for relinquishment.

The adoption professional should advise adult adoptees of their rights, where legally applicable, to have copies of all legal documents related to their births, including their original birth certificates and adoption (amended birth) certificates and adoption decrees. Where such legal rights do not exist, the adoption professional should advocate for such rights on behalf of adult adoptees who want this information.

Continue to serve the client. The adoption professional should not abandon or neglect the adoptee after an adoption has been finalized.

Respect the adoptee. The adoption professional should divest him or herself of adoption mythology and refuse to define the adoptee's reality for him or her by describing the adoptee as "chosen, lucky," or in negative terms, such as "ungrateful," or by using words like "illegitimate, bastard."

Principle 2: Integrity

Integrity is a foundational ethical concept, the cornerstone of all other ethical values. Integrity involves moral courage and the "elevation of principle over expediency or self-interest and requires a consistency between words and action" (Josephson, 1993, p. 15).

Over 75% of adoption groups and licensors say they have received complaints ab out misleading or dishonest behavior among adoption professionals (Babb, 1996). Among lay groups serving birth parents, adoptive parents, and adoptees, the lack of integrity among adoption professionals, including adoption attorneys, was cited as a major reason for disillusionment with and mistrust of professionals.

Integrity requires a professional to be, first and foremost, truthful with clients. Adoption professionals should not misrepresent adoption and its benefits, or disadvantages, to clients. In seeking to be honest with clients, the professional simply must have the "good faith intent to tell the truth" (Josephson, 1993, p. 13). Because adoption is a complex human service, professionals may find it impossible to serve clients honestly without being informed about current research and developments in the field. The truth as we know it in adoption continues to change as new information and research become available.

Integrity enjoins against any type of dishonesty or cunning aimed at depriving a client of anything of value, including a money, favors, or a child.

Birth Parents. Avoid undue influence. The adoption professional should recognize that parents considering adoption for a child are experiencing a crisis, and should recognize vulnerabilities that precipitated and were caused by the crisis.

The professional should regard the birth parent considering adoption, or under court supervision for child neglect or abuse, as a client who needs counseling, practical supports, or therapy before adoption is viewed as a solution.

Avoid exploitation of dependency or inexperience. Professionals should take extra care with younger clients who are making weighty decisions with little experience, be aware of their influence on parents considering adoption, and avoid exploiting or influencing the client in the direction they think best. The adoption professional should foster maximum client self-determination.

Support the kinship system. The extended family of the mother and father should be considered first when adoption is chosen as a plan for a child. The parents, siblings, aunts, uncles, and cousins of the expectant parents should be considered as possible guardians or adoptive parents of the child before strangers are asked to assume such responsibilities. If relative placement is not an option, the adoption professional should make every effort to preserve connections of some kind between children going into adoption and their birth families.

Be open about open adoption. Professionals who arrange open adoptions should provide birth parents with complete and accurate information, including the legal enforceability or unenforceability of such adoptions. When exploring open adoption with birth parents, professionals should be careful that the promise of open adoption does not become a coercive means of encouraging the surrender of a child. Professionals should continue to support the birth parents when a child is adopted and emphasize the need for birth and adoptive parents to keep their commitments to ongoing contact. Adoption professionals working with legal professionals and the birth and adoptive families party to open adoptions may also want to devise a legally binding open adoption contract between the parties when state laws do not protect open adoption arrangements.

Caution in use of time for consent to adoption and revocation of consent. Adoption professionals who work in infant placements should not expect or encourage expectant parents to make a binding adoption decision until after an infant is born. Such professionals should provide birth families with encourage-ment and the opportunity to spend time with their babies after birth, and should allow birth families sufficient time after birth to consider their options prior to legally committing to adoption plans. The Association of Open Adoption Agencies suggests at least a two-week time period (Catholic Charities USA, 1994). Other groups suggest that two weeks to six months is a reasonable time for consent to adoption or revocation of consent without cause (Babb, 1996).

Professionals working with parents who are under court supervision for child mistreatment should help parents understand the necessity of complying with court supervision and the consequences of noncompliance to themselves and their children. They should inform parents of time limitations for compliance with the service plan and of any statutory basis for the state's exemption from its obligation to make reasonable efforts to reunify children and their parents.

Professionals should encourage families to maintain contact with their children living in out-of-home placements and explain the importance of spending time with their children. Parents and extended families should be given sufficient time to consider the options before legally committing to voluntary termination of parental rights.

Adoptive Parents. Avoid undue influence. The adoption professional should recognize that prospective adoptive parents have probably come to adoption through crisis and loss and should recognize the vulnerabilities caused by infertility (if applicable) and by the adoption process itself, and avoid exploiting such vulnerabilities. The adoption professional should not pressure adoptive parents to accept a child that the parents feel unable to raise. The adoption professional should be aware that due to the competitive nature of U.S. adoptions, adoptive parents may be vulnerable to pressure from the professional and should refuse to exploit the adoptive parents in order to place a child.

Disclosure and truthfulness in recruiting. Adoption professionals should disclose complete and accurate information to prospective adoptive parents during the process of recruiting families for children awaiting adoptive placements.

While recruiting families for waiting children through the use of profiles, photo listings, "matching parties," or other means, the adoption professional should not exploit the emotions of the adoptive parents or their desire to have a child. Critical information about the needs of waiting children and the responsibility of raising them should not be minimized through the use of such recruiting tools or through exploitation of the prospective adoptive parents.

Full disclosure of adoptee history. Adoption professionals, workers, and agencies should disclose all known background information concerning the prospective adoptee to the adoptive parents prior to placement. The adoptee's history should include social, psychological, medical, educational, and emotional histories as well as information about and access to all former caretakers and the birth family of the child.

Be open about open adoption. Professionals who arrange open adoptions should provide adoptive parents with complete and accurate information about open adoption, including the legal enforceability or unenforceability of such adoptions, other legal means of enforcing open adoption agreements or contracts, and the moral obligation incurred by birth and adoptive parents who become party to an open adoption. The adoption professional should also educate adoptive parents about the risks, responsibilities, and benefits of open adoption.

Adoptees. Support the kinship system. The extended families of the mother and father should be considered first when adoption is chosen as a plan for a child. The parents, siblings, aunts, uncles, and cousins of the birth parents should be considered as possible guardians or adoptive parents of the child if adoption is chosen, before strangers are asked to assume such responsibilities. If relative placement is not an option, the adoption professional should make every effort to preserve connections of some kind between children going into adoption and their birth families.

Be open about open adoption. Professionals who arrange open adoptions should provide older waiting children with complete and accurate information about open adoption and guardianship, including the legal enforceability or unenforceability of such arrangements and the enforceability or unenforceability of continued contact with the children's birth and former foster families.

Avoid undue influence. The adoption professional understands the adoptee's search for his or her birth relatives as a normative aspect of having been adopted. The adoption professional avoids putting any responsibility on the adoptee for the feelings of the adoptive parents. Instead, the adoption professional provides printed resources and referrals to other professionals or groups who can help the adoptive parents cope with the adoptee's search, possible reunion, and possible ongoing contact with the birth family.

Principle 3: Diligence and Due Care

This ethical standard speaks to the professional's competence, improvement of knowledge, impairment, obligations, and maintenance of competence. The diligent professional is interested in excellence, in doing his or her best work in the service of adoptees, birth parents, and adoptive parents. The diligent professional maintains and improves his or her competence and works to improve the profession. Diligence and due care apply to services supplied to birth parents, adoptees, and adoptive parents and can be achieved through the following means:

Adoption-Specific Education and Training. Professionals who work in adoption should receive education and training specific to adoption in order to best serve their clients. Such preparation should include generalized education in a helping profession, in-service training, on-the-job training and experience, attendance at adoption conferences, and work with lay search and support groups.

Continuing education. Adoption professionals should maintain competence in the field of adoption and child welfare through adoption conferences and continuing education not only with those with whom they can agree philosophically, but also with those who are fundamentally different in their approaches to adoption and the treatment of women and families.

Competence and knowledge. Adoption professionals should maintain knowledge of current adoption research and literature, and base practice decisions on such information as well as on their professional codes of ethics. They should transmit current information to their clients in an understandable way.

Principle 4: Confidentiality

The ethic of confidentiality (sometimes called privacy) addresses disclosure of information obtained during the course of professional service. This ethic governs what information may be disclosed, under what circumstances, and to whom. Observance of this ethic requires a consistent commitment on the part of the professional to protect information obtained in client-professional relationships.

Disclosures regarding identifying information. Prior to an adoption, the adoption professional should tell birth parents and adoptive parents that in the future the adoptee may conduct a search for the birth parents, and that birth parent identifying information may be released to the adoptee either under court order or by law.

The adoption professional should inform adoptees of their right to search for their birth parents and what their responsibilities and rights are while conducting a search, including all rights or privileges regarding nonidentifying and identifying information. The adoptee should be told of limitations to the release of information, including any right of refusal the birth or adoptive parents may have under the law.

Limits to Confidentiality. The adoption professional should inform birth parents, adoptive parents, and adoptees of the limits of confidentiality in adoption practice both under current laws and, potentially, under future laws regarding release of identifying information and adoption records.

Use of Information. The adoption professional should inform birth parents, adoptive parents, and adoptees of the circumstances under which confidential information may be released, the use to which such information might be put, and the purposes for which it might be obtained.

Existence of Records. The adoption professional should inform birth parents, adoptive parents, and adoptees of the existence and extent of official records concerning them. Birth and adoptive parents should be informed of their rights and opportunities, if any, to obtain copies of the adoption home studies with appropriate releases or under the law.

The adoption professional should also sign releases allowing the adoptive parent(s) access to adoptee records and advocate for and with the adoptive parent(s) in obtaining such records from other professionals and agencies prior to the finalization of an adoption.

Access to Records. The adoption professional should give birth parents, adoptive parents, and adoptees reasonable and lawful access to all professional records concerning them, taking care to protect the confidentiality of others mentioned in such records. Observing confidentiality of professional records is not the same as barring the adult adoptee from access to his or her official birth certificate and records (Babb, 1996).

Assistance with Search. The adoption professional should inform adult adoptees, birth parents, and adoptive parents about legal barriers to the release of identifying information, where applicable, and how they may obtain help with adoption search and reunion apart from the adoption agency or adoption professional. Such help could include referral to an area search and support group for triad members, information about national triad or adoptee groups, or recommended readings.

Principle 5: Communication

This ethic governs disclosures and warnings of adverse consequences of a professional service rendered. It requires professionals to give clients accurate and complete information about the extent and nature of the services available to them. Communication is akin to integrity in that it requires candor, "the obligation to affirmatively volunteer information" that the client needs or wants to know

(Josephson, 1993, p. 14). The ethic includes a professional responsibility to allow and foster communication between the client and other professionals, community groups, or other supports who can provide information to the client about adoption (or the professional service rendered), including individuals and groups whose philosophies conflict with those of the professional. Ways in which professionals can operationalize this ethic include the following:

Define the Client. When an adoptee or parent (expectant, birth, or adoptive) presents him- or herself to the adoption professional for adoption-related counseling, whether voluntarily or, in the case of parents, under court-ordered supervision for child mistreatment, the professional should discuss with that person the definition of client, the standards identifying the client, the primacy of the client's interests, and the nature of the services to be provided to the client. If an adoption professional serves more than one client in an adoption, the professional should inform each client of the above and warn the client of the possibility of conflicting needs and values, offering solutions to possible conflicts of interest before they arise.

Explain Adoption Realistically and Fairly. The adoption professional should explain adoption realistically, along with its positive and negative outcomes, and give parents considering adoption, for their child or under court-ordered supervision for child mistreatment, the opportunity to learn from others who have faced similar situations or crises as well as from adult adoptees, former foster children, and adoptive parents.

The adoption professional should prepare adoptive parents for the part that grief and loss play in the formation of all adoptive families and for the reality that adoption is experienced differently by adoptive parents, adoptees, and birth parents. Both the positive and negative aspects of adoption for the adoptive parents and adoptee should be explained by the adoption professional. The adoption professional should give adoptive parents, birth parents, and adoptees the opportunity to learn from other adoptive parents, adult adoptees, and birth parents.

Warn of Adverse Consequences of Adoption. The adoption professional should completely explain the possible long-term effects of adoption surrender to parents, including the possible and probable emotional and psychological consequences of surrender or termination of parental rights (TPR), both for the birth parent(s) and for the child.

The adoption professional should warn prospective adoptive parents about the possible adverse consequences of adoption, especially in special needs and international adoptions. The adoption professional should completely explain the possible long-term effects of separation, loss, and adoption to prospective adoptive parents, including the emotional and psychological effects of adoption for both the adoptee and the adoptive parents. The adoption professional should provide written information, recommended reading, counseling, and other resources to help adoptive parents understand adoption dynamics.

Inform Birth Fathers of Their Rights and Responsibilities. Birth fathers should be full participants in the counseling process and in any prospective adoption proceedings. The adoption professional should inform birth fathers in writing of their rights and responsibilities and afford birth fathers every opportunity to participate in raising their children or participating in adoptive placements.

Utilize Lay Adoption Search and Support Groups. The adoption professional should encourage parents considering adoption for their child to attend support group meetings, not associated with an adoption agency or adoption attorney, of adult adoptees, former foster children, and postadoption birth parents as soon as possible as they consider their options. Birth parents should also have access to support groups for adult adoptees and adoptive parents who have positive outcomes.

Full Disclosure of Adoptee History. Adoption professionals, workers, and agencies should disclose all known background information concerning the prospective adoptee to the adoptive parents prior to placement. The history should include social, psychological, medical, educational, and emotional histories as well as information about and access to all former caretakers and the birth family of the child. This same information should be available to the adult adoptee.

Provide Information About Specialized Treatment. Many children who are older at the time of adoption and who have emotional or psychiatric problems will need residential treatment or other specialized mental health help. Prior to placement, the adoption professional should teach adoptive parents about such needs and about resources for treatment in the community, state, and surrounding regions. The adoption professional should tell adoptive parents about what financial assistance, if any, is available for such treatment, how much it will be, and its duration. The adoption professional should also inform adoptive parents about costs not covered by assistance programs, if any, and what the cost of such treatment would be in the event that adoption assistance payments, Medicaid, and other federal or state programs are reduced or eliminated.

The adoption professional should inform birth parents and adoptees about specialized services available in the community that will assist them with issues surrounding adoption, grief, loss, identity formation, and other adoption concerns.

Warn of Adverse Consequences of Adoption Search and Reunion. The adoption professional should completely explain the possible long-term effects of adoption search and reunion to adult adoptees, birth parents, and adoptive parents, including the potential negative reaction of the adoptive parents, or a rejection by the birth parents or family upon being found. Professionals should be able to provide their clients with information, resources, and referrals on how to assist family members in dealing with the positive and negative consequences of search and reunion.

Principle 6: Objectivity and Independence

Conflict of interest, adverse positions, and the duty of the professional to maintain objectivity are all issues arising from the ethic of objectivity and independence. This ethic requires the professional to avoid personal relationships with clients, students, supervisees, or research participants when such relationship might impair the professional's objectivity, interfere with the professional's ability to carry out his or her professional duties, or harm or exploit the other party. The objective professional avoids relationships or commitments that conflict with their clients' interests. When institutional or organizational commitments conflict with the professional's duty to clients, the needs of the client are of prime importance.

The following standards of professional conduct in serving adoption clients support this ethic.

Avoid Dual Roles. The adoption professional should avoid commitments or relationships that conflict with the interests of the client. If the client is a parent considering adoption for a child, or a parent under court supervision for child mistreatment, the adoption professional should avoid serving both the birth parents and prospective adoptive parents or others with a vested interest in the custody of the child.

Separate Legal Counsel. Adoption professionals should encourage birth and adoptive parents who are party to the same adoption to obtain independent legal counsel. Parents should be encouraged to retain legal counsel independent of the adoption professional or adoption agency. Adoption professionals should see to it that minor children entering adoptive placements are assigned a guardian *ad litem* or separate legal counsel from that of the birth or adoptive parents.

Principle 7: Fees and Finances

The ethical use of fees involves setting fees that are fair, reasonable, and commensurate with the service performed and with consideration of the client's ability to pay. In addition, the ethical professional acknowledges the real impact of finances on adoption clients and seeks to assist those clients with appropriate information and supports.

Discuss Financial Aid. Birth parents considering adoption for a child should be educated to know that they can receive financial assistance without any influence or intervention of an adoption agency, attorney, or professional.

Adoption professionals should tell adoptive parents about the financial burden they are likely to incur as a result of adopting a certain child and disclose accurate and complete information about adoption assistance payments, difficulty-of-care payments, Medicaid, crippled children's services, Social Security Income (SSI) availability, and other resources available to help the child and the adoptive family after the adoption is finalized.

Fees Should Not Be Charged for Providing the Service of Adoption. Children needing the service of adoption should be considered the responsibility of the local, state, and federal governments and service fees for their care and placements charged to the appropriate governmental agencies. The costs of adoption should be subsidized through tax deductions, adoption assistance, nonrecurring expense reimbursement, or other means. Adoption professionals should advocate for such legislative changes through their local, state, and federal governments.

Adoption professionals should see to it that financial limitations of the foster or adoptive family do not prevent the permanent placement of a child with special needs. Adoption outside a child's family should not be based solely on the inability of birth family members to pay adoption service fees or care for a child with special needs.

Fees for adoption search or release of identifying or nonidentifying information should not be charged by agencies.

Fees Levied. When adoption service fees are charged, they should be disclosed to the person responsible for paying them prior to matching with a child and should be based on the client's ability to pay.

Principle 8: Contractual Relationships

This ethic requires that professionals represent the client's interest first and foremost at all times. Professionals or others outside the client-professional relationship should be consulted when it is in the best interest of the client, and adoption clients should be allowed or encouraged to seek advice, information, or support from other groups even when the philosophy of the group differs from that of the primary counselor. Contractual relationships are closely related to the ethics of objectivity and independence, and also are influenced by that of communication.

Outside Consultation. Professionals or others outside the organization should be consulted when it is in the best interest of the adoption client or when the client requests such a consultation.

Encouragement to Seek Other Advice. Adoption clients should be encouraged to seek advice, information, or support from other professionals, even those with differing philosophies.

Information About Other Organizations. Adoption service recipients should be given written information about local, regional, and national adoption groups when they seek advice or counseling from the adoption professional.

Ongoing contact and representation of the client's interest. The adoption professional should serve his or her adoption clients on an ongoing basis or arrange for such service after parental rights have been terminated or an adoption has occurred.

In the event of the need for the disruption or dissolution of the child's adoption and subsequent adoptive placement, the adoption professional should apprise adoptive parents of their rights and responsibilities and continue to serve the adoptive family through family preservation services. Every effort should be made to preserve the adoptive family. In the event of a failed adoption, the adoption professional should continue to serve the adoptive parents through crisis and grief counseling and obtain separate professional counseling and supports for the adoptee.

If an adoption fails, the adoption professional should inform the older child about the rationale behind the decision and the options for the child's subsequent placement. The adoption professional should give the adoptee the opportunity to say good-bye to his or her adoptive parents, siblings, pets, neighbors and friends, and other loved ones as age appropriate.

In the event of the disruption or dissolution of the child's adoption, or other events (such as adoptive parents' divorce or death) leading to the child's subsequent availability for new adoptive placement, the adoption professional should, whenever possible, inform the birth parents about the situation, including the birth parents' rights, if any, to contact or adopt the child themselves.

If notified of the death of the surrendered child (adoptee), the adoption professional should make every effort to inform the birth parents about the child's death, the location of the adoptee's burial, and the opportunity, if any, for contact with the adoptive parents.

If notified of the death of the birth parent(s), the adoption professional should inform the adult adoptee, or the adoptive parents in the case of an adoptee who is a minor, about the birth parent's death and any opportunity for contact with the birth family as well as the location of the birth parent's burial.

CONCLUSION: CHALLENGES TO CHANGE IN ADOPTION VALUES AND ETHICS

It is not enough to identify our problems in applying values-based ethical codes to the professional practice of adoption, or to propose professional standards that may or may not ever be codified or formalized. Even when professionals train themselves with enough vigor to insure ethical competence, it is not enough to merely understand and apply ethical principles. These same ethical principles must be communicated to the larger society as professionals seek to fulfill their ethical responsibilities to that society.

The helping professions most often involved with adoption, social work, law, psychology and other counseling professions, nursing, and medicine—all acknowledge the professional's ethical obligations to society. Such obligations include social and political action to prevent and eliminate discrimination, to ensure that people have access to the resources, services, and opportunities they require to meet basic needs, and to foster respect for a diversity of cultures in society. The professional also has an obligation to act in ways that "expand choice and opportunity for all persons, with special regard for disadvantaged or oppressed groups and persons" (NASW, 1990, p. 9). Finally, this ethic of social responsibility also demands that professionals advocate changes in policy and legislation to improve social conditions and promote social justice, weighting requirements for professionals already working to apply professional standards in adoption as they compete with nonprofessional, lay practitioners of adoption who operate with a market mentality.

What challenges to change in adoption values and ethics do we face? The essential issues have been unchanged since early history and involve conflicting values. Such conflicts can be clearly seen in the controversy surrounding the failure of the United States to ratify the United Nations Convention on the Rights of the

Child, an international treaty defining minimum standards for the protection of children. On February 16, 1995 the U.S. representative to the United Nations signed the U.N. Convention on the Rights of the Child, signaling an intent to ratify. As of mid-1997 the United States had not yet ratified the Convention, expressing reservations about the Convention in several areas. Only six nations have failed to ratify the Convention (including the Cook Islands, Oman, Somalia, and the United Arab Emirates), whereas 187 other nations have ratified it, making the Convention the most rapidly and widely adopted human rights treaty in history.

The Convention provides for the protection of children from discrimination, torture, unlawful arrest, unlawful confinement, abuse, mistreatment, exploitation, and kidnapping and instructs states to consider the best interests of children in all actions and provide for the care of children when parents fail to do so. Provisions for access to information, education, and social welfare are also set forth. Regarding these provisions, Americans have no arguments with the Convention.

The Convention addresses areas specific to adoption, foster care, and child welfare. It recognizes the rights of children to a name at birth, the right to acquire a nationality, and, as far as possible, the right to know and be cared for by their own parents. If children cannot live with their parents, they have the right to maintain contact with one or both parents. Parents are given the right to raise their children, the state is instructed to assist them in doing so, and also to respect parents and the extended family. Children are to be protected when living away from their parents, and have the right to social security and social insurance. Minority race and indigenous children have the right to enjoy their own culture, religion, and language. It is these provisions that have been divisive for Americans.

In American adoption practice, we cannot agree that children have a right to a name at birth. Does this mean that the adoptee has a right to his or her birth name—identifying information that is concealed or altered under most of our state laws governing adoption? Americans cannot agree that children who cannot live with their parents have the right to maintain contact with one or both parents. Does this mean that adopted children have the right to open and ongoing contact with one or both birth parents? If so, do these values of identity and of blood relatedness conflict with the value of human relatedness in the context of families, including adoptive families? Does giving an adopted child the right to ongoing contact with his or her parent(s) compromise the right of that child to a safe, secure, and permanent adoptive family?

The Convention upholds the right of minority race and indigenous children to enjoy their own culture, religion, and language. Does such a right preclude transracial adoption, or challenge recent American legislation that specifically prohibits postponing an adoptive placement solely based on race?

The U.N. Convention asserts that adoption, when recognized or allowed, should be carried out in the best interests of the child, and then only with the authorization of competent authorities and safeguards for the child. Such safeguards include the following:

1. Children have the right to be protected from being sold.
2. Parents must give informed consent to adoption on the basis of competent counseling.
3. Intercountry adoption may be considered an alternative means of placement.
4. If adopted intercountry, the child should be given the same safeguards and adopted under standards equivalent to those in the country of origin.
5. If the child is adopted intercountry, the placement should not result in improper financial gain for those involved.
6. Bilateral or multilateral agreements between nations shall occur, ensuring that adoption is carried out by competent authorities or organs.

Whereas adoptions are accomplished in many nations solely through government agencies employing truly professional adoption workers, in America adoptions are facilitated through professionals, licensed public and private agencies, and lay facilitators. Does authorizing "competent authorities" threaten the unregulated, nonlicensed, or lay placement of children that has coexisted with professional adoption practice since America's first child welfare laws were passed? What does "informed consent to adoption on the basis of competent counseling" mean? When U.S. laws support adoptions through licensed and nonlicensed agencies, professionals, or facilitators, will the imposition of possibly higher or more demanding international standards on American adoption practice have an adverse effect on those who favor adoption as an industry (rather than adoption as a human service)?

Under the U.N. Convention, if adopted intercountry, a child should be given the "same safeguards and adopted under standards equivalent to those in the country of origin." Does this mean that children born in open-records countries such as South Korea but adopted by U.S. citizens in closed-records states should be given the right to have their birth records at the age of majority? Would imposition of such standards violate American interpretations of ethical values of confidentiality or privacy for the birth parents? Would violation of international standards conflict with the adoptee's right to self-determination and equal access to information under the law?

For intercountry adoption, the U.N. Convention states that the placement should not result in improper financial gain for those involved. How do other nations define "improper gain"? Are infant adoption fees of $20,000 or more considered improper? Who will set such standards? Will the imposition of such standards conflict with values respecting the legal processes of nations, including our own?

Professionals who work in adoption speak of adoption as a lifelong process. They spend years counseling, studying, and writing about birth parents, adoptive parents, and adoptees—becoming adoption experts. They pride themselves, usually, on their experience and understanding of the adoption triad and adoption dynamics. Many spend months and years working predominantly in adoption. They pay dues to professional associations, write articles and books, and collect salaries or fees based on adoption research, teaching, counseling, or placements. Yet many professionals who specialize in adoption are now realizing that what they have done has often only marginally served clients, and that adoption statutes and the institutions or agencies for which they work have done little to help professionals approach adoption work ethically.

While many have called for the professionalization of adoption through various means, these same professionals cannot seem to iron out their own philosophical differences with sufficient ease to establish adoption professionally. Many of these same professionals nevertheless counsel and admonish birth parents, adoptive parents, and adoptees to view one another as parts of an extended adoption kinship system that must somehow, together, work out their relatedness over a life-time—with or without professional help.

Adoptive parents, adoptees, and birth parents have done just that, many times giving up on professionals as any source of support, comfort, or guidance. They have established their own support groups and grassroots organizations such as Adopt a Special Kid, Adoptive Families of America, the North American Council on Adoptable Children, the American Adoption Congress, and Concerned United Birthparents, offering to one another what professionals have failed to give them: a means of living a lifetime with adoption, philosophically and practically.

While professionals debate in the pages of their publications over whether adoptees have a primal wound or birth mothers want to be found, adoptees and birth parents by the thousands have searched for and found one another. Adoptive and birth families have contacted one another and opened their families to each other by the thousands, largely without professional help. They have done it, often, not because professionals could not help them, but because they were told such contact was ill-advised or illegal. They have sometimes done it clumsily and at no small harm to themselves and their families because professionals stood back as if the obligation was complete the day the adoption was finalized. Often, profession-als did not trouble themselves to increase their expertise in adoption in order to serve adult adoptees and their families; clients had to become their own best experts.

Today in America, there are "adoption specialists" and "adoption workers," but it is unclear what qualifies a person to specialize in adoption. Individuals with no adoption-specific training at all are building adoptive families at the expense of birth families, and many times at the expense of children.

If adoption work in the United States is to professionalize, there must exist a uniform standard. Ethical codes and models for ethical decision making are necessary, specific to serving the various triad members. Ethics, values, and morality are inextricably bound to moral issues. Professionals have been unable to agree on how to work together to define, refine, and perfect adoption practice. Hopefully, professional commitment to helping and serving adoption clients to the best of one's ability will translate, eventually, into rules of ethical conduct that will assure clients that professionals are ultimately concerned with doing the right thing.

REFERENCES

Amadio, C. (1989). Wrongful adoption: A new basis for litigation, another challenge for child welfare. *Journal of Law and Social Work, 1*(1), 23–31.

Amadio, C. (1991). Doing the right thing: Some ethical considerations in current adoption practice. *Social Thought, 17*(3), 25–33.

Amlung, P. (1990). Conflicts of interest in independent adoptions: Pitfalls for the unwary. *Cincinnati Law Review, 59*, 169–189.

Anderson, P. (1989). The origin, emergence, and professional recognition of child protection. *Social Service Review, 63*(2), 222–244.

Babb, L. A. (1994, September 30). *Serving our clients, or serving ourselves?* Paper presented at the conference of the Council for Equal Rights in Adoption, New York.

Babb, L. A. (1996). A study of ethics in contemporary adoption practice in the United States. *Research Abstracts International, 21*(3), LD-03361.

Babb, L. A., & Laws, R. (1997). *Adopting and advocating for the special needs child.* Westport, CT: Bergin & Garvey.

Baran, A., & Pannor, R. (1990). Open adoption. In D. Brodzinsky & M. Schechter (Eds.), *The psychology of adoption* (pp. 316–331). New York: Oxford University Press.

Barth, R. (1987). Adolescent mothers' beliefs about open adoption. *Social Casework, 68,* 323–331.

Benet, M. (1976). *The politics of adoption.* New York: The Free Press.

Birmingham, J., Berry, M., & Bussey, M. (1996). Certification for child protective services staff members: The Texas initiative. *Child Welfare, 75*(6), 727–740.

Blanton, T. L., & Deschner, J. (1990). Biological mothers' grief: The postadoptive experience in open versus confidential adoption. *Child Welfare, 69*, 525–535.

Brodzinsky, A. (1990). Surrendering an infant for adoption. In D. Brodzinsky & M. Schechter (Eds.), *The psychology of adoption* (pp. 295–315). New York: Oxford University Press.

Cameron, J. (1989). The end of the beginning.   Address by the Campaign for Adoption Reform in Europe (CARE) conducted at the NORCAP Annual General Assembly of the Church of Scotland, Aberdeen, Scotland, June.

Campbell, T. (1988). Ethical issues in hepatitis B screening. *American Journal of the Disabled Child, 142*(1), 13–24.

Catholic Charities USA. (1989). *Perspectives on adoption.* Washington, DC: Catholic Charities USA Department of Social Services.

Catholic Charities USA. (1994). *Perspectives on adoption* (rev. ed). Alexandria, VA: Catholic Charities USA.

Child Welfare League of America. (1959). *Child Welfare League of America standards for adoption service.* New York: Child Welfare League of America.

Child Welfare League of America. (1960). *Standards for services to unmarried parents.* New York: Child Welfare League of America.

Child Welfare League of America. (1971). *Guidelines for adoption service.* New York: Child Welfare League of America.

Child Welfare League of America. (1973). *Standards on transracial adoption.* New York: Child Welfare League of America.

Child Welfare League of America. (1976). *Standards for adoption practice* (rev. ed.). New York: Child Welfare League of America.

Cole, E. & Donley, K. (1990). History, values, and placement policy issues in adoption. In D. Brodzinsky & M. Schechter (Eds.), *The psychology of adoption* (pp. 273–294). New York: Oxford University Press

Conrad, A. P., & Joseph, M. V. (1991). Ethical problem solving skills in social work practice. *Social Thought, 17*(3), 5–15.

Davie, L. (1984). Babes and barristers: Legal ethics and lawyer-facilitated independent adoptions. *Hofstra Law Review, 12*, 933–981.

DeWoody, M. (1993, May–June). Adoption and disclosure of medical and social history: A review of the law. *Child Welfare, 54*(3), 195–217.

Deykin, E., Patti, P., & Ryan, J. (1988). Fathers of adopted children: A study of the impact of child surrender on birthfathers. *American Journal of Orthopsychiatry, 58*(2), 240–248.

Dolgoff, R., & Skolnik, L. (1992). Ethical decision making, the NASW Code of Ethics and group work practice: Beginning explorations. *Social Work with Groups, 15*(4), 99–112.

Doxiadis, S. (1989). Children, society and ethics. *Child Abuse and Neglect, 13*(1), 11–17.

Dukette, R. (1984). Values issues in present-day adoption. *Child Welfare, 63*(3), 233–243.

Etzioni, A. (1969). *The semi-professions and their organization.* New York: The Free Press.

Feigelman, W., & Silverman, A. (1986). Adoptive parents, adoptees, and the sealed record controversy. *Social Casework, 67*(4), 219–226.

Fein, E., & Maluccio, A. (1992). Permanency planning: Another remedy in jeopardy. *Social Service Review, 66*(3), 335–348.

Fieweger, M. E. (1991). Stolen children and international adoption. *Child Welfare, 70*(2), 285–291.

Goldstein, J., Freud, A., Solnit, A., & Goldstein, S. (1973). *In the best interests of the child.* New York: The Free Press/Macmillan.

Gonyo, B., & Watson, K. (1988). Searching in adoption. *Public Welfare, 46*(1), 14–22.

Greenwood, E. (1957, July). The attributes of a profession. *Social Work, 2*, 45–55.

Hostetter, M., Iverson, S., Dole, K., & Johnson, D. (1989). Unsuspected infectious diseases and other medical diagnoses in the evaluation of internationally adopted children. *Pediatrics, 83* (4), 559–564.

Hughes, R. (1993). Child welfare services for the catastrophically ill newborn: A confusion of responsibility. *Child Welfare, 72*(4), 323–340.

Jones, M. B. (1993). *Birthmothers.* Chicago: Chicago Review Press.

Joseph, M. V. (1983, Fall & Winter). The ethics of organizations: Shifting values and ethical dilemma. *Administration in Social Work, 7*(3 and 4), 47–57.

Josephson, M. (1993). *Making ethical decisions.* Marina del Rey, CA: The Josephson Institute.

Kadushin, A. (1984). Principles, values, and assumptions underlying adoption practice. In P. Sachdev (Ed.), *Adoption: Current issues and trends* (pp. 3–14). Toronto: Butterworths.

Kristinsdottir, G. (1991). *Child welfare and professionalization.* University of Umea, Umea, Sweden: Umea Universitets Tryckeri.

Kugelman, W. (1992). Social work ethics in the practice arena: A qualitative study. *Social Work in Health Care, 17*(4), 59–80.

Levy, C. (1973). The value base of social work. *Journal of Education for Social Work, 9*(1), 34–42.

Melton, G. B., & Flood, M. F. (1994). Research policy and child maltreatment: Developing the scientific foundation for effective protection of children. *Child Abuse & Neglect, 18*(1), 1–28.

National Association of Social Workers (1979, 1987). Foster care and adoption. In *Social Work Speaks: NASW Policy Statement,* (2nd ed.). Washington, DC: Author.

National Association of Social Workers (1990). *NASW code of ethics.* Washington, DC: Author.

National Association of Social Workers (1996). NASW code of ethics. Washington, D C: Author.

National Council for Adoption, Ad Hoc Committee on Ethical Standards in Adoption. (1991, February). *Principles of good practice in infant adoption.* Washington, DC: Author.

National Council for Adoption (1996, March–April). Ann Landers under attack again. *National Adoption Reports, 17*(3/4), 1–2.

New American Standard Bible (1977). New York: Thomas Nelson Publishers.

Pine, B. (1987). Strategies for more ethical decision making in child welfare practice. *Child Welfare, 66*(4), 315–326.

Platt, A. (1969). *The child savers.* Chicago: University of Chicago Press.

Poppendieck, J. E. (1992). Values, commitments, and ethics of social work in the United States. *Journal of Progressive Human Services, 3*(2), 31–45.

Rest, J. R. (1988, Winter). Can ethics be taught in professional schools? The psychological research. *Easier Said Than Done,* 22–26.

Rompf, E. (1993). Open adoption: What does the "average person" think? *Child Welfare, 72*(3), 219–230.

Rosenberg, E. B. (1992). *The adoption life cycle.* New York: The Free Press/Macmillan.

Rosenthal, J. A., & Groze, V. K. (1992). *Special-needs adoption.* New York: Praeger.

Sachdev, P. (1984). *Adoption: Current issues and trends.* Toronto: Butterworths.

Sachdev, P. (1989). *Unlocking the adoption files.* Lexington, MA: D. C. Heath.

Sachdev, P. (1992). *Sex, abortion, and unmarried women.* Westport, CT: Greenwood Press.

Schechter, M., & Bertocci, D. (1990). The meaning of the search. In D. Brodzinsky & M. Schechter (Eds.), *The psychology of adoption* (pp. 62–90). New York: Oxford University Press.

Schmeiser, C. B. (1992). Ethical codes in the professions. *Educational Measurement Issues and Practice, 11*(3), 5–11.

Severson, R. (1994). *Adoption: Philosophy and experience.* Dallas, TX: House of Tomorrow Productions.

Silverman, A., & Weitzman, D. (1986). Nonrelative adoption in the United States. In R. Hoksbergen (Ed.), *Adoption in worldwide perspective: A review of programs, policies, and legislation in 14 countries.* Lisse: Swets & Zeitlinger; Berwyn: Swets North America.

Silverman, C. (1989). Regulating independent adoptions. *Columbia Journal of Law and Social Problems, 22,* 323–355.

Sinclair, T. A. (Translator). (1951). *Aristotle.* The politics (Book VII). Harondsworth, England: Penguin Classics.

Solinger, R. (1992). *Wake up, little Susie: Single pregnancy and race before Roe v. Wade.* New York: Routledge.

Sorich, C. J., & Siebert, R. (1982, April). Toward humanizing adoption. *Child Welfare, 61*(4), 207–216.

Sorosky, A., Baran, A., & Pannor, R. (1989). *The adoption triangle: The effects of the sealed record on adoptees, birth parents, and adoptive parents.* San Antonio: Corona Publishing.

Spencer, M. E. (1987). Post-legal adoption services: A lifelong commitment. *Journal of Social Work and Human Sexuality, 6*(1), 155–167.

Sutton, J. R. (1990, May). Bureaucrats and entrepreneurs: Institutional responses to deviant children in the United States, 1890–1920s. *American Journal of Sociology, 95*(6), 1367–1400.

Thomasma, D. C., & Pisaneschi, J. I. (1977). Allied health professionals and ethical issues. *Journal of Allied Health, 6*(2), 15–20.

U.S. Children's Bureau. (1961). *Legislative guides for the termination of parental rights and responsibilities and the adoption of children.* Washington, DC: Department of Health, Education, and Welfare.

Valentine, D., Conway, P., & Randolph, J. (1988). Placement disruptions: Perspectives of adoptive parents. *Journal of Social Work and Human Sexuality, 6*(1), 133–153.

Van Hoose, W. H., & Kottler, J. A. (1988). *Ethical and legal issues in counseling and psychotherapy.* San Francisco: Jossey-Bass.

Vitillo, R. (1991). International adoption: The solution or the problem? *Social Thought, 17*(3), 16–24.

Voss, R. (1985). A sociological analysis and theological reflection on adoption services in Catholic Charities agencies. *Social Thought, 11*(1), 32–43.

Walden, T., Wolock, I., & Demone, H. (1990). Ethical decision making in human services: A comparative study. *Families in Society, 71*(2), 67–75.

Watson, K. (1992, Winter). Providing services after adoption. *Public Welfare,* 5–13.

Watson, K. (1994). *Should adoption records be opened? YES.* Unpublished manuscript.

Weisman, M. (1994, July). When parents are not in the best interests of the child. *The Atlantic Monthly,* 43–63.

Zelizer, V. A. (1985). *Pricing the priceless child: The changing social value of children.* New York: Basic Books.

7

Treatment Issues in Adoption Practice from a Triad and Systemic Perspective

Joyce Maguire Pavao, Victor Groza,
and Karen F. Rosenberg

In this chapter, Joyce Maguire Pavao, Ed.D., Victor Groza, Ph.D., and Karen Rosenberg, L.I.S.W., discuss the lessons learned from trying to integrate the clinical issues, writing, and research about infant-placed and older-placed adoptions. There is significant overlap between the two populations. This concluding chapter examines the issues and implications for practice from a triad and family systems perspective.

BRIDGING THE GAP FROM A FAMILY PERSPECTIVE

While there are books on clinical practice in adoption, most divide into two poles, depending on whether the child was placed for adoption as an infant or as an older child. This book was developed to bridge the separate practice areas, accenting the similarities and differences in the two populations. This is the first endeavor to integrate these different areas and address the skills, values, and practice knowledge necessary in working with clients who are part of the adoption triad. This concluding chapter weaves together the previous chapters including topics such as treatment issues, implications of infertility, identity development of the adoptee, the search and reunion process, adoption supports, and ethics in contemporary adoption practice.

THE ADOPTIVE FAMILY

Adoption is a very positive way to create or expand a family. It is estimated that adoption affects the lives of 40 million Americans (Pavao, 1992). In a recent national public survey conducted by the Evan B. Donaldson Adoption Institute

(1997), 6 in 10 Americans have had a personal experience with adoption.[1] More than 100,000 adoptions occur each year (Stolley, 1993) and 2% to 5% of American households include adopted children (Bachrach, 1986; Bachrach, Adams, Sambrano, & London, 1989; Moorman & Hernandez, 1989; Stolley, 1993). Given these numbers, it is important for clinicians to be skilled in working with the unique issues that face adoptive family systems. Professionals with a family systems perspective can be of particular help to these complex families.

According to the family systems perspective, families are seen as dynamic, changing, interacting compilations of emotional and behavioral systems and subsystems. Family problems or difficulties are seen as connected to developmental processes or normative crisis in the development of the adoptive family (Falicov, 1988; Pavao, 1992). As part of a family system perspective for adoptive families, it is recognized that in the adoptive family life cycle, adoptive families may encounter more stressors than other types of family systems (DiGiulio, 1987; Groze, 1996; Talen & Lehr, 1984) and have unique life cycle issues (Pavao, 1992; Rosenberg, 1992). Therapists who take a systemic view and encourage empowerment instead of pathologizing the very normal and complex problems of families are best equipped to help adoptive families. Several models are available to assist professionals to apply a systemic perspective to families, including the Pavao systemic, developmental, and psychoeducational model of brief long-term therapy (1998), the Groze (1996) structural-ecological model, and the Hartman (1984) ecological family systems approach.

Regardless of the model employed, the family systems view proposes that a systemic approach is needed to work with the adoptive family system (which includes the birth family, foster family, and extended adoptive family). There is no identified patient; the whole system (from the wider context of adoption practices including the service system to the intricate relationships in the adoptive and birth families) is regarded as the client (Pavao, 1995). Crises are reframed and understood as normal; when they occur, they are opportunities that can lead to transformation and growth.

The family systems therapist can normalize and demystify the process of adoption and the typical issues faced by adoptive families throughout the life cycle. When this happens, the family can be treated honorably and can be prepared to handle the complex issues that are normal for infant adoptions and magnified in adoptions of older children, children placed across racial lines, or children placed from other countries.

With the media focusing frequently on adoption—and usually sensationalizing the problems unique to it—the public has developed an impression of a failed social arrangement and of an adversarial relationship between the birth family and the adoptive family. In fact, problems in adoption are the exception, not the rule.

---

1. The personal experience included either themselves, or a family member, or a close friend who was adopted, adopted a child, or made a plan of adoption for a child.

Most adoptions do not disrupt before legalization; over 80% remain intact. Most adoptions do not dissolve; over 98% are not terminated after legalization. Most children live in their adoptive home and are not placed in residential care or foster care after legalization; over 90% remain in the home. Families are overwhelmingly positive about the experience; over 70% of parents evaluate the experience in positive terms. Finally, very few cases of adoption are contested; less then .001 cases per year are contested (see Barth, 1988; Barth & Berry, 1988; Groze, 1996; Kadushin & Martin, 1988; Kagan & Reid, 1986; Rosenthal & Groze, 1992; Rosenthal, Schmidt, & Conner, 1988; Schaffer & Lindstrom, 1990). In the contested cases, it appears that neither set of parents can do what is in the best interest of the child. Fortunately, this is a rare problem. For the most part, the relationship between birth parents and adoptive parents is not adversarial. More recently, birth parents and adoptive parents collaborate together in open adoption arrangements as well as in advocacy and support groups, which often promote adoption policy reform.

Adoption is a successful, complex family arrangement. Even though the media have negatively portrayed adoption, most Americans have a favorable opinion of adoption. Less then 10% of Americans evaluated adoption as somewhat or very unfavorable (Evan B. Donaldson Adoption Institute, 1997).

THE BIRTH FAMILY

When women and their partners deal with an untimely pregnancy, the decision about whether or not to surrender a child for adoption should be an educated choice with all options known. Women who make a plan for adoption for their child in the 1990s do so in the belief that it will offer a better life for their child than they are able to provide (Chippindale-Bakker & Foster, 1996). In contrast, when children are removed for abuse or neglect reasons and the family has not succeeded with family preservation or reunification services, the plan of adoption is not usually voluntary. The birth parents have been evaluated by the court system and child welfare system as not able to parent their children. However, this does not mean that they do not love their children.

Whether children enter adoption as infants or as older children, they have a connection to the birth family. The psychological and emotional connection to the birth family is important for children and can be honored through a careful plan for some level of appropriate openness.

In both infant and older child placements, family preservation and kinship arrangements should be explored prior to any discussion of adoption by nonrelatives. Therapists should discuss with families the kinds of adoptions (open, closed, relative, nonrelative, etc.) available and the postadoption issues that they may encounter throughout the life cycle. There are many kinds of adoption arrangements.

Birth parents need to be educated, as do all families approaching adoption, about the different options. There are public and private agencies, private attorneys, closed, open, and semiopen arrangements for adoption—with many shades between very closed and very open. Birth parents feel more empowered when they feel they are being good parents by making a plan that will be best for their child, compared to those who feel like victims and who feel that they have no choice or input into the process.

The pain of loss is great for birth parents who voluntarily or involuntarily have placed a child for adoption. Birth parents need to speak with someone who has no invested interest in their decision at the beginning of their decision-making process. Once families have adequate education and counseling about the benefits and risks of adoption as well as the psychological and developmental issues that are normal throughout the adoption life cycle, then the possibility of a positive and healthy adoption is much more likely. Without the proper counseling for birth parents and their families, there is a greater chance of parental ambivalence, contested adoptions, and adjustment problems later. This is most true in older child placements where the attachment to the birth family is even greater than a psychological and emotional tie—there are conscious memories and connections from life in the birth family. In these cases, some openness in adoption is warranted.

Open adoption cannot be legally mandated. Families thinking of parenting an older adoptee who has had many emotional cutoffs and moves from family to family should consider that a way to avoid attachment difficulties is to keep some of the beneficial connections and to manage them in the best interest of the child. For example, it may not be safe or reasonable to allow a child to continue a relationship with a birth father who is an abuser and a violent person. However, if there is a grandparent or an aunt who has been a safe haven for that child and to whom the child has some attachment, a supervised visit to keep that relationship and to develop one between that person and the new family may help keep the child from feeling isolated and cut off once again. All the factors must be weighed as each situation is unique. It may be worthwhile to take risks to help the adoptee stay connected with important birth and foster family members.

Open adoptions can vary a great deal, from regular meetings to occasional written contact, telephone calls, and picture exchange. Chippendale-Bakker and Foster (1996) found that birth mothers were more likely to proceed with their adoption plan when they chose and met adoptive parents compared to those who do not, supporting openness in adoption practice. However, it is important to keep in mind that in open adoption as well as the other forms of adoption, birth parents terminate their parental rights, and the adoptive parents become the legal parents. Open adoption is not joint custody and it is not guardianship. The adoptive parents have all legal rights for caring for the child. They can sever the relationship with the birth parents if they so choose. The permanent plan for parenting of the child is that of the adoptive parents; the role of the birth parent is changed, and continues to change over time. The relationship must be built on trust and the child's best interest kept in mind.

One model of a semiopen adoption for infants is a one-time meeting of the birth and preadoptive parents. Often only first names are exchanged. A connection is made between both parties, and an agreement is made to have the agency or adoption professional act as an intermediary in the exchange of letters, pictures, and/or updated medical information. The agreement of exchange can be yearly or as otherwise decided by the parties involved. Semiopen adoption allows the birth parents to feel a sense of choice and connection to the child that they cannot parent. It is semiopen because it is not open to the child—the plan is not for an open relationship including the child and the birth parents—but an open beginning with the adoptive and birth parents. However, there are other models of semiopen adoptions. In some arrangements, ongoing, direct contact is arranged between the birth family and adoptive family for specific dates or celebrations.

As much as possible, the role of the birth family in the adoptive family should be negotiated and clearly defined as part of the preparation of placing an infant for adoption. Also, as life circumstances necessitate change, the families should plan how they will negotiate changes in their relationship. Although the birth mother and birth father will always be the ones who created this child, at the time of adoption their role changes from parent to extended family, or however the role is defined by the adoptive family.

A closed adoption—the traditional form of adoption since the 1930's—offers no identifying information, very little nonidentifying information, and no agreement for future meetings or a relationship. Closed adoption was created to protect children from the public's bias about illegitimacy. It was thought that if a new birth certificate were created and if the original birth certificate was sealed away rather than creating an adoption certificate, the general public would not chastise the child or ascribe negative characteristics to the child based on the circumstances of his or her birth. This was not done to protect the birth parent from the adoptive parent or vice versa.

Amended birth certificates are outdated at this point in time because single parents—even single fathers—can have a birth certificate issued that indicates that the father gave birth! Adoptees, adoptive parents, and birth parents are upset about this falsified document, calling it legal fiction. It is the only situation in this country where an adult does not have access to information about him/herself. For many, the issue is seen as a civil right violation that adoptees are not granted . More than any other contributing factor, it is believed that the system of closed adoption, and the secrecy and lies that are part of such an arrangement, causes or contributes to many of the problems and issues that evolve in birth families and adoptive families over time.

Older child adoptions are not closed adoptions in the traditional sense. It is not unusual for records of children to be given to adoptive parents before the placement is finalized, and even in those situations where records are not released, children often remember addresses, names, phone numbers, and so forth. However, older child adoptions may be closed to birth families in order to protect the child and adoptive family. It is unusual that birth families know identifying information about the adoptive family or for birth and adoptive families to have a relationship and exchange letters, cards, or photos.

In all of these forms of adoption it is important to know that the emotional and psychological connections between the birth parents and the child are never terminated. In order to avoid the cutoff that older children have experienced in their many moves in foster homes and relative placements, it is important to work with families to help children keep the positive connections. Many older children are separated from their siblings and it is essential that the visits between the siblings continue after the adoption is finalized. A relationship between the adopting or foster families must be developed and supervised in the initial stages by professionals. It is hoped that if this was a positive relationship for the child, this relationship will continue also. The same is true of grandparents who cannot take on the responsibility of parenting, but would like to continue to be the grandparent for the children and visit them. The more families and adoption professionals are helped to understand that although it is time consuming and labor intensive to deal with additional people, while at the same time trying to integrate a challenging child into the family, it will, in the long run, pay off for the child and the family. For example, the oldest, "parentified" child does not have the need to find out how his/her mother or siblings are if he/she has regular visitation and correspondence and knows that they are safe and doing well.

Childhood is very short. Children cannot wait for birth parents to be rehabilitated or to be out of jail. They must be parented consistently and with care. Hopefully, this can happen in the extended family or community, but when it cannot, adoption is a good option. An open arrangement, with permission by the birth family for the adoptive parents to do the parenting, helps an older child to feel that he or she is not being disloyal.

PREADOPTIVE PARENTS

Understanding what precedes the decision to adopt is important. A majority of couples who make the decision to adopt have struggled with infertility for years. The pain and loss that result from hoping for a birth child and undergoing invasive medical, pharmacological, and surgical procedures, as well as the strain on the couple's relationship, makes adoption seem like an additional hoop to jump through in order to obtain their goal of becoming parents. Like birth parents, adoptive parents can feel they are victims of the "process." For them, the process of the home study, the scrutiny of an adoption worker, and the inclusion or exclusion as being eligible to be an adoptive parent that is a part of the procedure can be frustrating and anxiety producing. Some become angry at the process, sometimes cutting themselves off from the education and support systems that might be useful and available to them post adoption.

Preadoptive parents sometimes suffer a lack of understanding and support from their family, friends, and community acquaintances. People sometimes do not understand why they want to adopt—especially if they are adopting an older child. They may question why a family would want to deal with the problems that are inherent in this type of adoption. This results in a subtle, but lifelong, experience of pain, guilt, shame, and loss, if these issues are not discussed and normalized. Most adoptive parents become educators about adoption as well as advocates. They learn that they have to stop and educate their extended family, friends, and community acquaintances about adoption. They work to help people in schools, social services, and churches/synagogues understand some of the unique issues in adoption.

In the past, there was a belief in American society that the panacea for infertility was adoption. Adoption does not "fix" infertility. It allows families to parent. However, for some adoptive families the issues of never seeing a child of "one's own" continue to exist. These issues exist for extended family members as well, particularly for grandparents.

Education and counseling prior to adoption for the parents of the couple or individual adopting and the extended family will lead to more support for the adoptive family, along with greater understanding of the participants' own feelings. They will have the opportunity to explore how their adult child's decision to adopt affects their lives. They may have to do some grief work around the loss of genetic continuity and the fantasy biological grandchild.

Single parents and gay and lesbian parents who plan to adopt also benefit from education about the added complexities that their families will face. A knowledgeable therapist can help families discuss and make sense of these issues in the preadoptive process.

THE ADOPTEE AS PARENT

Adoption is an issue throughout the life cycle and beyond, affecting not only past generations but the ones to come as well. Adoptees invariably grow up and most create families of their own. There are unique issues that adoptees encounter as they create families. Things that birth families take for granted may pose serious dilemmas for adoptees and adoptive families. One example is medical history—physicians say that dealing with an adopted person is like dealing with a coma victim, in the sense that critical and current family history information is often missing and impossible to get in a closed adoption. The lack of information can be problematic as the adoptee contemplates having children, causing anxiety or worry about health problems or genetic defects they may encounter.

As adoptees contemplate creating families, getting pregnant, or delivering their first child, issues of identity, belonging, connectedness, and identity emerge or reemerge. It is often during this developmental phase that adoptees contemplate a search or reunion. When adoptees choose not to search, their children often reflect the struggles they never resolved. Some even go on to complete a search on their own for their birth grandparents.

A MODEL OF SYSTEMIC FAMILY THERAPY FOR ADOPTIVE FAMILIES

This model of therapy is built on the assumption that adoptive families will need help at different developmental phases at different points in the family life cycle. Families need an inclusive, systemic approach that normalizes developmental crises. For example, it is clear that for many adoptive families of infants, the first crisis may be about the decision to adopt. Other crises often follow after adoption.

For families that adopt infants, the questions they must address at some point include: how to tell the child he or she was adopted, what to tell the child about the birth family, when to tell the child, how to deal with extended family members and neighbors, and how to work with the schools and with professionals who have little or no experience with adoption in general. For an older child, the crisis may be how to integrate a child who has a different history and often different values, beliefs, and behaviors into the adoptive family system.

In Pavao's therapeutic model (1992), called "brief long-term therapy," a family and various constellations (different family subsystems and extended family members) are seen during the crisis. The family intervention then involves transforming that crisis into an empowering and growth experience. If families come back for further therapy at a later stage of development, this is not seen as a failure. Rather, it is seen as a success in working through yet another stage of development. There is a completion of each stage of therapy but no "termination." The word "terminate" is too loaded for those who have suffered the losses associated with adoption. The therapist or team of therapists remain available for consultation and therapy. This avoids the emotional cutoff and loss that are primary issues in adoption.

Therapists who take a systemic view and encourage empowerment, instead of pathologizing the very normal and complex problems of adoptive families and birth families, are best equipped to help these families. Operating from the premise that families are not sick but current solutions have not solved the presenting problem, the therapist views the family as having the capabilities to successfully master the current crisis. The therapist's role is to help the family uncover and use the knowledge or skills they possess to solve the problem. For some families, the resource they need lies outside the family, such as a specialized service (e.g., counseling, educational testing, respite, etc.) in the social service system. Families are given information and taught new skills to help them gain access to new or different postadoption services. Postadoption services have historically been more available for families who have adopted older children. The reason has been an acknowledgment that older adoptees bring with them a separate history, including traumatic early life experiences, in addition to loss, separation, and attachment issues. As such, families who parent these children often enter the adoption knowing that there will most likely be a need for additional resources and postadoption services.

A systemic family therapy model acknowledges that also in infant adoptions there are critical times in the developmental cycle of the adoptee and family that put unique demands on the family. For example, as the adoptive family goes through "adaptive grieving" (Brodzinsky, 1987), the loss of the birth family becomes an issue for the adoptee who was placed even in the first few weeks of life. This may be a time that a family can be helped to understand that this is a typical adoptive family system developmental process.

In addition, adolescent adoptees, as they work on identity formation, start to look at their dual heritage and may become interested in their birth family in a different way than they did when they were younger. Adoptive families may need some help with these emerging issues, that is integrating the adoptee's past and not denying the importance of biological connectedness. By working with all of the family members, along with the agencies, courts, and schools, the systemic therapist can spread understanding and healing.

CONCLUSION

This book attempted to bridge the practice knowledge of infant-placed and older child adoptions. There is significant overlap between the two populations, as well as some differences. It is the hope of the editors and contributors that this book might begin a dialogue that will promote better integration of theory, practice, policy, and research between the different subgroups of adoptees, birth parents, and adoptive families.

REFERENCES

Bachrach, C. A. (1986). Adoptive plans, adopted children, and adoptive mothers. *Journal of Marriage and the Family, 48*(2), 243–253.

Bachrach, C. A., Adams, P. F., Sambrano, S., & London, K. A. (1989). *Advance data: Adoption in the 1980s. Advance data from vital and health statistics, no 181.* Hyattsville, MD: National Center for Health Statistics.

Barth, R. (1988). Disruption in older child adoptions. *Public Welfare, 6*(1), 323–329.

Barth, R. P., & Berry, M. (1988). *Adoption and disruption: Rates, risks, and response.* New York: Aldine De Gruyter.

Brodzinsky, D. (1987). Adjustment to adoption: A pyschosocial perspective. *Clinical Pyschology Review, 7*, 25–47.

Chippindale-Bakker, V., & Foster, L. (1996). Adoption in the 1990s: Sociodemographic determinants of biological parents choosing adoption. *Child Welfare, 75*(4), 337–356.

DiGiulio, J. F. (1987, November). Assuming the adoptive parent role. *Social Casework: The Journal of Contemporary Social Work,* 561–566.

Evan B. Donaldson Adoption Institute. (1997, November). *Benchmark adoption survey: Report on the findings.* Study conducted by Princeton Survey Research Associates. New York: Author.

Falicov, C. J. (1988). Family sociology and family therapy contributions to the family development framework: A comparative analysis and thoughts on future trends. In C. J. Falicov (Ed.), *Family transitions: Continuity and change over the life cycle* (pp. 3–54). New York: The Guilford Press.

Groze, V. (1996). *Successful adoptive families: A longitudinal study of special needs adoption.* Westport, CT: Greenwood Publishing.

Hartman, A. (1984). *Working with adoptive families beyond placement.* New York: Child Welfare League.

Kadushin, A., & Martin, J. (1988). *Child welfare services* (4th ed.). New York: Macmillan.

Kagan, R. M., & Reid, W. J. (1986). Critical factors in the adoption of emotionally disturbed youth. *Child Welfare, 65,* 63–74.

Moorman, J. E., & Hernandez, D. J. (1989). Married-couple families with step, adopted, and biological children. *Demography, 26*(2), 267–277.

Pavao, J. M. (1992). Normative crisis in the development of the adoptive family. *Adoption Therapist 3*(2), 1–4.

Pavao, J. M. (1995, December). Prediction and prevention in post adoption services. *Child Welfare Report.*

Pavao, J. M. (1998). *The family of adoption.* Boston: Beacon Press.

Rosenberg, E. (1992). *The adoption life cycle.* New York: The Free Press.

Rosenthal, J. A., & Groze, V. G. (1992). *Special needs adoption: A study of intact families.* New York: Praeger.

Rosenthal, J. A., Schmidt, D., & Conner, J. (1988). Predictors of special needs adoption disruption: An exploratory study. *Children and Youth Services Review, 10,* 101–117.

Schaffer, J., & Lindstrom, C. (1990). Brief solution-focused therapy with adoptive families. In D. M. Brodzinsky & M. D. Schechter (Eds.), *The psychology of adoption* (pp. 253–272). New York: Oxford University Press.

Stolley, K. S. (1993). Statistics on adoption in the United States. In I. Schulman (Ed.), *The future of children* (pp. 26–42). Los Altos, CA: Center for the Future of Children.

Talen, M. R., & Lehr, M. L. (1984). A structural and developmental analysis of symptomatic adopted children and their families. *Journal of Marital and Family Therapy, 10*(4), 381–391.

8

Transracial Adoptions

Karen F. Rosenberg, Kelli Steele Adams,
and Victor Groza

DEFINITIONS AND OVERVIEW

According to the Child Welfare League of America (1998), in 1995 there were over 32,000 children in the custody of public agencies who were legally free for adoption and over 25,000 who were adopted (78% of the children). One year later, there were over 51,000 children in the custody of public agencies who were legally free for adoption and only 23,100 who were adopted (45% of the children). By 1998 with data from only 30 states, over 90,000 children were awaiting adoption (DHHS, 1998) and about 70% of these children were minority children. As these numbers indicate, there has been an explosion of the number of children legally free for adoption but a reduction in percent of placements compared to waiting children. Public agencies, even with assistance from private agencies, have not been able to place the number of children available for adoption. In addition, since the U.S. government began tracking demographics, children of minority heritage (black, Latino, and Native American) have been over represented in the child welfare system and among those available for adoption. The result is that transracial, transcultural, and transethnic adoptions are a reality of current adoption practices in the United States.

A transcultural adoption is the adoption of a child from one culture by a family of a different culture. Culture includes language, history, values, foods, customs, rituals, folklore, and so on. All adoptions are transcultural adoptions—if for no other fact than even infants have an extended birth family history that is different from the family into which they are adopted. A transethnic adoption is an adoption where the child has a different ethnicity than either adoptive parent. Ethnicity means of or relating to large groups of people classed according to common racial, national, tribal, religious, linguistic, and cultural origin or background. An ethnic group is a social group or category of the population that, in a larger society, is set apart and bound together by common ties of race, language, nationality, or culture. Most children adopted internationally and many children adopted from the public child welfare system are transethnic adoptees. In the United States, the largest group of children placed transethnically are children of Latino origin. A transracial adoption is the adoption of a child of one race by a parent or parents who are of a different racial group. Transracial and transethnic adoptions have a long history in the United States including Native Americans adopted by Caucasians (Fanshel, 1972) and African American children adopted by Caucasian families (Grow & Shapiro, 1974; McRoy & Zurcher, 1983; Simon & Altstein, 1977, 1981, 1987; Simon, Altstein, & Melli, 1994). More recently, Latino children have been adopted by Caucasian families (Andujo, 1988).

Policy changes in the last decade have also supported transracial and transethnic adoption. The Multi-ethnic Placement Act of 1994 (MEPA) mandated that states could not delay or deny a child's placement based on the child's race, color, or national origin; that states could not deny the opportunity to become an adoptive parent on the basis of the prospective parents' race, color, or national origin, and that states must diligently recruit foster and adoptive parents who reflect the racial and ethnic diversity of the children in the system who need foster and adoptive homes. The amendment to MEPA with the Interethnic Adoption Provisions of 1996 (IEPA) went further stating that race, color, or national origin is not taken into any consideration in making placement decisions. Indications that states use any of these criteria result in economic sanctions and could lead to litigation.

These major policies were followed in 1997 by the passage of the Adoption and Safe Families Act (ASFA). The major provisions of this policy were to enhance the safety of children at home and in out-of-home care, and reduce foster care delays and move children quickly into permanent homes. In its essence, ASFA emphasizes concurrent planning, gives strict time parameters for permanency decisions, specifies situations in which family preservation or reunification need not be pursued, and allows foster families to participate in permanency planning hearings for the children in their care. It is beyond the scope of this chapter to detail the act. However, one of the consequences of these policies and their interpretation at the state level is an increase in transracial and transethnic adoptions.

In this chapter, given the expected increases in transracial adoptions, we focus specifically on transracial adoption. The discussion is also relevant for transethnic adoptions but we focus on this issue in the chapter on international adoptions. Therefore, the focus here is on both children placed as infants and children placed when they are older across racial classifications.

REVIEW OF RESEARCH ON TRANSRACIAL ADOPTIONS

The bulk of the research suggests that race or ethnicity plays little role in adoption outcomes (see Fanshel, 1972; Grow & Shapiro, 1974; Shireman, 1988; Shireman & Johnson, 1986; Silverman, 1993; Simon & Altstein, 1977, 1981, 1987; Simon, Altstein, & Melli, 1994). However, there have been a few studies that suggest that outcomes are not as positive for Native American children adopted by

Caucasians (Bagley, 1993; Green, 1983), but findings are not consistently negative (Fanshel, 1972). The preponderance of evidence is very positive toward transracial adoptions.

In one of the first studies of transracial adoptions, Fanshel (1972) examined Native American children placed in Caucasian families over a 5-year period. Initially there were 97 families and at the end of the 5 years, 60 families were still involved in the project. Overall, the children and families did remarkably well. The health, development, intellectual functioning, behavior, and family functioning were positive. Fanshel suggests that about 75% of the children were adjusting very well. However, he offers the caveat that the study was completed when the children were still quite young and difficulties would be expected to increase over time. Even with the increase, the adoption outcomes would remain very positive.

The seminal work in the adoption of African American children by Caucasians is the longitudinal study of Simon and Altstein (1977, 1981, 1987), and Simon, Altstein, and Melli (1994). These researchers followed children and the families that had adopted transracially over a 20-year period. The initial study (1977) included 206 families living in 5 different cities in the Midwest, most that had adopted an African American child. In the second stage of the study (1981), 71% of the original families participated. Surveys rather then interviews were used in the second wave of the study. In the third stage of the study (1987) when children were in adolescence, about half the original families were involved in the investigation. In the last stage of the study, Simon, Altstein, and Melli (1994) focused on the children, who were young adults at the time of data collection. At this stage, 55 transracially adopted children, 30 birth children, and 13 inracially (white) children participated in interviews.

In general, reports comparing white and transracial adoptees remained positive over time. Through the adolescent years transracial adoptees saw themselves as having the same type of family relationship as other children, did not evidence self-esteem or racial identity difficulties, and seemed to be performing well in most areas of their life. In addition, parents and children agreed on these issues. As young adults, the transracially adopted children had shifted close friendships from white to nonwhite peers, and after adolescence relations with parents and siblings improved dramatically. Results from the children as young adults did not negate the positive outcomes reported earlier. Most adoptive parents (63%) saw their children as identifying with the racial backgrounds of both their African American birth parents and Caucasian adoptive parents.

While failing to find profound negative effects of transracial placement on adoption, concerns that have clinical relevance have been raised by researchers. McRoy and Zurcher (1983) administered questionnaires to African American transracial and inracial adoptees. No difference was found in the self-esteem scores of the sample of transracially adopted youngsters and a sample of inracially adopted children. The adoptees also did not differ from the scale's norms (white, non-adopted individuals). They conclude that " . . . the adoptees had not been affected differently by the kind of adoptive family, nor had it been negatively affected by adoption" (p. 119). However, they caution that this is not to suggest that the adoptees were without challenges. They did indeed face challenges being black and adopted by Caucasian parents and had to endure the consequences from racism. In addition, McRoy and colleagues (1983) found that transracially placed black adoptees were more likely to report themselves as adopted than inracially placed black adoptees.

Only one study specifically focused on Latino children. Andujo (1988) found that Mexican American children adopted by Caucasian parents had less of a sense of ethnic identity than those adopted by Latino families.

Other concerns about the functioning of transracial adoptees have been documented also. Shireman (1988) found transracially adopted boys had more school difficulties. Falk (1970) suggests that families adopting transracially are less positive about adoptions than families adopting inracially.

While overall results about psychosocial adjustment are positive, the research findings do not necessarily address the issues most likely to come to the attention of practitioners working with transracial adoptees or their adoptive families. Clinical experience suggests that minority children adopted transracially are not prepared for the racism that they experience later on in their lives. During childhood, minority children are raised in and have access to the white dominant culture through their affiliation with their adoptive parents and have minimal experience with institutional and interpersonal racism. Once these children are out in the world separate from their adoptive parents, they can no longer rely on their adoptive status to defend against racism and must learn unique coping mechanisms to address society's racism. They struggle to create their own complex racial identity. One adoptee says, "Racism is something you have to deal with. Caucasian parents can't prepare you. I have not been able to escape the fact that I am a person of color and, therefore, regarded as a second-class citizen in the eyes of many people. As a mixed race person who has been rejected by people of all races, I feel pretty insecure about my heritage" (Lifton, 1994, p. 86).

In addition to perhaps not focusing on the issues likely to be of clinical relevance, the research conducted to date is limited, due to methodology and sampling, and has focused predominantly on children adopted transracially as infants and not as older children (Freundlich, 2000; Silverman, 1993). One study by Rosenthal and Groze (1992) focused on children adopted from the public child welfare system, many who were older at placement. They found that minority families experience greater closeness with those outside the family, their extended kin network, compared to families who adopt transracially. Factors that were expected to cause major problems in adoption outcomes did not apply for minority, inracial adoptive families (e.g., older age at adoption, child's emotional and behavioral problems, etc.). Similar to studies of transracial adoptions when children were adopted as infants, outcomes for both inracial and transracial placements of older and special needs children were overwhelmingly positive in this cross-sectional study.

While the findings to date are very positive, there are gaps in our research knowledge base. There is a dearth of thorough, longitudinal studies on the racial self-esteem of transracial adoptees. Transracial adoption is complex and there are often issues that may need to be resolved and addressed for both families and adoptees. These issues may not be reflected in most of the research conducted. The following sections highlight some of the clinical and practice issues in infant-placed and older children–placed transracial adoptions. The discussion is based on families in clinical populations who use professional intervention and should not be misconstrued as applicable to all families who adopt transracially or all transracial adoptees.

FAMILY FORMATION

Adopting transracially creates a multiracial and multicultural family system, lasting forever. Historically and currently, African American families have incorporated a wider definition of family and have a greater history of "taking in" children born to extended family members. Some of this history is consistent with tribal practices and part of it is the adaptation to slavery. Given their history and experiences, some African American families are more comfortable continuing ties to important biological "kin" of their adopted child and feel less threatened by those ties. In addition, African American families might feel more comfortable having a relationship with a same-race family. Caucasian families, particularly those with a socioeconomic status of middle class and higher, often have more rigid boundaries that define their families. Because of this difference, practitioners have reported more reluctance on the part of these families to encourage maintaining some kind of relationship with the extended biological family of the transracial adoptee. More research needs to be focused in this area. Is this resistance to connect to the biological family based more on socioeconomic class rather than racial background? Are middle- and upper-middle-class African American families less willing to maintain the same sort of openness as that of families from a lower socioeconomic class? Is it because it is more of a stretch and less comfortable for white families to connect with African American families, being from a different racial and ethnic background? These are important questions that need to be addressed both in research and clinical settings.

In pre-adoptive counseling sessions, families who are adopting both infants and older children transracially are encouraged to begin to view themselves as becoming a multiracial, multicultural, and multiethnic family. Though this concept may seem obvious to practitioners, many families are bewildered by the new identity of their family. Many families believe that, especially if the adoptee is an infant or toddler, the adoptee is a blank slate on which they will carve their own culture, ethnicity, religion, and so on. If the adoptive family itself is in denial about their new status as a multiracial family, one can imagine the denial that is reflected in their extended family. Adoption theory and practice maintains that families who accept and acknowledge differences fare much better than families that deny differences (Kirk, 1964, 1985, 1988). The issues are highlighted in this narrative from a mother who adopted transracially:

I didn't care about the race of my child but since we became an interracial family, my place in society has changed, and so has my consciousness. . . . People ask about being an interracial family. Or they don't ask. Part of what has happened in opening up my family this way is that my loyalties, my sense of who I feel connected with, has changed. I feel much more connected to African-American and Latino people than before, and much more aware of how pervasive racism is. It's my kid, after all, who is going out into a world in which people like her will not be seen for who they are. (Kinn, 2000, pp. 43, 45–46)

The concept of "belonging" is usually an issue that comes up in clinical sessions with adoptees placed transracially. It is even more felt by adoptees that join a family as an infant that also has biological children. Many such adoptees have shared that they never really feel like they belong to this family with children who have a biologic and genetic connectedness to the parents. They feel like they are on the outer boundaries of the family and at various times throughout their development behave as if they are not a part of the family. They may choose peer groups, particularly during adolescence and young adulthood, that reflect their birth family origins and not the culture they were raised in. Their values and behavior may also differ from their adoptive families, bringing them into individual or family therapy. These issues are often not explicitly processed by families, or are even denied by adoptive parents, who state that their relationship with all their children is equal. Even in biological families, parents have distinct, individual, and different relationships with their children based on many factors such as the pregnancy and birth experience, relationship during the infant and toddler years, temperament of both parent and child, and so on. The adoptee may feel reluctant or disloyal if he or she talks about feeling on the outer boundaries of the family or feels that there is something inherently wrong with them for having those feelings.

Another interesting dynamic occurs with the concept of belonging. Transracial adoptees, aware that they are different, want to look like they belong in their families. They want their families to understand that they belong in the family and they want their peer group and community to know that they belong as well. Behaviors that may surface include denying there is a skin-color difference (on the part of both the transracial adoptee and the adoptive parents) and not revealing painful racial incidents at school to the family for fear of enhancing their differences.

One unique parenting task in transracial adoptive families, regardless of whether they adopt children as infants or when older, is the ability to talk directly and candidly—appropriate to the adoptee's level of development—about race, racism, and prejudice (Chestang, 1983; Comer & Poussaint, 1975; Hopson & Hopson, 1990). Allen (1976) discusses how four families that adopted transracially felt helpless and guilty about their inability to protect their children when their children experienced prejudice. While a dated study, Allen's work highlights the importance of being able to deal with the issues of prejudice, discrimination, and racism in adoptive families. Freundlich (2000), citing Crumbley (1998), suggests that the content of the conversation should include:

- acknowledging prejudice and discrimination;
- explaining why the adoptee's minority group is mistreated;
- preparing the adoptee for discrimination, including providing a repertoire of response to discrimination;
- exposing the adoptee to role models and positive contacts in the minority community;
- teaching the adoptee the difference between responsibility to and for his or her minority group.

We would add to this list a focus on strengths, including:

- teaching the adoptee about the strengths of African American and Latino people;
- providing a history of minority groups in the Americas and the contributions they have made;
- explaining the differences and similarities of Afro-centric, Latino-centric, and Euro-centric approaches to life.

The specific elements of the task highlight how complex family formation and the issues across the life cycle are for transracial families. In addition to this cognitive approach to dealing with race, racism, and prejudice, rituals and family events celebrating diversity need to be a part of family formation and development. These rituals could include holidays and special events in history, incorporating members of the minority community to which the children are connected. Families have the most success over the long term with family formation when their social network is comprised of diverse families and friends as well as when they live in multicultural neighborhoods with multicultural school systems. When this is not possible, they must plan on how they will incorporate celebrations and diversity into their family's formation and development.

SEPARATION AND LOSS

Some practitioners in the field of adoption argue that all adoptees, even infants, experience separation and loss. Bowlby (1973) was one of the first researchers to write about the anxiety that infants experience when separated from their mothers. Verrier talks about the adopted infant being "traumatized" by his or her separation from the birth mother. She calls it the "primal wound" because this profound loss occurs so early in the mother–baby relationship. The wound may make an infant feel that part of itself has disappeared, leaving it with a feeling of incompleteness or lack of wholeness (Verrier, 1993). While this may be an issue for all adoptees, transracial adoptees may not begin to show issues related to their loss until they understand they are different from others. Being transracially adopted adds a new dimension to the separation and loss issues that all adopted children experience.

The following case exemplifies this point. The case involved an adoptive parent and her 6-year-old transracially adopted daughter who entered placement as an infant.

The daughter's longtime babysitter was saying good-bye because she had graduated from college and would be moving out of town. At first, the daughter seemed only somewhat sad about this pending separation, but then she broke down. She went to her mother and curled up in her arms, sobbing deeply. Her mother remarked about how deep her sobbing was, recognizing her child's deep emotional response to this impending loss and how it was connected with her adoption story.

Throughout childhood, transracial adoptees placed as infants may experience continual reminders about their losses. Because they look different, children and even adults ask questions such as: "Why do you look different from your family?," "Who is your real mother?," "What is your race/ethnicity?" These kinds of questions remind transracial adoptees that they have experienced loss: the loss of the birth mother, the extended family, and the loss of their culture. It also increases the emphasis on differences that can be denied with infants placed inracially. While questions continue for the transracial adoptee throughout his or her life, a young child can feel confused and perplexed by such questions. This is an additional dimension of growing up transracially, which inracial adoptees do not deal with in such an ongoing fashion. At the same time that this is an ongoing issue for the transracial adoptee, adoptive parents have to understand their own feelings about such questions and how those questions affect the children they love. The manner in which adoptees learn to deal with loss is largely dependent on the understanding, acceptance, and empathy of their adoptive parents, siblings, peers, and the adults that surround their lives.

Furthermore, losses may come from events that the transracial adoptee may never have experienced. The loss of culture, for instance, is a loss for transracial adoptees, yet they have no memory or knowledge of the culture they lost. This should be kept in mind when counseling both adoptees and their parents. The adoptive parents may do an exceptional job at presenting a diverse household and accepting the differences in their child, but they will never be able to give their child the memory of this loss. Adoptive parents will be more successful when they are able to help their children mourn their losses, whatever the loss means to the child. Adoptive parents need to have a firm sense of the losses in their own lives, so that they will be understanding, compassionate, and successful facilitators of the grieving process for their adopted children.

Children adopted transracially when older are usually conscious of the separation and loss that they experience. They have memories of their birth family and extended family and, depending on their age at placement, know a great deal of information about their birth family. They usually have experienced not one separation and loss, but multiple ones. These are the children that often languish in our child welfare system, having multiple placements from biological families to foster families and eventually to an adoptive family. When adopted transracially, they lose not only their families, but often ties to their genetic past, racial heritage, history, and culture. They struggle with the loss of identity, feeling alienated from the white community and not a part of the black community.

Separation from and not knowing about one's racial or ethnic identity can be a roadblock for transracial adoptees. Practitioners report that many of these adoptees go underground with their feelings of loss, powerlessness, and rage. As Lifton (1994) writes, "There is no question that adoptive parents feel a profound love for their transracial children. Yet all too often that love denies the child's need for connection to his roots. Taking in a child . . . should not mean taking away her heritage, but rather should mean helping the child to integrate one with the other" (p. 83).

Practitioners need to pay attention to these feelings of separation and loss and help adoptees and their families create rituals to say good-bye to their birth families and birth cultures, while also integrating the healthy pieces of their histories into their present lives. Families also need to understand that loss is cumulative and that they may see rather extreme reactions to the normative developmental tasks around separation and loss.

ATTACHMENT

According to Bowlby (1969, 1973, 1988) and Ainsworth and colleagues (1978), one way to classify certain behaviors of children is as an attachment behavior system. These behaviors function to maintain or increase proximity of a child to a mother or mother figure, or cause the mother figure to move toward the child (Hinde, 1983). The behavior system promotes and is affected by relationship experiences; as a child interacts with the primary caregiver and other people, he or she develops a sensitivity to and expectation about others (Hinde, 1983). Or, as Bowlby suggests (1969), a working or cognitive model of themselves, their caregivers, others, and the world.

An attachment behavioral system changes as a child grows and develops. While initially there is little coherence in behavior patterns, by the middle of their first year of life, these patterns become organized (Bowlby, 1969; Hinde, 1983). These organized patterns have been classified into three main topologies: secure, anxious-resistant (ambivalent), or anxious-avoidant (Ainsworth, 1973; Bowlby, 1988). Anxious-avoidant attachment patterns include displaying minimal affect or distress, and avoiding attachment figures under circumstances that would elicit interaction from those who are securely attached. Anxious-ambivalent attachment patterns include eliciting ongoing interaction with attachment figures while simultaneously lacking the ability to be comforted or calmed when distressed. Main and Weston (1981) suggest another classification of attachment patterns as a result of maltreatment; they suggest that some children evidence a disorganized/ disoriented pattern of attachment. This pattern blends contradictory strategies for dealing with separation and reunion. Zeanah and colleagues (Zeanah, Mammen, & Lieberman, 1993) offer a different typology of attachment disorders. They suggest that children may demonstrate no attachment preference, indiscriminate attachment, insecure attachment, aggressive attachment, and role-reversal attachment. While various classifications of attachment problems are offered, attachment is a significant practice and clinical issue in adoption.

Infancy to age two is a critical time for the parent–child attachment, but up to age six lays a strong foundation for the future. Those parents who were able to adopt their children at a very early age usually have an advantage in promoting secure attachment. Those who adopt later often have more challenges. Much has been written in the popular press about how to promote healthy attachments between parents and their infant or toddler children (see Brazelton, 1992; Sears, & Sears, 1993; Spock, Parker, Parker, & Scotland, 1998). In essence, children need a caregiver or caregivers who consistently, appropriately, and in a timely fashion respond to their needs. If these practices are experienced during early childhood, it is usually easier for a transracially adopted child placed as an infant to attach. A secure attachment then lays the groundwork to allow the transracial adoptee to develop healthy racial identity past the age of six.

During latency, ages six through twelve, attachment issues continue to be significantly influenced by life circumstances. For those children who had the opportunity to develop healthy, secure attachments with their adoptive parents before the age of six, it is often easier for them to go to their parents or family for support, help, or guidance when older. They will have the sense of trust that was built from a healthy and secure attachment, especially if the adoptive parents are able to accept the differences in their children. Sometimes adoptive parents are unable to adequately address the differences apparent within the family system, yet are still able to create a successful attachment to their child. Transracial adoptees may feel loved by their parents, yet are unable to talk with their adoptive parents about their race, or how they experience being transracially adopted. Transracial adoptees, feeling a deep attachment to their parents and knowing that their adoptive parents feel uncomfortable talking about their differences, go underground with their feelings. To talk about differences means that the balance within the family system will be upset. While this can be problematic, the fact that the adoptive parents and transracial adoptee successfully attached will be of great help to the adoptee as he or she navigates and develops understanding of what it is like to be transracially adopted.

Attachment during adolescence is problematic for most parents. During this time, it is common for adolescents to become more independent. Transracial adoptees are no exception. At this stage transracial adoptees often begin to explore different ways of expressing themselves. This is healthy, but it can be an extremely painful loss for the adoptee. They need to make sense of their attachment to their adoptive parent, their need to develop their independence, and their need to belong outside their family.

For transracial adoptees placed when older, the early years often did not lay a strong foundation for secure attachment. Many of the transracial adoptees placed when older have experienced inadequate parenting, family violence, neglect, abuse, and even severe trauma. Once removed from their biological families, these children have spent time in the child welfare system or even residential placements. Many of these children display behaviors that reflect developmental delays, attachment problems, and a lack of basic trust. The result is children that have attachment difficulties, unless there are radical improvements in care, may develop attachment disorders or problems (Keck & Kupecky, 1995). Fortunately, Bruer (1999) suggests that later experiences are just as powerful as early experiences in shaping developmental outcomes, although he offers a caveat that this might not always be the case when the early care is extremely negative. Still, research and experience to date is hopeful about the ability of most children to recover from early attachment trauma (see also James, 1994). In addition, the culture that these children have experienced prior to adoption may be significantly different than that of the adoptive families. Most of the families that adopt these children typically function at adequate and high levels emotionally and socially. The introduction of two systems with such divergent histories and levels of attachment, in addition to distinct cultures and belief systems, can threaten the stability of the family system and the placement.

Attachment for transracial adoptees placed when older will be and feel very different from the attachment that occurs with a child who is adopted at a younger age. Many times these transracial adoptees have such a clear sense of their birth family history that they see their adoptive parents more as caregivers until they reach the age of 18, when they will fantasize about reuniting with their birth family. Also, the sense of needing to belong to the adoptive parents and family system will probably not be of central importance. It will be important that these adoptive parents be able to accept detached or distancing behaviors and not expect many emotional rewards from the older-placed transracial adoptees.

Adoptive parents who have adopted older children report that their situations were successful when birth family and birth history was openly discussed within the family. For example, adoptive parents may feel perplexed that their child has loyalties toward birth parents who may have neglected or abused him or her. The fact that the transracial adoptee is of a different race compounds the dynamic of misunderstanding between all family members. What may occur is the transracial adoptee feeling that the adoptive parents have negative feelings toward their birth parents because their race is different. Conversely, the adoptive parents may also begin to attribute negative behaviors to the child's race. Therefore, it is of great importance for the adoptive parent to create a sense of openness, to accept the adoptee's feelings, and to cultivate awareness of their own prejudices.

IDENTITY DEVELOPMENT

How transracial adoptees experience life depends largely on their age at placement, the circumstances of the birth parents and adoptive parents, the social service agency preparation and support of the adoptive family, the community in which the child grows up, and the family's knowledge and comfort about transracial adoption. All of these factors work together to create the identity and values of the transracial adoptees. The process is different for each transracial child. Some are quite capable of holding themselves in this world in a very impressive way. Others have a more difficult time. It is impossible to put every transracially adopted person into a neat box, as their experiences are all different. However, there are different stages of identity development from a transracial perspective that are important to consider.

It is not unusual for transracial adoptees placed as infants to feel different from their adoptive family while growing up (Howe & Feast, 2000). While it has to be acknowledged that they are different, the difference doesn't have to be alienating. Yet, some transracial adoptees feel alienated. Reflecting back on their childhood, many adoptees have been painfully aware of the difference in skin color. From a developmental perspective, children under the age of five conceptualize identity in concrete terms. In order not to look different than their parents, some attempt to "scrub" the color off their skin. It is further complicated if they live in all-white communities. If other children, other families, and the institutions that are part of their lives are predominantly white, who wouldn't try to look like everyone else? Looking at their families and others while not seeing their own features reflected back is disconcerting.

Grade school marks the beginning of a child's social perspective on life. Children begin to think about how others perceive them, and they can form categories about themselves and others according to multiple criteria (Cole & Cole, 1993). As children enter these more complex social situations in the school setting, issues surrounding their adoptive status and race begin to surface in a new arena. Two very important issues are playing out during this time. The issues for the transracial adoptees are the developmental task of understanding how others perceive them, and an intense need to belong or fit in with those around them. At this stage, children begin the development of a social identity (related to themselves in the context of their communities), a psychological identity (how they identify with and relate to others), and an intrapersonal identity (how they think about themselves).

One mother who adopted transracially offers insight into the identity issue. Speaking about her biracial daughter, she writes:

I hope when Anna gets to high school and people choose up sides by ethnicity, she'll know in her bones that everyone within these groups is only an individual in an ethnic outfit. That doesn't mean these ethnic outfits don't serve some purpose. Anna sees herself as African American rather than as biracial. . . . What's moving to me and important is that Anna has an expansive sense of what her identity is. . . . Anna is making herself up. That's what all kids have to do, even if their families look ordinary. And it's very touching to see how kids become themselves in the world. The culture you hand them doesn't work without all kinds of modifications for the next go-round. Anna is a rich, idiosyncratic person, not predictable in any sense. It will be her job to teach people how to see her. It's a huge thing, to have to face people who assume they know who you are, in the most shallow sense, and to be able to say, "No, I am this and this" and not allow yourself to get smaller to suit their uninformed ideas.

I'm not a black mother and I haven't experienced what Anna's going to experience, so I can't share that with her: I've never felt overt racism. (Kinn, 2000, p. 46)

One difficult situation that many infant-placed transracial adoptees experience during latency age is enduring racist comments from family, friends, and those that are insensitive or want to hurt them. Some transracial adoptees' friends and family make racist comments about the transracial adoptees' race and then say, "you aren't one of them." From these incidents transracial adoptees learn that they are different, that others will like them but deny their race, and that some people will blatantly not like them because of their race. Couple this with the sense of wanting to belong within their family and their peer groups. This sets up a kind of "cognitive dissonance" for the child. At the child's level of development, this can be extremely confusing because at this stage most children are unable to think abstractly. They also will not be able to infer the sense of injustice either, so they often are not able to put words to their confusing feelings or stand up for themselves because they want to belong. Many transracial adoptees try to make themselves "white" by acting "white" or denying the "dark-skinned" side of themselves. By repressing or denying their "dark skin," transracial adoptees then can attain a false sense of "sameness" with their family and peers, thus helping them feel like they belong. If transracial adoptees have no sense of their minority heritage, then it is inevitable they will feel shame and hurt for themselves and their minority race and culture. The children need "scripts" to respond to racism and racist remarks. Of course, this means that race has to be an open topic and discussion in the family.

In theory, both being adopted and being ethnically different from most people make the identity tasks of adopted adolescents more difficult (Bagley, 1993). The biggest concern about the issue of identity is whether children will have a secure sense of who they are as a racial and ethnic minority and whether they can learn the skills to deal with discrimination and prejudice if they are placed in a family that has not experienced discrimination or prejudice. Allen (1976) asserts that the child is confronted with subtle pressures to conform to white assumptions, and does not know how to deal with these pressures. In general, until adolescence, many transracial adoptees placed as infants see themselves as white, or feel white even when they are black/brown. This dissonance becomes minimized in order to conform or belong to their family, friends, and community. They might not see racism or discrimination because they see themselves as white—unless the racism is blatant.

In adolescence, other issues emerge for the transracial adoptee placed as an infant. Part of the work of the middle and high school student is forming and honing identity. The understanding of how they fit in the world is created by their more complex thought processes. They begin to see how they judge others, how others judge them, how they judge the judgment processes of others, and how all this corresponds to social categories available in the culture (Cole & Cole, 1993). One of the categories that transracial adoptees may put themselves into is their ability to feel secure by maintaining their "other-ness" (Kelley, undated). They become the person who is "different" or "other" because that is where they feel most comfortable.

Some adoptees at this stage may actually find a sense of satisfaction in being adopted because it is different. Furthermore, transracial adoptees may seek out and integrate with other minority groups outside of their race because there is no expectation for belonging. Some transracial adoptees placed as infants feel like imposters in their adoptive families, and at the same time feel like they don't fit in with the race and culture of their biological ancestry. They may ironically find belonging in not belonging, by embracing the "other" identity. Issues of loyalty are often raised with these children. They are betwixt and between and may even ponder what racial category to mark on school forms and such. Some adoptees live in the context of incongruence—who they look like on the outside is incongruent with who they are on the inside. In particular, adoptees that are biracial feel particularly confused, in part because often our society insists on classifying people by race in a rigid way.

While there is an overlap in the issues faced by the transracial adoptee placed when older, identity issues are more complicated. They are complicated by the child's history before placement. As stated previously, most of the older-placed transracial adoptees have endured chaos and trauma before adoption. Their experience with their birth family has often been unstable. Many have suffered the trauma of neglect, physical abuse, sexual abuse, and/or exposure to domestic violence. These children often have an identity, but one that is based on negative role models. Oftentimes, the only pieces of information that they have are the dysfunctional pieces.

Identity in the older-placed transracial adoptee is intricately linked with survival behaviors that are often problematic in an adoptive family. These behaviors and the child's responses to daily living, changes, or conflict developed in response to their history before adoption. The coping style of these children and how they view themselves is influenced both by their trauma experiences as well as the various placements they were in while in their birth family and in the child welfare system. Sexually abused children may not have good boundaries about their bodies, both with people inside the family and with people outside the family. The physically abused and neglected child may not respect personal space, including property. It is not unusual for them to destroy their own belongings or the possessions of others. The child who experienced neglect may hoard items or not place much value on property, impulsively taking things that are not his own for no particular reason or "stealing" within the family. These behaviors often last many years after adoptive placement. The difficulty is to help these children develop their identity while dealing with survival behaviors, and not have the way the adoptive family deals with problematic behaviors negatively affect an already problematic identity.

In adolescence, the older-placed transracial adoptee has multiple paths that he or she can take to further develop his or her identity. If a child feels conflicted about loyalty to one's birth family, the adoptee may emulate what he or she remembers or what he or she has constructed from memories of the birth family. These memories are often faulty, as most children do not remember sequences and details of their childhood. On the other hand, they may continue to distance themselves from their memories and recollections of their birth family but be at a loss in trying to develop both autonomy from the adoptive family and their identity. These children may be attracted to groups and activities similar to their birth families, or what they perceive as "their people" based on media images or the groups available to them in their schools and communities. These children are the most at-risk for difficulties and for entering juvenile justice systems based on their early negative experiences.

There is a dearth of good longitudinal studies on the racial self-esteem and identity of transracial adoptees. Their identity-formation experience is complicated, based on their vulnerability of internalizing our race-obsessed culture. Transracial adoptees are not only racial minorities in mainstream culture, but they are racial minorities in their own families. Because our society does not readily accept the idea of a multiracial identity, one that combines influences from two or more racial backgrounds, identity formation is particularly complex for transracial adoptees.

RECOMMENDATIONS

Having a strong sense of ethnic identity is a strength. On the other hand, the lack of a strong ethnic identity is not a deficit. It means that the person has one less resource on which to draw as he or she navigates through life. If one of the tasks of parenthood is to give children as many strengths and resources as possible to maximize their successes, then families must consider how to best build strong ethnic identity in their children. For children adopted transracially as infants, that means giving serious consideration about the neighborhood/location of housing, places of worship, social activities, and friends who are part of the family in order to assure that their child is exposed to appropriate role models and opportunities for building a strong ethnic identity. This commitment to opportunities must be considered throughout the child and family life cycle. Older-placed transracial adoptees usually have some sense of identity, although they may have negative or incomplete perceptions of themselves. As with children adopted when infants, families must make the same commitment to embrace diversity in their lifestyle as one mechanism of building this strength in their child. While McRoy and Zurcher (1983) conclude that the quality of parenting is more important than whether the child is adopted inracially or transracially, it does not preclude thoughtful parenting about building strong multiracial identity in children. It also underscores, as Brodzinsky and Schechter (1990) indicate, that adoptive families need strengths that are different than those involved in biological parenting.

Keefer and Schooler (2000) offer some strategies for enhancing positive cultural identity in transracial adoptive families. They suggest that families should be a bridge to the adoptee's cultural/racial group and that families get help from people in the adoptee's cultural/racial group. They also recommend that families make sure that children learn the "rules" of their birth culture by making sure the adoptee has opportunities to learn these skills at school, at church, in neighborhood groups, and with friends of the family.

Adoptive families fare better when support groups are available. For transracial adoptees, there are two kinds of support groups that are particularly helpful. One is the group that focuses on the adoption issues of transracial adoption and the other is the support group that focuses on the issues of raising children in a multiracial family. The latter group includes both biological and adoptive parents.

As practitioners, we encourage families who adopt transracially to incorporate the child's traditions and cultures into their family in meaningful ways. The emphasis is to celebrate differences. We have to take into consideration that even when this is done, each individual resolves his or her search for racial identity in different ways, even in the context of the same family. Other factors are in play, including gender, personality, biology, and relationship to birth family history.

There are many layers of complexity in transracial adoption. Children pick up cues from parents and significant others in their social environment that affects how they see themselves as a racial and ethnic person.

Life books, or photo scrapbooks with a narrative about the child's history, are particularly valuable for the older-placed adoptee. In order to feel whole, children need to see their life history as continuous, and for children who have had multiple placements, this is a difficult and complex task. It is essential, however, for identity formation in the context of a fragmented personal history.

Another variation of the life book for older-placed adoptees who have had multiple moves are "life maps" (Pinderhughes & Rosenberg, 1990). This tool facilitates the narrative of the adoptee's past history and relationships with birth family members, foster families, staff at residential treatment centers, and so on. This process gives the child a chance to review and clarify his or her life story, making his or her identity continuous. It also gives the adoptive family an opportunity to hear and validate the child's past without denying facts and events. To construct a life map on poster-size paper, the social worker and adoptee make a chronological outline (like a road on a board game) of all the places the child has lived, dating each transition as accurately as possible with names, dates, significant events, locations, and so on. The life map might reflect a move back with the biological family after a foster care placement, only to be removed again later on in the child's history. The adoptee illustrates each event with a drawing that has significance for him or her and that symbolizes that time of his or her life. In cases of abuse, the adoptee may even draw the experience, using this tool as an art therapy technique to help process the trauma and tap into unconscious material. The adoptive family can join the experience when the life map is at the point of their connection in the adoptee's journey. Making a life map may take many weeks and can be used as a way to process experiences, heal wounds, acknowledge important relationships, and hopefully move on.

The social environment of the family is also critically important in promoting successful transracial adoptions. As Bagley (1993) writes, " . . . inter-ethnic . . . adoption can work when the wider community does not . . . hold negative stereotypes about the ethnic group in question, and the adoptive parents have the intellectual and emotional resources (including the support of a peer group of adopters) which can [help them] cope with most of the problems [that] are likely to arise . . ." (p. 212). Children need playmates who are similar to their race/ethnicity, and have dolls, books, toys, games, greeting cards, calendars, artifacts, audiovisual media (videos, CDs, DVDs) that reflect their culture and ethnicity. Services and service providers must be culturally diverse. Families must be thoughtful and plan out these issues if they want to maximize success and minimize difficulties in a transracial adoption.

Post-adoption services are of utmost importance to facilitate the process of becoming a multiracial family. Support groups, family therapy with sensitivity to the unique issues of being a transracial adoptive family, and practitioners with experience with adopted children are needed throughout the life cycle of the adoptive family. Older children have years of separate histories, rituals, and traditions that need to be incorporated into their adoptive family's life. During the honeymoon phase, these children may appear attached but they actually have little or no emotional involvement. As the adoptee becomes attached, the child begins to test the family, act out, and distance themselves in order to defend against another potential/possible loss. This is positive because it signifies that the child is making a significant emotional connection to the family.

As transracial adoptive placements continue to increase, there needs to be more longitudinal studies on the outcomes of these placements. How one defines success is an important question. Is success defined by a lack of disruption in transracial adoption, by the experience of the adoptive parents, and/or by the healthy racial self-esteem of the transracial adoptee? How successful can transracial adoption be in our racially polarized society's paradigm of rigidly defining race? Transracial adoption raises many issues, not only for the adoptee and the family, but for society in general.

SELECTED INTERNET RESOURCES ON TRANSRACIAL ADOPTION

There are several Web sites that address the issues of transracial adoption. Parents, adoptees, and birth parents will need to navigate the following resources to find information pertinent to their situation. Perhaps the first place to begin is by checking state and/or county child welfare Web sites in your area. Also check Web sites of local private and nonprofit agencies. After you have checked your local area, you may then want to browse through the following Web sites:

North American Council on Adoptable Children (NACAC)
This organization is committed to meeting the needs of waiting children and the families who adopt them. NACAC conducts trainings and workshops related to child welfare and special needs adoptions, through a newsletter and national conference. Many of the families this agency helps are transracial.
www.NACAC.org

National Adoption Information Clearinghouse (NAIC)
This is a comprehensive resource on all aspects of adoption.
www.calib.com/naic

Pact: An Adoption Alliance
This organization serves all members of a triad through national conferences, books, educational events, crisis consultations, and programs that support and inform adopted children and adopted adults of color.
www.pactadopt.org

RainbowKids
Rainbow Kids (RK) is an online magazine for parents of children adopted internationally.
www.rainbowkids.com/transrace.html

Multiracial Family Circle
MFC provides multiracial families (not necessarily all families are adoptive families) with a network of support and a safe place to mutually explore issues surrounding multiracial relationships of all kinds.
www.cdiversity.com/mfc

Tapestry Books
This site is a resource for books related to adoption.
www.tapestrybooks.com

Voices of Adoption
An Internet site serving adoption triad members. It offers a wide range of resources, a chat line, and links. Look in the "adoption" section for transracial adoption information.
www.ibar.com/voicesofadoption

Shades of Love
An Internet site for the network of interracial, multiracial, transracial adoption, and the biracial community.
www.shadesoflove.com

American Counseling Association
The Web site includes a paper with a vast amount of information of Web sites, articles, children's books, and so on for multiracial families. There is plenty of information on this page that focuses on transracial adoption.
www.counseling.org/conference/advocacy6.htm

REFERENCES

Ainsworth, M. D. S. (1973). The development of infant-mother attachment. In B. M. Caldwell & H. N. Ricciutti (Eds.), *Review of Child Development Research* (Vol. 3, pp. 1–94). Chicago: University of Chicago Press.

Ainsworth, M. D. S., Blehar, M. C., Waters, E., & Wall, S. (1978). *Patterns of attachment.* Hillsdale, NJ: Erlbaum.

Allen, W. E. (1976). *The formation of racial identity in black children adopted by white parents.* Dissertation Abstracts International, 37(4–B): 1888.

Andujo, E. (1988). Ethnic identity of transethnically adopted Latino adolescents. *Social Work, 33,* 531–535.

Bagley, C. (1993). *International and transracial adoptions: A mental health perspective.* Brookfield, VT: Ashgate Publishing Company.

Bowlby, J. (1969). *Attachment and loss: Attachment*. New York: Basic Books, Inc.

Bowlby, J. (1973). *Attachment and loss: Separation, anxiety and anger*. New York: Basic Books, Inc.

Bowlby, J. (1988). *A secure base: Clinical applications of attachment theory*. London: Routledge, A Tavistock Professional Book.

Brazelton, T. B. (1992). *Touchpoints: Your child's emotional and behavioral development*. Reading, MA: Addison-Wesley.

Brodzinsky, D., & Schechter, M. (Eds.). (1990). *The psychology of adoption*. New York: Oxford University Press.

Bruer, J. T. (1999). *The myth of the first three years: A new understanding of early brain development and lifelong learning*. New York: The Free Press.

Chestang, L. (1983). The policies and politics of health and human services: A black perspective. In A. E. Johnson (Ed.), *The black experience: Considerations for health and human services* (pp. 13–25). Davis, CA: International Dialogue Press.

Child Welfare League of America (1998). *Children's legislative agenda*. Washington, DC: Author.

Cole, M., & Cole, S. R. (1993). *The development of children* (2nd ed.). New York: W.H. Freeman and Company.

Comer, J. P., & Poussaint, A. F. (1975). *Black child care: How to bring up a healthy black child in America*. New York: Simon & Schuster.

Crumbley, J. (1998). Training on transracial adoption: Impact of transracial adoption on the adopted child and the adoptive family (Tape A); Parental tasks, goals, and challenges in transracial adoptions (Tape B). Philadelphia: Author, as cited in Freundlich, M. (2000). *Adoption and ethics: The role of race, culture, and national origin in adoption*. Washington, DC: Child Welfare League of America.

Department of Health and Human Services, Children's Bureau (1998). *Child welfare outcomes 1998, annual report*. Washington, DC: DHHS.

Falk, L. L. (1970). A comparative study of transracial and inracial adoptions. *Child Welfare, 49*, 82–88.

Fanshel, D. (1972). *Far from the reservation: The transracial adoption of American Indian children*. Metuchen, NJ: The Scarecrow Press, Inc.

Freundlich, M. (2000). *Adoption and ethics: The role of race, culture, and national origin in adoption*. Washington, DC: Child Welfare League of America.

Green, H. (1983). Risks and attitudes associated with extra-cultural placement of American Indian children: a critical review. *Journal of the Academy of Child Psychiatry, 2*, 63–67.

Grow, L. J., & Shapiro, D. (1974). *Black children, white parents*. New York: Child Welfare League of America.

Hinde, R. A. (1983). Ethology and Child Development. In M. M. Haith & J. J. Campos (Eds.), *Handbook of child psychology. Vol. II: Infancy and developmental psychobiology* (pp. 27–93). New York: Wiley.

Hopson, D. P., & Hopson, D. S. (1990). *Different and wonderful: Raising black children in a race-conscious society*. New York: Prentice Hall Press.

Howe, D., & Feast, J. (2000). *Adoption, search and reunion: The long term experience of adopted adults*. London: The Children's Society.

James, B. (1994). *Handbook for treatment of attachment-trauma problems in children*. New York: The Free Press.

Keck, G. C., & Kupecky, R. M. (1995). *Adopting the hurt child.* Colorado Springs: Pinon Press.

Keefer, B., & Schooler, J. E. (2000). *Telling the truth to your adopted or foster child.* Westport, CT: Bergin & Garvey.

Kelley, M. (undated). Creating an "other" identity. http://www.mavinmag.com/v3_adopt.html

Kinn, G. (2000). *Be my baby.* New York: Artisan, Workman Publishing Company.

Kirk, H. D. (1964). *Shared fate. A theory adoption and mental health.* New York: The Free Press.

Kirk, H. D. (1985). *Adoptive kinship: A modern institution in need of reform,* revised and enlarged. Port Angeles, WA: Ben-Simeon.

Kirk, H. D. (1988). *Exploring adoptive family life.* Port Angeles, WA: Ben-Simeon.

Lifton, B. J. (1994). *Journey of the adopted self.* New York: Basic Books.

Main, M., & Weston, D. (1981). The quality of the toddler's relationship to mother and to father: Related to conflict behavior and the readiness to establish new relationships. *Child Development, 52,* 932–940.

McRoy, R. G., & Zurcher, L. A. (1983). *Transracial and inracial adoptees: The adolescent years.* Springfield, IL: Charles C. Thomas.

Pinderhughes, E. E., & Rosenberg, K. (1990). Family bonding with high risk placements: A therapy model that promotes the process of becoming a family. In L. M. Glidden (Ed.), *Formed families: Adoption of children with handicaps* (pp. 209–230). New York: Haworth Press.

Rosenthal, J., & Groze, V. (1992). *Special needs adoption: A study of intact families.* Westport, CT: Praeger.

Sears, W., & Sears, M. (1993). *The baby book: Everything you need to know about your baby from birth to age two.* New York: Little, Brown & Company.

Shireman, J. F. (1988). *Growing up adopted: An examination of some major issues.* Chicago: Chicago Child Care Society.

Shireman, J., & Johnson, P. (1986, May-June). A longitudinal study of Black adoptions: Single parent, transracial, and traditional. *Social Work,* 172–176.

Silverman, A. R. (1993). Outcomes of transracial adoption. *The Future of Children, 3*(1), 104–118.

Simon, R. J., & Altstein, H. (1977). *Transracial adoption.* New York: John Wiley & Sons.

Simon, R. J., & Altstein, H. (1981). *Transracial adoption: A follow-up.* Lexington, MA: Lexington Books.

Simon, R. J., & Altstein, H. (1987). *Transracial adoptees and their families: A study of identity and commitment.* New York: Praeger.

Simon, R. J., Altstein, H., & Melli, M. S. (1994). *The case for transracial adoption.* Washington, DC: American University Press.

Spock, B., Parker, S. J., Parker, S., & Scotland, S. (1998). *Dr. Spock's baby and childcare.* New York: Dutton.

Verrier, N. (1993) *The primal wound: Understanding the adopted child.* Baltimore: Gateway Press.

Zeanah, C. H., Mammen, O., & Lieberman, A. (1993). Disorders of attachment. In C. H. Zeanah Jr. (Ed.), *Handbook of infant mental health* (pp. 342–439). New York: Guilford.

9

International Adoptions

*Victor Groza, Lindsey Houlihan,
and Karen F. Rosenberg*

REVIEW OF RESEARCH

Since 1990 there has been a 110% increase in the number of children adopted
internationally. In 1999 about 16,000 children entered the United States from other
countries, representing about 15% of all adoptions in the United States.
Cumulatively, over a 10-year period, there have been over 100,000 children adopted
from other countries. Summarizing from data provided by the State Department on
immigrant visas issued to orphans entering the United States from the top countries
of origin, in 1999, 47% of the children came from Asia, 35% came from Russia and
other USSR/Eastern European countries, 8% came from Central/South America, and
10% were not listed. The children from Asia were predominantly from China
(4,101), the children from the USSR/Eastern Europe were predominantly from
Russia (4,348), and the children from Central/South America were predominantly
from Guatemala (1,002). The children adopted from other countries, for the most
part, enter their adoptive families from institutions/orphanages (Groza, Ileana, &
Irwin, 1999; Harrison, Rubeiz, & Kochubey, 1996; Sloutsky, 1997). While there have
been media reports suggesting that the children from China are dramatically different
than children from other countries, recent research (Miller & Hendrie, 2000) documents
that Chinese adoptees display a similar pattern of medical and developmental difficulties
as seen in other groups of children adopted internationally.

Institutionalization brings unique health, developmental, and behavior risks that
may not be mitigated after adoption. To understand the risks to children, it is
important to understand the orphanage/institutional environment. Institutional life
is regimented—schedules are not flexible. You cannot change the routine for a
group of children in order to suit a particular child. Relationships between adults
and children are usually superficial and brief, with little continuous warmth and
affection. Often, there are too many children and not enough staff, with the result
that few children receive any individualized attention or care and suffer emotional

neglect (Miller, 2000), if not physical neglect. In Romania, children in orphanages were exposed to child-to-staff ratios ranging from 8:1 to 35:1 (Groza, Ileana, & Irwin, 1999). Institutional life does not provide children with the quality of life, or the experiences they need, to be healthy, happy, fully functioning adults.

The negative effects of institutionalization are compounded by other significant risks in a child's pre-adoptive life. It is clear that one of the main reasons children enter institutions is poverty. Prenatal care is often compromised for poor mothers in developing countries. In a review of records of children presented to parents as candidates to adopt internationally, Jenista (2000) found that when parental issues were mentioned as the reason children were free for adoption, 28% of the time the issue was poverty. The conclusion is that many of the children adopted internationally have high medical and social risks that are often exacerbated by institutional care. In essence, the international adoptee experiences many similar traumas as do children adopted from the public child welfare system in the United States.

However, it also has to be recognized that in many countries, social policy about population control and cultural attitudes play a role in children being abandoned. For example, China's one child per family policy and a cultural tradition of preference for male children have been often cited as reasons that families abandoned their female children. In Romania, during the communist era pronatalist policies—including the outlawing of abortion, taxation for childlessness, rewards for large families, and decreasing resources to raise children—resulted in families abandoning their children (Groza, Ileana, & Irwin, 1999). Post-communism mentality that children do better in institutions than in poor families because they have access to medical care contributes to the ongoing use of institutions.

While there are many risks, the effects from early experiences in institutions are not uniform. For example, from one-fifth (Groza, 1997; McGuinness, 1998) to one-third (Jenista, 1997) of the children are very resilient; they have been able to navigate extreme circumstances and do not demonstrate profound negative effects from the trauma in their lives. A second group, representing 30% to 60% of the children (Bascom & McKelvey, 1997; Groza, 1997; McGuinness, 1998), have significant developmental delays resulting from institutionalization. However, these children recover dramatically after they enter adoptive homes. They make up for many of the delays they exhibit at placement and, even though they may be somewhat behind in their development compared to those children who had not been exposed to this type of trauma, they get on a developmental path toward change and growth. The third group is severely affected by institutionalization, and many have profound developmental delays. Although they show progress in some areas of development, they continue to have considerable difficulties. Groza (1997) and McGuinness (1998) suggest that one-fifth of the children fall into this category; Jenista (1997) suggests one-third of the children fall into this category; and, Rutter and his colleagues (1995) suggest less than 10% of the children fall into this category.

There are two ways to describe the effects of institutionalization on children. From a strengths perspective, most of the children either recover from early negative experiences or are relatively unaffected by the traumas they encounter.

From a pathology perspective, most of the children are negatively affected by institutionalization. While seemingly contradictory, both views are correct. In understanding children and families that are created through international adoption, practitioners need to understand both the strengths and vulnerabilities that children bring to their families as well as the unique issues these families bring to the new adoptive family system. In this chapter, we highlight the issues regarding children adopted as infants and as older children from other countries.

Additional policies have also affected the information on children. In Russia and other USSR/Eastern European countries, where there is no criminal prosecution for abandonment, there is often information about the birth families. However, gathering an extensive history is not a priority. The professional and lay staff in the child welfare field do not have the skills or training to systematically gather a comprehensive history. So, the information is often scant and may be inaccurate, but there is information available. In contrast, in China, where abandonment is illegal, children will have virtually no information about their background. They may be given a birth date or name that was pinned to them, but virtually no other information is available until they are placed in an orphanage.

In summary, children adopted internationally have many risks. The different experiences of children have implications for practitioners working with them and their families.

ADOPTION PROCESS

Many families perceive that adopting internationally is easier than adopting domestically. This may be true if the family does not want to (a) parent a child documented to have special needs from the public child welfare system, (b) meet the age or other personal qualifications of agencies dealing with infant adoptions, or (c) participate in an open adoption. The paradox is that many international adoptees have risk factors that would classify them as special needs children in the public child welfare system but much less information is available about them than the children in the U. S. public child welfare system. However, families are willing to take these risks, because most of the children are infants or toddlers.

Other families adopt older children internationally because they (a) are unaware of the older children waiting for adoption in the United States, (b) have a misunderstanding of their eligibility to adopt, or (c) have had negative experiences with agencies. For example, a family many contact adoption agencies and, based on the initial contact, perceive that the agency is not interested in their family or the bureaucracy is overwhelming. The family then begins to pursue other options. The members of one family, who are now advocates for older children in the public child welfare system, talked about how they were discouraged from adopting domestically because they were a white, professional family, middle aged, and living in a rural area. They went on to adopt older children from Central America because an international agency did not prejudge them on the basis of their demographics, and worked with them in thinking about the issues they would encounter in their unique situation.

For some families who adopt from Eastern Europe, Russia or former Russian republics, there is also an issue of racial preference. Some Caucasian families prefer these children because they more easily blend into their families and communities. They would not consider adopting through the public child welfare system because they do not feel that they can parent a child from a different racial or ethnic background. These families are often at-risk because some of them want children who blend in, so they can deny the differences about being a multicultural family or even that they are an adoptive family.

Increasingly, we also hear that families choose international adoption because they fear the birth parents will come back to claim their children or want an open adoption if they adopt domestically. Even though a very small percentage of adoptions are contested and the children are returned to their birth mothers, the fear of birth parents reclaiming their children is so strong that families prefer international adoption. Many adoptive families have a bias or anxiety about open adoption.

The adoptive process requires involvement with several federal bureaucracies. To adopt internationally, families need the Application for Advanced Processing of Orphan Adoption Petition and the Petition to Classify an Orphan as an Immediate Relative. The I-600–A form indicates the family's desire to adopt abroad and prompts Immigration and Naturalization Service (INS) to begin a file of its own on the family; copies of the forms are sent to the National Visa Center and the consulate of the country of adoption. Once a child has been picked and the adoption paperwork has been completed, the I-600 is filed at the appropriate consulate. This is in addition to the home study.

While most agencies or individuals facilitating international adoption are helpful in the logistics, few are adequately preparing families for the reality of international adoption. There is no mandated pre-adoption training; the decision is left up to the agency or the parent to find information and prepare for the adoption. Too often, families are not adequately prepared for the adoption experience. The risk information is either not presented or minimized. Unless they actively educate and prepare themselves, most agencies do a less than adequate job of adoption preparation. This lack of preparation increases the stress families experience after placement and may result in more negative adoption outcomes, including disrupting the adoption.

Increasingly, families receive videotapes and/or medical histories of their adoptive children while waiting for the paperwork to be completed in the pre-adoptive stage of the process. They are able to take these tapes and histories to pediatricians, developmental psychologists, or staff at one of the international adoption clinics, to review and give a preliminary assessment of the health and development of their children. When told of the risk factors that institutionalization has created, or concerns are raised from viewing records or videos, many families go into denial, not wanting to hear the risk factors or concerns. Often, by the time families get to this stage, they have bonded to the photos or videos of the children and cannot hear or evaluate realistically the information they receive. Practitioners agree that informed adoptive parents fare better, and have more realistic expectations, in addition to having services lined up as soon as they return home. However, by the time they have obtained photos or videos, for some families, they cannot change their decision.

Post-placement support can also be problematic. Some families may have never established a rapport with the home study agency—they see the home study as a means to an end rather than a time to gain helpful information. In such cases, families do not turn to the home study agency for help post-placement. In other cases, while most agencies complete the post-placement visits as required, they are unwilling or unable to provide case management if families need access to services. In addition, if problems arise or get recognized later, most families are left on their own to navigate locating and securing help. Added to this stress is the fact that all financial burdens for services are the total responsibility of the adoptive family. Finally, for families residing in rural areas, often the services they need are not easily obtainable. This places an additional burden on the developing family.

The lack of adequate preparation and the failure to provide post-placement support highlight the need for standards in service delivery in the international adoption process. The Hague Convention may assist with these standards but with such a decentralized, state-based approach to adoption, the quality of services is very uneven from state to state and throughout the adoption process.

FAMILY FORMATION

Families who adopt infants and toddlers and families who give birth experience similar life cycle issues. For example, there are the stresses and strains of changing routines to accommodate a new person in the family. There are adjustments to (a) the marital/relationship system to make space for the child, and (b) parental roles as well as the realignment of the relationships with the extended family to include parenting and grandparenting roles. Of course, these alterations in the family system become extremely stressful and problematic when the child has health, developmental, attachment or other difficulties.

Families who adopt older children from other countries are often not prepared for the number of transitions and adoption-related issues that place stress on these families. The older children often have difficulties in school and are not motivated to achieve high grades. Some demonstrate problematic communication skills—in particular, older children do not disclose information about their past before adoption or their feelings. Some families feel that these children should be grateful, while, in fact, the children can feel somewhat resentful. The following case is an example of this issue:

The adoptive family was a working-class family who adopted two teenage boys from South America. The boys were the youngest of five in their birth family. The spouses of the older biological brothers in South America had refused to adopt or parent these boys. With little preparation, an American family adopted them. Six months after placement, the agency that facilitated the adoption left town, leaving the family with no post-adoption support. The boys were very independent as a result of spending several years together on the streets, and had infrequent school attendance in their country of origin. Once in the United States, they quickly learned English and within two years, at the ages of 15 and 17, both were employed. They did not perform well in school, and, when disciplined, would tell their adoptive parents they were saving their money to return to their homeland. They refused to acknowledge the adoptive mother as their parent. The adoptive parents both were unhappy about how the boys treated the adoptive mother and the boys' poor school performance. In addition, the adoptive parents didn't understand the boys' longing for their homeland.

Some adoptive families choose to adopt internationally because they may be unwilling or feel unprepared to adopt transracially. This always brings an interesting perspective in the family's use of denial in family formation, in that same-race families can "pass" for biological families, unlike families that adopt transracially. Of course, families that adopt from India, Korea, and Latin America are challenged by all the issues of international adoption compounded by the issues of adopting transracially.

SEPARATION AND LOSS

For older international adoptees, little attention is paid to preparing them for adoption. It is not unusual for children to go from their routine of group living into the arms of a parent or parents who don't speak their language and who will be taking them to a culture and environment far from which they are familiar. There are a few agencies that have established procedures to prepare older children. However, for the most part, no attempt is made to help these children say good-bye to peers and significant adults, aside from perhaps a few moments saying good-bye to staff before leaving with the new adoptive parents.

Familiar possessions are few. It is important to recognize that children often do not distinguish between what is good and what is bad for them. Children experience what is familiar and what is unfamiliar. The change is traumatic, and older adoptees experience obvious loss, grief, and mourning. Often, the cues are missed or hard to distinguish, because too much happens at one time—they go from a group to a family, then from one country to another. These children may be so overwhelmed, as are the adoptive parents, that the adjustments they undergo may not be interpreted as loss, grief, or mourning.

It is also difficult to help older children sort through the losses and grief they have experienced. Language plays a major factor. Infants and younger children were pre-verbal at adoption and never had words to describe their experiences. For older adoptees, as they lose their native language, they lose the experiences and history that the language described. Some occupational therapists and social workers are using body work to help these youngsters sort through their complicated history, using the theory that they have cellular or body memories.

A child, seen in a private practice, spent the first 18 months of life with his biological family, including two older siblings. The birth mother was alcoholic and not much is known about the biological father. When the child was about 18 months old, the birth mother committed suicide. The children were placed in different institutions. The two older siblings were separated from the younger sibling. The youngest child was adopted at age 3 from the orphanage, has no conscious memory of his first 18 months, and no memory of his siblings who have been adopted by a European family. Issues of loss, neglect, and separation were woven throughout the child's history as he attached to different primary caretakers in his family of origin, followed by the orphanage, only to experience another loss and separation when adopted by an American couple.

This case reflects many of the same clinical issues and symptomatology of older-placed children in our public child welfare system.

However, loss is not unique to those international adoptees that are placed at an older age. For adoptees placed as infants or toddlers, it may be more subtle. A particular event may trigger a loss and grief reaction, as the following case illustrates.

An adoptee from Central America had been adjusting well in her family, school, and community until an earthquake occurred in her native country. She began to show symptoms of anxiety and preoccupation with trauma. She told her family that even though she had been living in the states since infancy and was very much a part of her adoptive family, she was preoccupied with thoughts and images of her birth family being killed by this devastating earthquake. Her family was able to get a letter to members of the religious community who lived and worked in the Central American community and who the adoptive parents worked with to adopt this youngster. The family eventually received information that her birth family was safe, which brought great comfort and relief to the adoptee.

This experience reflects two issues. One, even children adopted as infants have loss issues. Two, the ties to biological and cultural roots are strong even when children are adopted as infants and have no conscious memory of their birth families. The following is a different example but also highlights this point.

When Maria was 3 years old, a little boy in her class drowned. That tragedy seemed even more complicated for her than it would have been for a non-adopted kid. She has a keen sense of abandonment and loss. We had to spend a lot of time on it; she kept talking around it. At first she said, "A bad witch is gonna come and take me." She was upset and it was hard to tell what it was about. Then it became clear that she was upset because she realized that a child could disappear forever.

We saw that Maria's response to the death of her classmate was an expression of loss for her biological mother: For her there's anger and sadness, and curiosity. Somewhere inside of her, Maria seems to know what it's like for a parent and a child to be permanently separated. A child who isn't separated from his or her biological parents doesn't know grief like that. For us that was a terrible sorrow. To love your child more than anything and then to feel that you can't replace something she's lost in her life is very painful. But we are her parents, and I don't think this sadness causes an unbridgeable gap between us. We're very close.(Kinn, 2000, pp.7, 9)

Some children deal with loss through an active fantasy life. They fantasize what their lives would be like if they had not been adopted. One adoptee from India imagined himself being a beggar in the streets. Another adoptee from Latin America imagined himself as a great soccer star. Many adoptees imagine themselves living in poverty and feel guilty about having a comfortable life, while their biological families are living a less comfortable life. Some have rescue fantasies about their birth families, particularly concerning siblings. It is important to recognize that fantasies are a normative part of a child's life in general, and an adoptee's life in particular. The adoptive family who fears openness or dreads talking about the birth family usually does not handle this situation well. In particular, if the adoptive family entered international adoption because of fear of the birth family, they will face crisis and be unable to deal with the loss issues that inevitably emerge.

IDENTITY DEVELOPMENT

Forming an identity is important for children who are adopted. Those who are adopted internationally are not only faced with the adoption issue, but are often faced with being a different race than the adoptive parents. Racial and ethnic identity issues may often surpass the adoption issue for international adoptees (Freidlander, 1999). It is particularly difficult for international adoptees to form their identities with little or no biological histories. Adoptive families can teach them about their cultural origins, expose them to rituals and traditions of their ethnic culture, and even take trips back to their homelands to see the people and experience the culture. But, all this information is theoretical and not personal. Internationally placed adoptees have the largest gap in real information about their birth families.

A Korean adoptee in clinical practice had some information about her birth mother, only to find out at age 11 that the woman who abandoned her at the orphanage was really an imposter, a woman hired by her birth family to take her to the orphanage. All the information that she carried around with her for many years was fiction and there was no way that she could find out the true facts of her origin. Her adoptive parents knew this but were reluctant to share this information with her until she began treatment at age 11. Her trust of her adoptive parents was shaken dramatically and she was in a crisis due to genealogical bewilderment and a sense of betrayal of the truth.

Families are the most important vehicles for children in terms of early identity development. Families who adopt internationally are faced with many choices and challenges as adoptive parents. How parents choose to deal with adoption and racial/ethnic differences within their families impacts the early identity development of their young children. Parents can either deny the differences between adoptive and biological family formation or acknowledge the differences (Kirk, 1964, 1985, 1988). Families who deny the differences do not acknowledge that adopted children differ from biological children. Many of the families who deny the differences do not adopt to help children but to fill their own needs, and the denial of difference continues to meet their needs. Adoption is an acceptable way to build a family and denying the differences is not helpful to children. While many of the daily tasks of parenting are similar for adoptive and biological parents, one of the differences is the communication style of how issues such as adoption and race are handled by the family.

Families who deny the differences regarding the adoption issue often tend to hold the same stance toward denying racial differences in the family. Parents who choose to define the adoptee's status in the family as "just like all the other kids in the family"also assume a color-blind stance in regards to ethnic issues (McRoy et al., 1984). If differences cannot be acknowledged and discussed, adoption and racial diversity cannot be addressed as identity development issues. If families do not talk about the adoption, the racial/ethnic identity issue cannot be discussed either. Children are often left with the message that if they cannot talk about their adoption from their country of origin, something must be wrong with them. Research on Korean international adoptions has found that children long for discussions about their adoptions and birth cultures as well as developing an ethnic identity as they mature into adults (Freundlich & Lieberthal, 2000).

On the other hand, adoptive families who acknowledge and celebrate the differences are open about diversity. Adoptive parents face the reality of becoming a multicultural family. The recent proliferation of adoptions from China over the past decade provides an example of how adoptive families are acknowledging diversity. Many families are choosing to incorporate their children's Chinese identity into the identity of the family. Adoptive parents are acknowledging and socializing their Chinese children as Chinese American. The process of raising a child in both cultures is called acculturation or bicultural socialization (LaFramboise et al., 1993). In the case of adoptive parents of Chinese children, families have developed strategies to include Chinese ethnic identity into the new family identity. Many families include their children's Chinese names as a way of welcoming their new children. Some learn a great deal about Chinese culture before they travel to China. The long-term goal of bicultural socialization is to provide an emotional, social, and psychological foundation to empower self-esteem about the ethnic identity and assist children in developing tools to address prejudice and racism (Tessler, Gamache, & Liu, 1999).

The parents of a 4-year-old girl adopted from China are committed to raising their daughter to know her Chinese heritage. Each week they take their daughter to a Chinese culture class at a local library. The parents take turns presenting topics about Chinese culture. The theme for this week is the history of fans in Chinese culture. All the girls participate in an arts and crafts project to make a fan and pose together waving their fans for a group picture.

The family can best begin the positive internalization of their child's native culture when they travel to the country of origin to get their child. This experience can set the stage/tone for all that is to follow. The strengthening of ethnic and cultural identity for adoptees continues when the child is physically present in the family. Families are the primary vehicle for socializing children, especially during their early years (to age 3). Children adopted as infants and even as toddlers do not remember their birth parents or the country of their birth. It is incumbent upon the adoptive family to help the child maintain an image of his or her country of origin. Family activities such as attending international adoption support groups, celebrating cultural holidays with other adoptive families, and having a reunion with members of the travel group will help parents and children become acquainted with other families who look just like them.

Children around the age of 3 begin to notice physical differences between themselves and other people as part of the developmental process (Aboud, 1987; Katz, 1987). International adoptees can be particularly aware of physical differences between themselves and their parents (Brodzinsky, Schechter, & Henig, 1992). This stage begins at age 3 and ends around the age of 6. The development of a positive self-identification of racial/ethnic identity by the child is proportional to the level of engagement in racial or ethnic promotion by the parents (Huh & Reid, 2000). It is important for parents not to be afraid of and to recognize the ethnic and racial differences between their children and themselves. It is not necessary for the parents to provide detailed explanations. A basic explanation would be fine and it may be incorporated with elements of the adoption story as well, if it is appropriate at the time.

A pre–school-age adoptee was playing with his father and comparing arms. "I'm brown," said the boy. "Yes," said the father, "brown is a great color." The boy looked at his father's freckles and said, "Spotted is a great color, too."

The beginning of school is an important milestone for internationally adopted children. Developmentally, children begin to separate slowly from their parents and build an emotional connection with their peer groups at school. Children will be challenged with questions about racial differences and adoption, and will relay the responses given by the parents. If parents are comfortable and can set appropriate boundaries with questions about racial/ethnic differences and adoptions, children will most likely share this confidence. This is a sign of healthy self-esteem. The cognitive development of children at this stage suggests that they are beginning to understand what adoption really means psychologically. They are beginning to think abstractly—that is, in order to gain a family they had to loose a family.

The hallmark of adolescence is the search for identity. It is one of the most important developmental tasks. Research on minority children has shown that teens who have pride in their ethnic/racial identities have increased self-esteem (Phinney, 1990). Adolescents should be encouraged to continue activities supporting their ethnic identity development. At this stage, many adolescents also have issues relating to identity which come to life at the beginning of search issues. In many cases, searching for the birth parents may be unrealistic, so a search for foster parents may be the focus of the search. A few international adoption agencies sponsor an adoption-focused homeland tour.

A group of Korean-American adopted adolescents attend an adoption agency—sponsored trip to their birth country. The first part of the trip is emotional for some of the adoptees, since it involves a visit to a facility for unwed mothers, similar to what may have occurred with their birth mothers. The next part of the tour involves searching for birth mothers or foster mothers. A few are reunited with birth mothers, a few with foster mothers, and some are unable to find the link they were looking for. The final part of the trip involves learning about Korean culture by exploring family life, art, language, and education. As they return to the United States, a flurry of new feelings have emerged.

A young adult adoptee from Colombia who grew up in a Jewish family recalls his experience:

Last year, my mother and I went back to visit my orphanage. When I was younger, I was afraid to go back because I thought they would leave me there—at least that's what my parents told me I said. As an adult, I felt very much at home. I definitely didn't feel like a tourist. . . . I can safely say that while I was in Bogota, I wasn't looking for my birth mother. I wasn't looking at every supermarket cashier, thinking, "Maybe she's my birth mother." Though if I found out a month from now that my parents could arrange for me to meet her, I definitely wouldn't shy away. I identified with all the kids in the orphanage, and felt connected to the place. It was a beautiful home, not the nightmarish image we have from stories. (Kinn, 2000, pp. 104–105)

As international adoptees move through different developmental stages, their needs and feelings change in regards to their connection with their birth cultures. Some adoptees have a different response than the case above.

During latency, an adoptee from Central America was very involved in such activities as culture camp, learning Spanish, and connecting with other Latino adoptees. She told her therapist that she felt proud and special about her Latino heritage. As she entered adolescence, her wish was to "blend in" with the mainstream culture of adolescents she knew, and even though her family had always expected her to have a "quince anero" celebration at age 15, which is traditional for Hispanic girls, she resisted. She wanted to have a "sweet 16" party instead, like her many girlfriends. When she was invited to participate in a special education program for minority youth in her middle school, she refused at first, not identifying with being a minority, even though she was a person of color from an indigenous Indian culture in Central America. Her family was white and that was how she was identifying herself, now that she was entering adolescence.

Children who are adopted when they are older have memories of their birth countries. International adoptees often have to relinquish their language as the first step toward adjusting to their new homes and new countries. As they relinquish their language, often memories will also fade. What still appears to be a statement toward assimilation needs to be challenged for the older adoptee. As with children who are adopted as infants and toddlers, parental recognition and acceptance of the adoptee's birth culture includes socializing with people with cultural/ethnic similarities as the adoptee, choosing to reside in a neighborhood with diversity, and celebrating holidays and traditions related to the birth culture.

The adoptive families from an orphanage in China organized a reunion in the mountains of Colorado. Enough money was raised to bring the orphanage director and the overseeing official to Colorado to see the 60-plus girls and their families traveling from throughout the United States. The orphanage director surprised two families by stating that their two girls were in the same crib until they were adopted. The orphanage director remembered this from hearing their Chinese names. The two girls, now 5, were born months apart from each other and adopted within one year. The two girls became fast friends and played together all weekend. The parents were surprised that they bonded so quickly, but happy for their daughters. The weekend continued with Chinese dance lessons, crafts, picnics, and family dinners. The girls put their hands on a banner to be hung at the orphanage with their Chinese names, their American names and the day they were adopted. The one girl still thinks about her crib-mate from China: "She's my Chinese sister."

During childhood, minority adoptees gain access to mainstream the white majority through their parents. However, when they leave home they are minorities in a white world. White parents have little knowledge about this challenge since many international adoptive parents belong to the majority culture. Oftentimes they are unaware of the importance of ethnic or cultural issues for adoptive children. While adoptive parents of infants and toddlers may have begun to incorporate their children's birth culture into family life at an earlier age, adoptive parents of older internationally adopted children might follow the same practice of acknowledging their birth culture. Many adoptive parents fear talking about adoption and birth culture because such discussions raise the issue of birth parents. Others may view the grief issues of the adoptee as rejection of them as parents, which is not the case. Parents need to see that honest and open communication about adoption can impact the adoptee's identity. The message is that, "we can talk about this as a family and it is a part of our family history." The openness will support a feeling of belonging to the adoptee that will translate into good healthy self-esteem.

A teenage Amerasian adoptee, that was older at placement eventually realized that her birth father was an African American GI stationed in Viet Nam. This was the only information she knew about her origin besides the memories she had of her birth mother socializing with many American soldiers. As she attempted to form her identity, she put together the only two pieces that she knew and became sexually active only with African American young men, eventually getting pregnant and having a baby. The urge to repeat one's family of origin experience is strong, even when raised in the context of an adoptive family with different values and cultural expectations.

One adoptee offers a life course/developmental perspective on his identity journey.

I grew up in Queens, a bastion of Italian American life . . . but I was born in Seoul, South Korea. Finding my way through this background—Korean-Italian-American adoptee—has been like swinging on a pendulum. At different stages of my life the pendulum has swung from my identification with my Italian American roots over to my Korean birth and then back again. Being Korean was never an issue with my good friends. But sometimes, other kids would give me a hard time. I remember coming home from school one day when I was 6 and asking my mother, "What does chink mean?" Having to learn about issues of racism at the age of 6 was often difficult. . . . I didn't want to always have to explain myself, but I went through life thinking I had to. Being able to choose privacy when you want to is crucial to an adopted child, who may sometimes feel that his life is an open book.

When I was younger and then when I was a teenager, there were times when I saw myself as an American more than anything else. I didn't even consider myself Asian. . . . But soon the pendulum started swinging toward things Korean. I began noticing more hate crimes against Asians, and I realized that no matter who I was, people were going to identify me from the outside, because that's what they generally do. Then, during the L.A. riots in 1992, I watched the largest community of Korean Americans living in the United States burning down. That's when it really got to me that as much as I assert myself as a person of a multicultural background, my race is going to be the first perception people are going to have of me. I began to think, "I'm Korean and I have to acknowledge that."

It was in college that I had my first frightening experience with overt racism. One day I came back from class and found one of my architecture projects destroyed. Things were stolen from my room. It was like living through a freshman hazing, a rite of passage, but much worse.

Participating in the Korean American church opened up my understanding. I learned more about the culture . . . I got a bit more radical. Little by little I grew distant from my Italian culture. . . . At one point everyone was calling me by my Korean name, which at first I thought was great. But then I realized that I really didn't feel comfortable answering to that name. . . . I'm adopted and I have this whole other side of me. My face shows I'm Korean but it doesn't show everything else. Once again, the pendulum swung, now the other way, toward Queens.

The pendulum is finally losing its momentum altogether and coming to a place of rest. If I can't find the precise words to define who I am, that's okay. In aspects of culture and ethnicity, we assume that we all have to be put in one category or another. But, I'd have to say, "Well, I'm Korean, but I'm also Italian American, I'm a son, but I'm also an uncle and so on." Adoption is not something to get over. It's part of who I am. . . . Over time, I've found that I've had to create a special space for myself, a place where all the different aspects of my personality would be validated. I've found this in many corners of my life but particularly in my involvement with a group of other adoptees in an organization called Also Known As, Inc., which is an association of adult Korean adoptees.

Prospective parents of international adoptees often ask me "How much cultural background should I give my child?" And my answer is, "Until they reject it." For kids, it's great to participate in cultural events, but what they really want is to go out and play with their friends. They want and need to fit in. Make their background available but don't push it on them. And don't discount the fact that your culture is as important to them as any other. Culture is learned; it's a gift that's passed on from generation to generation. Connections are not automatic, they have to be worked at.

In the end, I think I had to grow up in order to take whatever aspect of Korean culture I cared about for myself. My ownership of it is what matters. I don't know how it would have worked if my parents had learned Korean and tried to pass it on to me; it would have felt secondhand. It's difficult to know what to do. Every family is different. (Kinn, 2000, pp. 96–101)

ATTACHMENT

It is clear that children coming from institutions are at great risk for attachment problems. It is also clear that most of the attachment difficulties can be successfully resolved in the adoptive family without professional intervention.

It is important to distinguish between bonding—which is a biological event of emotional connection—and attachment, which is a complex, developmental process. Many families bond with a picture of their adopted children before they actually meet them. Most of the children become attached to their parents over time. For internationally placed infants, the attachment issues are similar to those experienced by infants adopted domestically. However, since children respond to familiar sights, sounds, and taste, most internationally adopted children experience a radical change in these areas, while the change for domestic children is often less radical. Since continuity and familiarity, as well as a responsive adult, lay the foundation for secure attachment, in general the earlier children achieve this the more likely they are to attach securely in their adoptive families. Still, the change is traumatizing for children; some children deal with it more resiliently than others.

Older children adopted internationally have often experienced prolonged periods of inadequate caregiving. The regimentation of living in an orphanage or institution, plus the few staff compared to the number of children needing care and attention, has resulted in inconsistent caregiving, and often extreme neglect/deprivation. O'Connor, Rutter, and colleagues (2000) found a close association between duration of deprivation and attachment disorder behaviors in a sample of Romanian adoptees. In addition, over time, there was little decrease in the attachment difficulties. While deprivation that is neglectful negatively affects attachment, caregiving may have also been neglectful or abusive prior to the child entering an institution. Jenista (2000) found that when parental issues were mentioned in the records of international adoptees, about 25% of children entered the institution/orphanage due to parental abuse or neglect and 14% entered due to parental substance abuse. This risk can be further compounded by abuse in the institutions. However, the incidence of physical and sexual abuse among institutionalized children is unknown (Miller, 2000). The conclusion is that many of the children adopted internationally have high risks for attachment difficulties that are often exacerbated by institutional care. In addition, the older the child, the greater the risk.

RECOMMENDATIONS

For older children, it is important for parents to look for naturally occurring opportunities for promoting attachment with their children. There are four prime times when this occurs—when children are anxious, fearful, fatigued, or ill. One of the first opportunities for attachment to occur is when children are removed from the familiarity of orphanages to the unfamiliarity of families. The children may be anxious or fearful; once they recognize that they are not going back, they may become anxious in addition to fearful about the strangeness. This is an opportune time for the family to comfort and connect to the child. This opportunity presents itself from the time of family placement through the plane ride and into the first few weeks to months the child is in the home. It is not unusual to hear that the child developed his or her first attachment to an escort, if the family did not travel themselves to bring the child to the United States, or for an intense connection to form between only one parent and the child if a single parent makes the international trip.

The attachment is solidified between the traveling parent and the child. Of course, this can also be quite stressful since the child may be inconsolable on the trip—but this should not be confused with bad behavior. It is a grief reaction and traumatic—a naturally occurring response to the change and an opportunity for the parent and child to build an emotional connection. Any new situation may invoke anxiety or fear and can be used as a naturally occurring event to promote attachment.

A third opportune time is when the child is tired or sleepy. It is at this time, when they are fatigued, that they are vulnerable and an attachment connection can be made between parent and child. It is not unusual to hear of parents and children sleeping together after placement, as they use this time to make a different type of attachment connection, replacing a developmental phase that they may have missed.

Many of the children become ill—either from the change in food and routine or from the medical treatment/inoculations they receive abroad or at home. An ill child presents itself as an opportune time to nurture, cuddle, hold, and take care of while the child gets well, regardless of the age of the child at placement. An illness in many ways replicates the stimulation-relaxation cycle that enables the parent to provide fundamental caretaking. Pampering goes a long way to building connections, particularly when children are vulnerable from illness.

Activities to support a positive ethnic identity include enrollment in a Chinese cultural program, taking Korean-language lessons, or a visit to a Russian Orthodox Church. Families who encourage and participate in ethnic and/or cultural activities will not only socialize children around their birth culture, but will be able to talk with their children about family inclusion of their ethnic identity. A good family activity is to discuss how the ethnic identity will be included in other family activities on a regular basis. Parents will also have an opportunity to discuss the birth culture during the planning sessions. Similar to the adoption issue, if the children and parents are secure and comfortable about discussing the ethnic and cultural identity issues on a regular basis, then the foundation is set for more in-depth and complex questions as the child matures into school age and adolescence. However, parents should expect that children may not always be so eager or willing to participate in enrichment programs. The following is a case in point.

Because Maria is Chinese, we have a Chinese baby-sitter who is teaching her Mandarin. . . . But Maria's relationship to things Chinese is tricky. She resists and rejects it on some level. Though Maria is beginning to understand some Mandarin, she behaves like many first-generation American kids: she wants to speak only English. I know that her resistance doesn't come solely because she wants to be just like her mom and dad, but because she knows English is the dominant language here. Her Chinese culture class, though, gives her the chance to enjoy speaking Mandarin with her peers. This could all backfire, of course, and she'll be upset with us for making her pay so much attention to her native culture. But if we didn't start helping her to learn about China now, when she reaches the age of eighteen she might turn around and scream at us, "Why didn't you give me Mandarin lessons?" As adoptive parents, particularly of a racially different child, you have to consider how much attention to draw to the issues of adoption and ethnic differences. It's not only the kids who have trouble with these distinctions, but parents as well. (Kinn, 2000, p. 6)

Parents need to recognize that they do not have all the answers, especially in identity issues. Enlisting support from the community is a strength. One recommendation is that parents seek out other adults from their child's birth culture and begin socializing with them. Other parents have moved to neighborhoods that reflect multicultural diversity. Many obtain referrals to speak to family therapists or social workers. Adoption agencies have groups for teen international adoptees for social as well as educational purposes. Parents often need to educate teachers about the complexities of international adoption, particularly around assignments like the family tree.

Children who have been adopted transracially need clear boundaries in terms of psychological as well as ethnic and cultural identities. It is very important to recognize identity issues in order to give children a better sense of who they are, instilling in them a sense of pride and appreciation. Families must feel confident to prepare minority children for the realities of discrimination and inequality in today's world. Helping children develop healthy and flexible bicultural identities will assist international adoptees to navigate the life course in productive ways. As the adult adoptee from Colombia who grew up in a Jewish family writes:

I've experienced prejudice hundreds of times. It was easier to deal with when I was younger because my brother and sister were there to protect me. As I got older, I was able to protect myself. One time I was pulled over by the police while driving my sister's BMW with my fiancée, Janice, who is Irish American. They asked her if she was okay, at which point she became enraged. Then they asked, "Whose car is this?" They never would have stopped me if I wasn't with a white girl. . . . I was most upset because all he could see was this Hispanic male driving a white girl in a BMW, and that didn't seem right to him. Sometimes I use these terrible situations as opportunities to educate. My feeling is that if you explain how your life situation came about, the next time they come across a Hispanic Jew, they'll have a context for it. (Kinn, 2000, p. 105)

Many international adoptees are older when adopted and have memories of the places they have lived and the important people in their lives. Identity development is continuous and to help these youngsters tell their story practitioners can make a "life map" with the adoptee (Pinderhughes & Rosenberg, 1990). This exercise facilitates the narrative of the adoptee's past history and relationships with his or her biological family, the staff at the orphanage, foster families, and so on. This process gives the child a chance to review and clarify his or her life story, reducing confusion and helping the child separate fantasy from reality. It also gives the adoptive family an opportunity to hear about and accept the child's past without denying the facts and events. On poster-size paper, the therapist and the adoptee create a chronological outline (like a road on a board game) of all the places the child has lived, dating each event, as accurately as possible, including names of people, if known. The adoptee illustrates each event with a drawing that symbolizes that time of his life. The adoptive family members can join the project when the life map is at the point of their connection.

A "life map" was created with an Amerasian adoptee who was adopted around age 5, although her age was a mystery as she didn't have any papers with her birth date. She drew pictures of the orphanage where she lived before being adopted, her grandmother's home in the mountains where she would often visit, the "village" where her birth mother and other Asian women were living together, an area frequented by American GI soldiers, memories of other important people in her life, including a brother who was younger. As she drew these pictures, more memories were recovered and more feelings emerged. She remembered feeling loved and safe in her grandmother's house and wondered what became of her. She connected with feelings of anger and betrayal at her birth mother's deception when she was brought to the orphanage. Her birth mother told her that she was bringing her to a boarding school because she was so smart that she deserved to be educated, but in fact, she was abandoned at an orphanage. She talked about the longing she felt for her family and the tears that she shed missing her younger brother while in the orphanage. She wondered about his whereabouts and fantasized that her mother eventually brought him to the orphanage, too, and that maybe he was adopted by an American family. She talked about the "village" where she lived and came to the realization that her mother was probably a prostitute with drug and alcohol problems. She was able to mourn and grieve the many losses she had experienced on a different level of intensity once the memories were activated by making her life map.

Adoptive families need to be encouraged during the pre-placement phase to gather as much information as possible when traveling to get their youngsters from the orphanages. One family who adopted a youngster from Russia was told that the child had two siblings who were adopted by a family in France. They were unable to gather much information about the biological family in Russia, but did manage to get the address of the adoptive family in France. Letters and e-mails have gone back and forth and there is a plan for the siblings, and their adoptive families to have a reunion next summer. The siblings are older and have more memories of their birth family that they will be able to share with the youngest child, as she is now developmentally ready to hear them.

Many post-institutionalized children are developmentally uneven. One practitioner describes seeing 5- and 6-year-old children in her practice who appear as if they have no "boundaries" with their adoptive parents. They are constantly touching their parents, attempting to sit on their laps, playing with their hair, and touching their faces, presenting a very regressed manner. If you think of them as 9 month olds, or even young toddlers, this behavior seems developmentally on target. Most of these children never received the kind of touching and cradling that infants need and are attempting to make up for those lost developmental tasks. In addition, some children experience developmental regression. Once completing the missed developmental tasks, they are able to move and develop on a typical trajectory. An example of this is school-age children who return to "baby talk." As they fill the gap in their development, they move on. Their need for order and ritual is striking, at home and at school. For those youngsters who appear to have more serious diagnoses such as Obsessive Compulsive Disorder or Pervasive Developmental Disorder, sensory integration sessions with an occupational therapist can be very useful. More research is needed, particularly in the area of longitudinal studies of international adoptees. In addition, practitioners in domestic and international adoption need to be working together since so many issues are the same.

SELECTED INTERNET RESOURCES ON INTERNATIONAL ADOPTION

Adoption About (www.adoption.about.com) gives general information about international adoption.

Families with Children from China (www.fwcc.org) is a network of chapters supporting Adoption from China.

International Adoption Resources (www.calib.com/naic/pubs/index.htm#inter) gives information on international adoption maintained by the National Adoption Information Clearinghouse.

Korean American Adoptee Adoptive Family Network (www.kaanet.com/)

International Special Needs Adoption (www.homes.4kids.org/int.htm)

Families with Russian and Ukrainian Adoptions (www.fura.org/)

Issues to Consider before Pursuing Intercountry Adoption (www.adoption.org/race.html)

Latin American Parents Association (www.lapa.com)

International Adoption Alliance (www.i-a-a.org/)

The Hague Convention on Protection of Children and Cooperation in Responsibility of Intercountry Adoption (www.jcics.org/haguetext.html)

Guidelines and Documents from U.S. State Department (http://travel.state.gov/adopt.html)

Comeunity (www.comeunity.com/)

United States Immigration and Naturalization Services (INS) (www.ins.usdoj.gov/)

Especially for Adoptees (www.adopting.org/adoptees.html)

International Concern Committee for Children (www.iccadopt.org)

Families with Children from Vietnam (www.fcvn.com)

Parent Evaluation of Adoption Agencies (Eastern European Adoption Coalition) (http://eeadopt.org)

REFERENCES

Aboud, F. E. (1987). The development of ethnic self-identification and attitudes. In J. Phinney & M. J. Rotheram (Eds.), *Children's ethnic socialization: Pluralism and development* (pp. 32–55). Newbury Park, CA: Sage Publications.

Bascom, B. B., & McKelvey, C. A. (1997). *The complete guide to foreign adoptions.* New York: Pocket Books.

Brodzinsky, D., Schechter, M., & Henig, R. (1992). *Being adopted. The lifelong search for self.* New York: Doubleday.

Freidlander, M. (1999). Ethnic identity development of internationally adopted children and adolescents: Implications for family therapists. *Journal of Marital and Family Therapy, 25*(1), 43–60.

Freundlich, M., & Lieberthal, J. (2000). *The gathering of the first generation of adult Korean adoptees: Adoptee's perception of international adoption.* New York: The Evan B. Donaldson Adoption Institute.

Groza, V. (1997). International adoption. In R. L. Edwards (Ed.), *Encyclopedia of social work, 19th edition, 1997 supplement* (pp. 1–14). Washington, DC: NASW Press.

Groza, V., Ileana, D., & Irwin, I. (1999). *A peacock or a crow? Stories, interviews and commentaries on Romanian adoptions.* South Euclid, OH: Willes e-press.

Harrison, L., Rubeiz, G., & Kochubey, A. (1996). Lapsele oma kodu (bringing abandoned children home): A project from Tallinn, Estonia to reunite institutionalized children with families. *Scandinavian Journal of Social Welfare, 5,* 35–44.

Huh, N., & Reid, W. (2000). Intercountry transracial adoption and ethnic identity. *International Social Work Journal, 43* (1), 75–87.

Jenista, J. (1997). Romanian review. *Adoption-Medical News, 3*(5), 1–6.

Jenista, J. (2000). Preadoption review of medical records. *Pediatric Annals, 29*(4), 212–215.

Katz, P. (1987). Developmental and social processes in ethnic attitudes and self-identification. In J. Phinney & M. J. Rotheram (Eds.), *Children's ethnic socialization: Pluralism and development* (pp. 92–100). Newbury Park, CA: Sage Publications.

Kinn, G. (2000). *Be my baby.* New York: Artisan.

Kirk, H. D. (1964). *Shared fate. A theory adoption and mental health.* New York: The Free Press.

Kirk, H. D. (1985). *Adoptive kinship: A modern institution in need of reform,* revised and enlarged. Port Angeles, WA: Ben-Simeon.

Kirk, H. D. (1988). *Exploring adoptive family life.* Port Angeles, WA: Ben-Simeon

LaFromboise, H. L., Coleman, K., & Gerton, J. (1993). Psychological impact of biculturalism: Evidence and theory. *Psychological Bulletin, 114* (3), 395–412.

McGuinness, T. M. (1998). *Risk and protective factors in internationally adopted children from the former Soviet Union.* Dissertation: University of Pittsburgh.

McRoy, R. G., Zurcher, L. A., Lauderdale, M. L., & Anderson, R. E. (1984). The identity of transracial adoptees. *Social Casework, 65,* 34–39.

Miller, L. C. (2000). Initial assessment of growth, development, and the effects of institutionalization in internationally adopted children. *Pediatric Annals, 29* (4), 224–232.

Miller, L. C., & Hendrie, N. W. (2000). Health of children adopted from China. *Pediatrics, 105* (6), 1–6.

O'Connor, T. G., Rutter, M., & the English and Romanian Adoptees Study Team. (2000). Attachment disorder behavior following early severe deprivation: Extension and longitudinal follow-up. *Journal of the American Academy of Child and Adolescent Psychiatry, 39* (6), 703–712.

Phinney, J. S. (1990). Ethnic identity in adolescents and adults: Review of research. *Psychological Bulletin, 109,* 499–514.

Pinderhughes, E. E., & Rosenberg, K. (1990). Family-bonding with high risk placements: A therapy model that promotes the process of becoming a family. In L. M. Glidden (Ed.), *Formed families: Adoption of children with handicaps* (pp. 209–230). New York: Haworth Press.

Rutter, M., Quinton, D., Hay, D., Dunn, J., O'Connor, T., & Marvin, R. (1995). *The social and intellectual development of children adopted into England from Romania.* Report prepared for the Department of Health, United Kingdom.

Sloutsky, V. M. (1997). Institutional care and developmental outcomes of 6- and 7-year-old children: A contextualist perspective. *International Journal of Behavior Development, 20,* 131–151.

Tessler, R., Gamache, G., & Liu, L. (1999). *West meets East: Americans adopt Chinese children.* Westport, CT: Bergen & Garvey.

Index

About the Contributors

KELLI STEELE ADAMS, M.S.W., is a transracial adoptee and social worker. She has worked in the areas of child welfare, child mental health, and international adoption over the past 10 years. Ms. Steele Adams has presented to many pre- and post-adoptive parent groups in both the United States and the United Kingdom about transracial adoption and fostering issues. Currently she is a board member with Adoption Network Cleveland and is staying home taking care of her son.

KAREN J. ANDERSON, M.S.W., is the Director of Foster and Adoption Services at Bellefaire Jewish Children's Bureau in Shaker Heights, Ohio. She has worked with triad members for 13 years. Ms. Anderson has presented on adoption and permanency planning issues at conferences throughout the United States. She is a consultant to public child welfare agencies and private social service agencies.

L. ANNE BABB, Ph.D., is the author of *Ethics in American Adoption* (Bergin & Garvey, 1999) and co-author of *Adopting and Advocating for the Special Needs Child: A Guide for Parents and Professionals* (Bergin & Garvey, 1997). She writes and lectures about parenting, child welfare, adoption, and ethics. Anne and her husband of 20 years parent 13 children in Norman, Oklahoma. Ranging in age from two to 25 years, their children entered the family through marriage, birth, and adoption.

VICTOR GROZA, Ph.D., has 18 years of practice experience in child welfare and continues to work with adoptive families. Dr. Groza has been involved in training, research, and consultation with public and private child welfare agencies. His research focuses on the institutional care of children and adoption as a resource for children who cannot reside in biological homes. Since 1991, he has been leading teams of social workers and social work students to Romania to provide consultation, training, and technical assistance. He is author of *Successful Adoptive Families: A Longitudinal Study of Special Needs Adoption* (Praeger, 1996) and co-author with James Rosenthal of *Special Needs Adoption: A Study of Intact Fam-*

ilies (Praeger, 1992), and co-author with D. Ileana and I. Irwin of *A Peacock or a Crow: Stories, Interviews and Commentaries on Romanian Adoptions* (1999).

LINDSEY HOULIHAN, M.S.S.A., has over 10 year's experience in social service administration and clinical practice in the area of substance abuse. She is an adoptive parent of a daughter from China who has inspired Lindsey to contribute to the knowledge base of international adoption. Ms. Houlihan has been active in the adoption community by teaching a pre-parenting class for adoptive parents and supporting a Chinese cultural program for pre-school-age adoptees and their families. She is currently enrolled in doctoral study at the Mandel School of Applied Social Sciences at Case Western Reserve University.

REGINA KUPECKY, L.S.W., has a Master's degree from John Carroll University in Ohio. She has worked in the field of adoption for over 28 years. Currently she works as a co-therapist at the Attachment and Bonding Center of Ohio, working with children with attachment disorders. Her services to children were recognized by the Ohio Department of Human Services in 1990 when she was the recipient of an "Adoption Worker of the Year" award. She authored a resource guide *Siblings Are Family Too*, and is co-author with Dr. Gregory Keck of the book *Adopting the Hurt Child* (1995). She has presented at local, national, and international conferences.

RITA LAWS, Ph.D., is co-author of *Adopting and Advocating for the Special Needs Child* (Bergin & Garvey, 1997) and has written for adoption magazines for the last 18 years. She currently volunteers as one of Oklahoma's Representatives to the North American Council on Adoptable Children (NACAC) and on the Education and Policy Council of Adoptive Families of America (AFA). She has 11 children, 9 of whom are at home. Three of these children were born to her, 8 are adopted.

BETTY JEAN LIFTON, Ph.D., is as a writer, adoption counselor, lecturer, and children's rights advocate. Among her books on the psychology of the adopted child/adult are *Journey of the Adopted Self: A Quest for Wholeness*, *Lost and Found: The Adoption Experience*, and *Twice Born: Memoirs of an Adopted Daughter*. Her other books include *The Kings of Children: The Life and Death of Janusz Korczak*, *A Place Called Hiroshima*, and *The Children of Vietnam*. She has an adoption counseling practice in Cambridge, Massachusetts, and lectures and gives workshops in this country and abroad.

JOYCE MAGUIRE PAVAO, Ed.D., L.C.S.W., L.M.F.T., is the founder and director of the Center for Family Connections, Inc. (est. 1995), The Adoption Resource Center (ARC est. 1973) and the Pre-Post Adoption Consulting Team (PACT est. 1978). Dr. Pavao has done extensive training nationally and internationally. She has developed models for treatment and for training using her systemic, intergenerational, and developmental framework. She is author of *The Family of Adoption* (1998) and co-author with Susan Dillard of *Joining Forces/Joining Families: Making and Mediating Open Adoptions from a Clinical and Legal Perspec-*

tive (in press) and co-author with Penny Callan Partridge of *The Power of Story* (in press). She believes her most valuable credential is that she has experienced life as an adopted person, and she has love and great respect for both her birth and adoptive families.

KAREN F. ROSENBERG, M.S.S.A., L.I.S.W., is a clinical social worker who has been in practice for 26 years. In addition to her clinical work, Ms. Rosenberg is a consultant for private and public mental health and adoption agencies. She has presented adoption-related workshops at national conferences, particularly in the areas of special needs adoption, family therapy with adoptive families, and clinical issues of adoption triad members. She has also contributed articles on adoption to professional journals.

JAYNE SCHOOLER, B.A., is affiliated with the Institute of Human Services, Columbus, Ohio, as a trainer in child welfare and adoption education for both professionals and families. Her publications include *The Whole Life Adoption Book* (1993), *Searching for a Past* (1995), and co-author with Betsy Keefer of *Telling the Truth to Your Adopted or Foster Child* (Bergin & Garvey, 2000). She also has had the experience of speaking on over 3 dozen radio stations on adoption issues and publishing over 300 articles on family life issues in magazines, newspapers, and journals.